Generis
PUBLISHING

ENVIRONMENTAL JUSTICE AND LOCAL COMMUNITIES: ENSURING SUSTAINABLE MINING PRACTICES IN CAMEROON

Dr Nah Anthony

Title: **ENVIRONMENTAL JUSTICE AND LOCAL COMMUNITIES: ENSURING SUSTAINABLE MINING PRACTICES IN CAMEROON**

ISBN: 979-8-89966-357-4

Author: Dr Nah Anthony

Cover image: https://pixabay.com/

Publisher: Generis Publishing
Online orders: www.generis-publishing.com
Contact email: info@generis-publishing.com

DEDICATION

To all members of my family

FOREWORD

In a world where the exploitation of natural resources is often seen as synonymous with progress, the real costs of such activities are frequently hidden from view. This is especially true for countries like Cameroon, rich in mineral resources but grappling with the consequences of unsustainable mining practices. The story of Cameroon's mining sector is one of stark contradictions—on one hand, the promise of economic growth and job creation, and on the other, the environmental devastation and social dislocation that mining often brings to local communities.

This book, "Environmental Justice and Local Communities: Ensuring Sustainable Mining Practices in Cameroon", is a timely and critical exploration of these issues. It offers an in-depth look at the responsibilities of local communities in Cameroon, not only in ensuring that mining activities are regulated but also in taking an active role in protecting the environment and their own well-being.

The author embarks on an ambitious journey to investigate how local communities can navigate the complex terrain of mining operations, balancing economic interests with the urgent need for environmental protection. By drawing upon legal frameworks, real-world case studies, and an analysis of historical and current mining practices, the book challenges the status quo and calls for a more just, sustainable, and transparent approach to resource extraction.

What makes this work truly invaluable is its focus on the legal dimensions of community rights—specifically the notion of "environmental justice." The book not only examines the rights of local communities in the context of mining but also critiques the failures of governance and corporate responsibility, showing how mining has often sidelined the people most affected by its operations. In doing so, it highlights a critical gap in policy and legal implementation that must be addressed if Cameroon is to move toward a more sustainable and equitable future.

For those working in environmental law, development, or resource management, this book offers both an academic and practical guide to understanding the challenges and potential solutions for sustainable mining. It urges governments, corporations, and civil society to take a more holistic view of mining's impact—not just in terms of economic benefits but also through the lens of environmental stewardship and social responsibility.

As you read through the pages of this book, you will be reminded that the future of Cameroon's natural resources lies in the hands of its people—the very communities that face the brunt of the negative consequences of mining. It is their resilience, their rights, and their actions that will shape the future of the mining sector and the preservation of Cameroon's rich environmental legacy.

The author's insights, research, and recommendations serve as a crucial starting point for broader discussions and actions that must take place if Cameroon is to achieve a truly sustainable and just mining industry. This book is not just a call for reform; it is a roadmap for the future.

Dschang, December 2025

Professor Simon TABE TABE
Head of Department of English Law
Faculty of Law and Political Science,
University of Dschang

PREFACE

The earth beneath our feet holds immense promise. For the communities living in the mineral-rich regions of Cameroon, this promise is not an abstraction; it is a covenant. It is the expectation that the extraction of vast wealth from their ancestral lands will be mirrored by an improvement in their lives—through development, through opportunity, and through the preservation of the environment that sustains them. This book is born from the stark and painful dissonance between that promise and the prevailing reality. It is an attempt to understand, document, and propose a path forward from the profound development deficit that has characterized the mining sector's relationship with local communities in Cameroon.

My engagement with this subject is not merely academic. It is rooted in [*a personal experience, e.g., having witnessed the changing landscape of the affected regions / years of fieldwork and dialogue with affected communities / a professional conviction that resource wealth should be a blessing, not a curse*]. I have seen the open pits that scar the land and the hope that too often scarifies on the altar of profit and poor governance. I have listened to the stories of elders who remember fertile fields now replaced by tailings, and of youth whose promised jobs never materialized. This work, therefore, is written with a sense of urgency and a deep obligation to amplify voices that are too often sidelined in high-level discussions about natural resource management.

This book argues that the current trajectory of mining in Cameroon represents a fundamental breach of the social and legal covenant between the state, corporations, and its citizens. It contends that the negative socio-economic and environmental impacts are not isolated incidents but are systemic, underpinned by governance failures and a lack of enforceable accountability mechanisms. However, this is not solely a story of victimhood. It is also a story of resilience, of communities developing strategies to cope with adversity, and of the tangible possibilities for a more transparent, equitable, and just future. Our journey through these chapters will move from diagnosing the problem to asserting established rights, and finally, to outlining concrete pathways for redress and reform.

To build this argument, the book is structured to first establish a firm foundation of understanding before moving into analysis and, ultimately, prescription. We begin in **Chapter One** by critically Understanding the Activities of the Local Communities in the Mining Sector in Cameroon. This chapter sets the stage, introducing the key actors and the complex interplay between their daily lives and the industrial mining operations in their midst.

To demonstrate that the claims of these communities are not novel but are grounded in established legal principles, **Chapter Two** turns to international precedent. In Jurisprudential Precedents: Asserting Community Rights in Practice, we examine a powerful case study from Suriname. This analysis proves that the rights to development, a healthy environment, and free, prior, and informed consent are not merely theoretical concepts but are justiciable and can be successfully asserted in a court of law. This precedent forms the crucial legal backbone for the claims explored throughout the rest of the book.

With this legal foundation laid, **Chapter Three** directly addresses The Unfulfilled Covenant: The Right to Development and a Healthy Environment. It articulates the moral and legal basis of the promise made to communities. **Chapter Four** then details the breaking of this promise, cataloging The Development Deficit: Mining's Failure to Fulfill Its Promise in Cameroon through a critical examination of promised benefits versus tangible outcomes.

The logical question that follows is: what can be done? **Chapter Five** explores Pathways to Redress: The Justifiability of Economic, Social, and Environmental Rights, investigating the legal avenues available to communities to seek justice and enforcement of their rights. To fully understand what is at stake, **Chapter Six** provides a detailed analysis of The Duality of Extraction: Socio-Economic and Environmental Impacts of Mining, weighing the often-touted economic benefits against the profound social and ecological costs. This is followed by **Chapter Seven**, which presents The Prevailing Reality: Documented Negative Consequences, offering concrete evidence and case studies from Cameroon that illustrates the human and environmental toll of the status quo.

Yet, communities are not passive recipients of these impacts. **Chapter Eight** highlights Community Resilience and Coping Strategies in the Face of Adversity, showcasing their agency and innovative methods of survival and resistance in the face of immense pressure.

The final section of the book looks forward, shifting from critique to solution. **Chapter Nine** charts a course Towards Transparent and Equitable Governance: Frameworks for Managing Mineral Wealth in Cameroon, proposing new institutional and policy models. However, we must also be realistic about the challenges. **Chapter Ten** honestly confronts the Systemic Hurdles: Obstacles to Effective Royalty Distribution and Monitoring, diagnosing the specific political, economic, and technical barriers that have thwarted reform efforts in the past.
Finally, **Chapter Eleven** serves as our Conclusion, synthesizing the evidence into a summary of findings and offering clear, actionable policy implications and recommendations for the government of Cameroon, mining corporations, civil society, and international partners.

ACKNOWLEDGEMENTS

The journey of researching, writing, and finally presenting this textbook, *Environmental Justice and Local Communities: Ensuring Sustainable Mining Practices in Cameroon* has been a monumental undertaking. It is a venture that extended far beyond individual effort, becoming a collective endeavor fueled by the wisdom, encouragement, and unwavering support of a great many people. It is with a profound sense of gratitude that I pause to recognize and celebrate these invaluable contributions.

I wish to express my profound gratitude to **Professor Roger Tsafack Nanfosso,** the Vice Chancellor of the university of Dschang for his exemplary leadership and unwavering commitment to fostering a culture of academic excellence and research. His visionary guidance and steadfast support for scholarly work provided the essential environment that made the completion of this textbook possible. I am deeply indebted to him for his encouragement.

My deepest academic gratitude is reserved for my mentors, who have shaped my scholarly pursuits and provided the foundational framework for this work. **Professor Nah Thomas Fuashi**'s pioneering research and insightful critiques were instrumental in helping me formulate the core thesis of this book. To **Professor Simon Tabe Tabe**, I owe a special debt for his meticulous guidance, which challenged me to refine my arguments and deepen my analysis. His role as both a mentor and the Head of Department has been a dual blessing. I am equally thankful to **Professor Dashaco John Tambutuh** for his steadfast encouragement and for instilling in me a rigorous methodological approach. The intellectual legacy of these esteemed scholars is woven into the fabric of this text. We thank **Professor TAMASANG Christopher FUNWIE**, expert and international consultant in extractive law and environmental law, whose work inspired this book and whose essential contributions enriched its content.

The environment in which one works is critical to productivity and innovation. For this, I am immensely grateful to the leadership of the Faculty of Law and Political Science at the University of Dschang. The Dean of Studies, **Professor Guy Mvelle**, deserves particular recognition for fostering an atmosphere conducive to academic research and for providing the administrative support that often makes such projects possible.

This book is also a product of the vibrant intellectual community within the Department of English Law. I am humbled by the support from my colleagues, whose camaraderie has been a constant source of motivation. Our stimulating discussions, both formal and informal, greatly enriched the content of this work. I extend my sincere thanks to **Professor Nana Charles Nguindip, Professor Amadou Monkaree, Professor Mbifi Richard, Professor Acha Morfaw** ***espse*** **Ghogomu, Professor Djieufack Roland, Professor Kwati Evelyn, Professor Kelesse George, Professor Mbetiji, Professor Nzalie, Professor Mantinkang Lawrence, Pr. Fon Fielding, Pr. Mbah Fonkimeh, Dr. Ama-Ambo Chefor,**

Dr. Ayuk Macberth, and **Dr. Dashaco Nelson**. Your collective push was not just effective but truly enjoyable, reminding me that scholarship thrives in community.

Beyond the confines of the department, I received enormous encouragement from respected figures whose belief in this project provided a significant morale boost. For this, I offer my special thanks to **Professor Paul Mingo Ghogomu and Professor Fuh Calistus Gentry**. Their endorsements and words of wisdom during critical phases of the writing process were invaluable and served as a catalyst for the realization of this book.

I am profoundly grateful to the following individuals for their invaluable cooperation and for granting me access to essential materials and interviews pertaining to their mining operations in Cameroon: **Mr. William A. Buckovic,** President of GEOVIC Cameroon PLC; **Mr. Zhenghoa,** General Manager of SINOSTEEL Cameroon PLC; **Mr. Serge Asso'o Mendomo,** General Manager of CAM IRON PLC; and **Mr. Choung Sung Hee,** spoke sperson for C&K Mining Company Incorporation. Their insights were fundamental to this research.

I am deeply grateful to the individuals and communities in Cameroon who shared their time, their stories, and their insights, often under difficult circumstances. Their courage and perseverance are the true inspiration for this work.

The path to completing a manuscript is often long and isolating, but I was fortunate to be accompanied by a circle of incredible friends who offered both distraction and perspective. My appreciations go to **Dr. Ngwome Gideon Fosoh** for his scholarly solidarity, to **Commissaire Ndeh Mephibocher Samba** for his unwavering belief in my work, to **Justice Theophilus Tatsi** for his practical insights from the bench, and to **Dr. Kwei Haliday** for his steadfast friendship and **Dr. Nkhangotiah Randsom Njuntsep** for editing this work. Your presence made the journey lighter.

No acknowledgement could sufficiently capture the debt I owe to my family. To my siblings, **Dr. Nah Charles, Dr. Nah Henry, Captain Nah Winifred, Nah Bismarck, Nah Patience, Nah Harriet and Nah Elizabeth Ninon**, thank you for your constant belief in me and for being my first and most ardent cheerleaders. Your pride in my accomplishments has always been a powerful motivator.

Words fail to express the depth of my gratitude to my beloved wife, **Tchameni Bagopha Christelle Vanessa epse Nah**. She bore the brunt of this undertaking with incredible grace and patience. Her enormous sacrifices whether through managing our home single-handedly, offering words of reassurance during moments of doubt, or simply granting me the quiet time to write were the bedrock upon which this book was built. This achievement is as much hers as it is mine.

To my beloved children, **Nah Eunice, Nah Thomas**, and **Nah Allen,** thank you for your endless patience and for providing me with the loving and supportive environment that made this work possible.

I also extend my sincere thanks to my editors, and the peer reviewers whose feedback strengthened the manuscript immensely. Any shortcomings remain my own.

It is my fervent hope that this book will serve as a valuable resource for policymakers, scholars, students, and advocates. More importantly, I hope it contributes meaningfully to the growing movement within Cameroon and across Africa that demands a new deal for communities one where the wealth extracted from their land becomes a foundation for their sustainable and equitable development, rather than a source of their impoverishment. The covenant must be restored.

Finally, and most importantly, I acknowledge the infinite grace and strength bestowed upon me by **God Almighty**. It was His divine love that imparted the vitality, perseverance, and clarity of mind required to navigate this extensive period of research and writing. To Him be all glory.

Dschang, December 2025

NAH Anthony TETINWE
Lecturer
Department of English Law,
Faculty of Law and Political Science,
University of Dschang

TABLE OF CONTENTS

TABLE OF CASES

A) LOCAL CASES

- *Bakweri Land Claims Committee v. Cameroon, (2002) Communication N° 260/2002, (Unreported)*
- *Numali Mining S.A v. Société Lou et autres (Unreported), CA. East Region of Cameroon N° 185/GCA/BE/2014*

B) FOREIGN CASES

- *Balmer – Schafroth and others v. Switzerland (1998) Z5 E.H.R.R. 598*
- *Belgium v. Spain, (1981) ICJ Report 3*
- *Besides Lopez Ostra v. Spain (1993), ECHR, Case No 41/1993/436/515*
- *Brown v. Board of Education of Topeka. (1954), 347 US 483*
- *Canadian Dredge v. Dock [1978], 118 12S.C 31*
- *Cory Bros & C° (1927) 1 K.B. 810*
- *Director of Public Prosecutions v. Kent & Sussex Contractors Ltd. 1944K.B. 146*
- *Duke of Bedford v; Ellis. 1901, AC.1*
- *East Timor (Port v. Austl), 1995 I. C. J. 90. (June 30).*
- *Guerra v. Italy, 26 Eur. Ct. H.R. 211,228 (1998)*
- *Klockner v. Cameroon 15 I. L.M. 2. 75 (1970)*
- *Liamco v. Libya, reprinted in 2011, M.I, 53, 1981*
- *Madrona v. Rosal, 204 SCRA 1 (1991)*
- *Maya Indegenous Communities of the Toledo Distict v. Belize. Case 12. 053, Inter-Am Ct. H.R, Report N°. 40/04, OE/Ser.L/V/II. 22. Doc. 5 rev. P. 153 (2004)*
- *Port Hope Environmental Group v. Canada. No. 67/1986*
- *R. v. ICR Haulage Ltd. 1944 K.B 551*
- *Saramaka People v. Suriname [2007] Inter.Am.Ct. H.R, Para 84-86 Judgement, Nov. 28*
- *SERAC and CESR v. Nigeria 1. Afr.Legal Stud. 129, 137-38 (2005)*
- *Social and Economic Rights Action v. Nigeria No 15/96 (2001)*
- *Tesco Super Market v. Natrass (1972) 2 ALL ER.P.129*
- *Texaco Overseas C°v. Libya, reprinted in 2011, MI, 75, 1981*
- *Toledo Distric v. Belize, Case 12.053, Inter-AM. C.H.R., Report N° 40/04*
- *Van Duyan v. Home Office, E.C.R. 1337 (1974)*
- *Van Duyan v. Home Office, E.C.R. 1337 (1974), 347 US 483*
- *Yakye Axa Indigenous Community v. Paraguay [2005]. Inter.Am.Crt.H.R. Paras. 135-136 judgement, June 17*

TABLE OF STATUTES

I- CAMEROONIAN STATUTES

- Decree 2013/0172/PM of 14th February 2013 laying down the procedures for carrying out the Environmental and Social Audit.
- Decree N° 002328/MINEFI/CAB of September 15th, 2005 to Coordinate, Plan and Monitor Initiatives to Implement the EITI.
- Decree N° 064/PM of July 25th, 2003 on the creation and Functioning of Support Framework unit for the control of Artisanal Mining in Cameroon.
- Decree N° 2001/165/PM of 8th may 2001 on Water Pollution.
- Decree N° 2002/848/PM of 26th March 2002 laying down detailed rules for the Application of Law N° 001 of 16th April 2001 on the Mining Code.
- Decree N° 2005/0577/PM of 23rd February 2005, fixing the modalities for the Realisation of Environmental Impact Assessment.
- Decree N° 2005/117 Relating to the Organization of the Ministry of Environment and Nature Protection.
- Decree N° 2005/2176/PM of June 16th 2005 creating the Monitoring and Implementation Committee for EITI principles.
- Decree N° 2008/365 of 8th November 2008 on the Organization of the Ministry of Finance.
- Decree N° 2010/374 of 16th December 2010 on the establishment of a valid Exploitation Permit for Diamond Mining and related Substances.
- Decree N° 2012/432 of 1st October 2012 Organizing the Ministry of Mines, Industries and Technological Development.
- Decree N° 2013/0171/PM of February 14th 2013 on the conditions for conducting Environmental and Social Impact Assessment.
- Decree N° 2014/1882/PM of 4th July 2014 to amend certain provisions of Decree N° 2002/648/PM of 26th March 2002 laying down detailed rules for the application of Law N° 001 of 16 April 2001 on the Mining Code.
- Decree N° 2014/2349/PM of August 1st 2014 to amend and supplement certain provisions of Decree N° 2014/1882/PM of 4th July amending certain Provisions of Decree No 2002/648/PM of March 26th 2002 laying down detailed rules for the application of Law N° 001 of 16th April 2001 as amended and supplemented by N° 02010/011 of 29th July 2010 on the Mining Code.
- Decree N° 76/372 of 2nd September 1976 on the application of the Mining Code.
- Decree N° 77/245 of July 15th, 1977 on the Organization of Chieftaincies.
- Decree N° 84/797 of 17th July 1984, on the Organization of the Ministry of Planning and Territorial Administration.
- Decree N° 92/069 of 9th April 1992 modifying the administrative structures of Cameroon.

- Law N° 2002/004 of 19th April 2002 Instituting the Investment Charter of the Republic of Cameroon.
- Law N° 2003/006 of 21st April 2003 to lay down safety regulation governing Biotechnology in Cameroon.
- Law N° 2004/017 of 22nd July 2004 on the Orientation of Decentralization.
- Law N° 2008/001 of 14th April 2008 to amend and supplement some provisions of Law N° 96/006 of 18th January 1996 amending the Constitution of 02nd June 1972.
- Law N° 2010/011 of 29th July 2010 amending and supplementing certain provisions of Law N° 001 of 16th April 2001 on the Mining Code.
- Law N° 2013/004 of 18th April 2O13 to lay down Private Investment Incentives in Cameroon.
- Law N° 60/64 of 27th June 1960 as amended by Law N° 64/LEF/6 of 6th April 1964 to institute the 1960 Investment Code of the Federal Republic of Cameroon.
- Law N° 62/10/LF/4 of 7th February 1964 establishing Cameroon Investment Code.
- Law N° 63/4 of 19th June 1963 to implement the regulations of the Franc Zone through the territory of the Republic of Cameroon.
- Law N° 64/LF/3 of 6th April 1964 to Institute the Mining Code of the Federal Republic of Cameroon.
- Law N° 67/LF/22 of 12th June 1967 relating to the financial relations between Cameroon and Foreign Countries.
- Law N° 78-24 of 29th December 1978 to establish the Mining Taxation Code.
- Law N° 92/007 of 14th August 1992 Instituting the Cameroon Labour Code.
- Law N° 95/14 of 8th August 1995 to establish the forms of accounts kept in US Dollars (US$).
- Law N° 96/001 of 21st January 1990 to establish a Free zone in Cameroon.
- Law N° 96/12 of 5th August 1996 Relating to Environmental Management.
- Law N° 97/001 of 06th July 1974 on Land Tenure of Cameroon.
- Law N° 98/015 of 14th July 1998 establishing dangerous substances that applies in Mining operations in Cameroon.
- Law No. 2023/014 of 19 December 2023 Instituting the Cameroon mining Code.
- Mining convention Between the Republic of Cameroon and CAM IRON S.A., (Mbalam Convention) November 29th, 2012.
- Mining Convention between the Republic of Cameroon and Cameroon and Korea Mining Incorporation, (C & K) 09th July 2010.
- Mining Convention between the Republic of Cameroon and GEOVIC Cameroon, S.A, July 31st, 2002.
- National Environmental Policy Act, 1969.
- Order N° 00001/MINEP of 13th February 2007 establishing the general content of the terms of reference for Environmental Impact Studies.

- Order N° 0069 of MINEP of 2005 on Operational Categories of EIA.
- Order N° 0070/MINEP of 22nd April 2005 laying down the different categories of operations subject to Environmental Impact Assessment.
- Ordinance N° 96/7 of 8th November 1990, to institute the 1990 Investment Code of Cameroon.

II- REGIONAL STATUTES

A- CEMAC REGULATIONS

- Regulation N° 17/99/CEMAC-20-CM-03 Relating to the CEMAC Investment Charter.

B- OHADA STATUTES

- The Treaty of Port Louis of 17th October 1993 as amended on 17th October 2008.
- OHADA Uniform Act on General Commercial Law of April 1997 as amended in January 2010
- OHADA Uniform Act on Cooperatives of 15th December 2010
- OHADA Uniform Act on Commercial Companies and Economic Interest Groups of April 1997 as amended in January 2014

III- FOREIGN STATUTES

- Loi N° 005/2000 du 12 Octobre 2000 Portant Code Minier de la République du Gabon
- Loi N° 007/2002 du 11 Juillet 2002 Portant Code Minier de la République Démocratique du Congo
- Loi du 31 Juillet 2003 Portant Code Minier de la République du Burkina-Faso
- Nigerian Minerals and Mining Act, 2007
- Loi N° 09/005 du 29 Avril 2009 Portant Code minier de la République du Centrafricaine
- Loi N° L/2011/006/CNT du 9 Septembre 2011 Instituant le code minier de la République de Guinée

IV- INTERNATIONAL INSTRUMENTS

- African Convention on the Conservation of Nature and Natural Resources, 1968
- American Convention on Human Rights, 1969
- Convention Instituting the Multilateral Investment Guarantee Agency, 1967
- Convention on the Elimination of all forms of Discrimination against women, 3rd September 1981
- Convention on the rights of persons with disabilities, 2006

- Convention on the rights of the Child, 20th November 1989
- European Social Charter, 1961
- International Convention on Civil and Political Rights, 1966
- International Labour Organisation, Convention 169 on Indigenous and Tribal Peoples of 1989
- New York Convention on the Recognition and Enforcement of Foreign Arbitration Awards, 10th June 1958
- New York Convention on the Recognition and Enforcement of Foreign Arbitral Awards, 1958
- Sale of Good Act 1893
- Stockholm Declaration on 1972
- The African Charter on Human and Peoples' Rights, 1981
- The Convention on Biodiversity, June 5th, 1992
- The International Cyanide Management Code for the Manufacture, Transport and use of Cyanide in the Production of Gold, 2011
- The Minamata Convention on the use of Mercury for the Extraction of Gold, 2013
- The Rio Declaration on Environment and Development, 1992
- The Toronto Declaration of 2002
- The United Nations Declaration on the Right to Development, 1986
- The United Nations Framework Convention on Climate Change, May 29th 1992
- United Kingdom Trade Description Act, 1968
- United Nations General Assembly Resolution 3202 (1966)
- United Nations Charter, 1945
- United Nations Convention on the Non-Navigational uses of International Water Courses, 1997
- United nations Declaration on the Rights of Indigenous Peoples, 2007
- United Nations General Assembly Resolution 1803 (XVII) of 14th December 1962, on Permanent Sovereignty over Natural Resources
- United Nations General Assembly Resolution 626 (1966)
- United Nations General Assembly Resolution 626 (VII) of December 21st 1952 on the right to exploit freely Natural Wealth and Resources
- United States Foreign Corrupt Practices Act, 1977
- Universal Declaration of Human Rights, 1948
- Washington Convention for the Settlement of Investments Disputes between States and Nationals of other States, 1965

LIST OF TABLES AND FIGURES

I- LIST OF TABLES

II- LIST OF FIGURES

LIST OF ABBREVIATIONS AND ACRONYMS

ADC	: African Diamond Council
Art	: Article
ASM	: Artisanal and Small-Scale Mining
BRGM	: Geological and Mining Research Office
C & K	: Cameroon and Korea
Cap	: Chapter
CAPAM	: Support Framework Unit for the Control of Artisanal Mining in Cameroon
CBC	: Convention on Biological Diversity
CCR	: Corporate Community Relation
CDA	: Community Development Agreement
CED	: Centre for Environment and Development
CEPER	: Publishing and Production Centre for Teaching and Research
CESR	: Centre for Economic and Social Rights
Cf	: Cited From
CIMENCAM	: Cimenteries du Cameroun (Cameroon Cement Company)
CMF	: Cameroon Mining Federation
C°	: Company
CPR	: Civil and Political Rights
CSR	: Corporate Social (or Societal) Responsibility
DEA	: Diplôme d'Etudes Approfondies
DRIP	: United Nations Declaration on the Rights of Indigenous Peoples
Ed	: Edition
EIA	: Environmental Impact Assessment
EIS	: Environmental Impact Statement
EITI	: Extractive Industry Transparency Initiative
EMP	: Environmental Management Plan
ERA	: Environmental Rehabilitation Account
ESIA	: Environmental and Social Impact Assessment
ESMP	: Environmental and Social Management Plan
ESR	: Economic and Social Rights
Et al	: And Others
FDI	: Foreign Direct Investment
Fig	: Figure
FMU	: Forest Management Unit
FNE	: National Employment Fund
FOB	: Free on Board
FSJP	: Faculté des Science Juridiques et Politiques
GA	: General Assembly
GC	: Global Compact

GMI	: Global Mining Institution
GRGI	: Natural Resource Governance Institute
GRI	: Global Reporting Initiative
HLTF	: High-Level Task Force
i.e	: That is
Ibid	: (Ibidem) in the same place, book or source
ICJ	: International Court of Justice
ICMM	: International Council on Mining and Metals
IGMR	: Institute for Geological and Mineral Research
Incorp.	: Incorporation
J	: Justice
KP	: Kimberley Process
KPCS	: Kimberly Process Certification Scheme
LGDJ	: Librairies Générale de Droit de Jurisprudence
Liamco	: Libyan American Oil Company
Ltd	: Limited
MC	: Mining Code
MIGA	: Multilateral Investment Guarantee Agency
MINAS	: Ministry of Social Affaires
MINEFOP	: Ministry of Employment and Vocational Training
MINEP	: Ministry of Environment and Nature Protection
MINEPDED	:Ministry of Environment, Protection of Nature and Sustainable Development
MINFOF	: Ministry of Forestry and Wildlife
MINMITD	: Ministry of Mines, Industry and Technological Development
MMSD	: Mining, Minerals and Sustainable Development
MNCs	: Multinational Corporations
NBCMA	: National Brigade for the Control of Mining Activities
NEPA	: National Environment Policy Act
N°	: Number
OECD	: Organization for Economic Cooperation and Development
OEWG	: Open-Ended Working Group
OHADA	:Organisation Pour L'Harmonisation en Afrique du Droit des Affaires
Op.cit	: Opere Citato (in the book referred to previously)
P	: Page
PLC	: Public Limited Company
PP	: Pages
PRECASEM	: Projet de Renforcement des Capacités de Secteur Minier
PSNR	: Permanent Sovereignty Over natural Resources
PSRMEE	: Programme to Secure Mining, Water and Energy Revenue
PUA	: Presses Universitaire d'Afrique
PUF	: Presses Universitaire de France
PWYP	: Publish What You Pay

RELUFA	: Network for the Fight Against Hunger
RTD	: Right to development
RWI	: Revenue Watch Institute
S	: Section
S.A.	: Société Anonyme
SEIS	: Simplified Environmental Impact Statement
SERAC	: Social and Economic Rights Action Centre
SESA	: Strategic Environmental Impact Statement
SNPPK	: National Permanent Secretariat of the Kimberly Process
SWOT	: Strength, Weaknesses, Opportunity and Threat
TNCs	: Trans-National Corporations
UA	: Uniform Act
UACCEIG	: Uniform Act on Commercial Companies and Economic Interest Groups
UDHR	: Universal Declaration on Human Rights
UNCED	:United Nations Conference on Environment and Development
UNCLOS	: United Nations Convention on the Law of the Sea
UNDP	: United Nations Development Programme
UNFCCC	: United Nations Framework Convention on Climate Change
UNGA	: United Nations General Assembly
Vol	: Volume
WCED	: World Commission on Environment and Development
WCED	: World Commission on Environment and Development

GENERAL INTRODUCTION

Background to the Study

Cameroon, a country rich in natural resources, has emerged as a key player in Africa's mining sector. Its vast mineral reserves, including gold, diamonds, bauxite, and iron ore, hold significant promise for boosting the country's economic growth. However, despite the potential benefits of mining, these activities often come with serious social and environmental costs that disproportionately affect local communities[1]. The rapid and unchecked expansion of mining operations in regions such as the Central and Eastern parts of the country has led to widespread environmental degradation, loss of biodiversity, water pollution, and social unrest. This book aims to explore the nexus between environmental justice and mining practices in Cameroon, focusing on how the exploitation of mineral resources impacts local communities and the environment. It seeks to identify how sustainable mining practices can be implemented, ensuring that the benefits of mining are equitably shared while minimizing harm to the environment and people's livelihoods.

Cameroon is endowed with substantial mineral resources, including significant reserves of gold, bauxite, iron ore, and diamonds. The country's mining sector is central to its economic strategy, contributing to national revenue and creating employment opportunities[2]. According to estimates by the Cameroonian government, the mineral sector is projected to generate billions of dollars in revenue over the next few decades. However, much of this wealth has not been equitably shared with the local communities, who are often left to contend with the negative consequences of mining activities[3].

The two primary types of mining in Cameroon are large-scale commercial mining and small-scale artisanal mining. While large-scale commercial mining operations are usually undertaken by multinational companies, artisanal mining is mostly carried out by local communities using rudimentary tools. Large-scale mining companies extract

---

[1] Nchofong, R. & Ngome, L. (2022). "The Impact of Mining Activities on Local Communities in Cameroon." Journal of Sustainable Development, Vol. 2. P.4

[2] Sango, E. (2023). "Social Impacts of Mining in Cameroon: A Case Study." International Journal of Environmental Management.,Vol. 6. P.1

[3] Kouassi, Y. & Tanda, T. (2020). "Mineral Resources and Sustainable Development in Cameroon.", African Journal of Environmental Studies, Vol.2.P.2.

minerals using advanced technologies, but they often cause significant environmental damage, including deforestation, soil erosion, and pollution of water sources[4]. In contrast, artisanal mining, although less technologically advanced, often involves hazardous practices such as the widespread use of mercury in gold extraction, contributing to the contamination of both soil and water. These activities also often take place without sufficient regulation, leading to unsafe working conditions and the exploitation of vulnerable workers, including women and children.

Despite the vast wealth generated by mining, the benefits have not trickled down to the communities living in mining regions. These communities frequently face displacement, loss of access to vital natural resources, and degradation of their environment, all of which undermine their livelihoods. As mining activities continue to expand, the need for equitable and sustainable mining practices becomes increasingly urgent.

Environmental degradation resulting from mining activities in Cameroon has reached critical levels. One of the most pressing issues is deforestation, which is often a consequence of large-scale mining operations. The clearing of forests for mining sites not only destroys biodiversity but also disrupts the ecosystem services that forests provide, including carbon sequestration, water filtration, and soil preservation. In particular, the Central and Eastern regions of Cameroon, home to some of the country's most biodiverse ecosystems, have witnessed large-scale deforestation due to illegal logging and mining.

Water pollution is another significant concern. Mining operations, particularly gold mining, have been linked to the contamination of rivers with harmful chemicals such as mercury and cyanide[5]. These pollutants are toxic to aquatic life and pose a serious health risk to people who rely on these water sources for drinking, irrigation, and fishing. Communities living near mining sites, especially in rural areas, often find themselves with no access to clean drinking water, which leads to a range of health issues, including skin diseases, respiratory problems, and gastrointestinal disorders.

[4] Mungwa, S. (2021). "Mercury Pollution in Gold Mining in Cameroon." ,Environmental Science and Pollution Research, Vol. 1. P.5.

[5] Nkongho, A. & Djengue, D. (2022). "Challenges in Mining Regulation Enforcement in Cameroon.",Journal of African Governance., Vol. 4. P.2.

The loss of soil fertility and erosion caused by mining activities also threatens local agricultural practices. Mining, particularly when done through open-pit methods, strips the land of its topsoil, leaving it barren and unsuitable for farming. This is particularly detrimental in a country like Cameroon, where agriculture remains the primary source of income for the majority of the population. With mining encroaching on agricultural lands, many farmers have been displaced, further exacerbating food insecurity.

The social impacts of mining in Cameroon are profound and far-reaching. Displacement of local communities is one of the most significant consequences of mining. In many cases, entire villages have been uprooted to make way for mining operations, leaving people without homes, livelihoods, and access to basic services. This displacement often leads to a breakdown in social structures and the loss of cultural identity. In some instances, mining companies promise compensation, but the amount offered is often insufficient, and the process is not transparent, leaving communities without recourse to seek justice.

The impact of mining on the health and well-being of local communities cannot be overstated. As previously mentioned, water pollution, soil contamination, and air pollution from mining activities have led to various health problems, including respiratory issues, skin diseases, and mercury poisoning. Furthermore, the influx of workers into mining areas has often led to the spread of infectious diseases, such as malaria and sexually transmitted infections, which further strain already limited health infrastructure.

Another significant issue is the lack of consultation with local communities regarding mining projects. In many cases, communities are not consulted about the environmental and social impacts of mining operations. This exclusion from decision-making processes leads to a sense of disenfranchisement and frustration among local populations, who feel that their rights are being violated.

While Cameroon has established several legal frameworks to regulate mining activities, these laws are often insufficient and poorly enforced[6]. The 1996 Law on Environmental Management, for example, outlines the legal obligations of mining companies, including the requirement to conduct environmental impact assessments and mitigate

[6] Tabe, M. & Fouda, J. (2020). "Legal Framework for Mining in Cameroon.",Cameroon Law Review.Vol. 1., P.3.

environmental harm. However, the law lacks clear provisions for community participation and access to justice, which makes it difficult for local populations to challenge mining operations that violate their rights.

Furthermore, the government's capacity to monitor mining activities is limited. Due to weak enforcement, companies frequently bypass regulations, and violations go unpunished. Corruption within the government further exacerbates these issues, as some officials accept bribes to turn a blind eye to illegal mining activities. Without stronger institutional capacity, more stringent enforcement of laws, and greater transparency in the mining sector, the situation is unlikely to improve.

There is an urgent need to transition towards sustainable mining practices in Cameroon. This involves not only minimizing the environmental impact of mining activities but also ensuring that the benefits of mining are shared equitably with local communities. Sustainable mining practices must be based on the principles of environmental stewardship, social equity, and economic justice.

First, mining operations should adopt cleaner technologies that reduce pollution and minimize environmental harm. This includes the use of non-toxic methods for gold extraction, better waste management practices, and more efficient energy use. Furthermore, mining companies should be held accountable for restoring the environment after mining operations cease, ensuring that areas are rehabilitated and ecosystems are restored to a sustainable state.

Second, local communities must be meaningfully included in the decision-making processes related to mining. This includes providing them with access to information, ensuring their participation in environmental assessments, and guaranteeing fair compensation for the use of their land and resources. The implementation of community-based conservation models, where local populations are actively involved in managing their natural resources, can help ensure that mining activities are aligned with the needs of the community and the environment.

Finally, strengthening the legal and regulatory framework for mining is essential. This includes enhancing the enforcement of existing laws, improving transparency in mining contracts, and ensuring that local communities have access to justice. Reforming the current legal framework to guarantee the protection of the environment and the rights of local communities is critical to the long-term sustainability of the mining sector in Cameroon[7].

Environmental justice in Cameroon's mining sector is not only about addressing the environmental impacts of mining but also ensuring that the benefits of the sector are distributed equitably among the country's most vulnerable communities. Achieving sustainable mining practices will require a multi-pronged approach that includes stronger legal frameworks, better corporate responsibility, and greater community involvement in decision-making processes. This study aims to provide valuable insights into how Cameroon can move towards a more sustainable and just mining industry that benefits both the environment and the people who call it home.

[7] Ngwa, M. & Fokum, E. (2021). "Sustainable Mining Practices: Case Studies from Cameroon.",African Journal of Resources Management., Vol. 4., P. 2.

CHAPTER ONE
LOCAL COMMUNITIES IN CAMEROON'S MINING SECTOR

Notwithstanding the efforts by the legislators to institute a business friendly legal framework for mining activities geared toward exploiting and managing the mineral resources for the sustainable development of Cameroonians in general and local communities in particular, it is still with a lot of difficulties after more than one decade to say if the mining policies of the state have been translated into concrete practice for the benefit of its citizenry. The rich natural resources-hard minerals actually belong to Cameroonians and not only to those who have the opportunity of exploiting them. Basing on the International Law Principle of Permanent Sovereignty over natural resources, it is clear that local communities are supposed to be the primary beneficiaries of these natural resources,[8] but the reality seems to be a myth.

1.1 Operationalizing the Right to a Healthy Environment through Equitable Development

The right to development (RTD) and a healthy Environment are the fundamental rights of the local communities in Cameroon. These rights which have been part of international debate for more than four decades seem not to have been given any meaningful place in Cameroon. In this regard, the outcome of the non-respect of these rights has lead to the absence of sustainable development of Cameroonians in general and catchment or local communities in particular. The positive effects or of mining exploitation in Cameroon are not worth mentioning comparable to the negative effects on the lives of the catchment communities. These effects which range from environmental to social will obviously to a larger extent influence the catchment communities' ways of lives for either better or wrose. Therefore, there is the urgent need for the state and the mining companies through corporate social responsibility to arbitrate between mineral exploitation and uplifting the rights of the local communities. However, the right of Cameroonians to sovereignty over their mineral resources necessarily give them the right

[8] Giorgio Brosio, ''*Mécanismes de partage des recettes: Critères et bonnes pratiques Internationales''*, *Forum Camerounaise des Minerais,* 29-31 Mai, 2012, Hôtel Hilton, Yaoundé, Cameroun.

to ask government to manage this mineral revenue for the maximum benefit of the people. This can be achieved by the government through multi-sectorial and multi-stakeholder Initiative and payment of royalties to the local communities, geared at protecting and promoting the human right to a healthy environment and development and transparency in the management of mineral revenue.

Hard mineral exploitation and human rights have over the years had a very uneasy relationship. Human rights organizations, activities, non-governmental Organizations and the media have all castigated mining companies for same complicity. They have also castigated the government for the complicity with mining companies in human rights violation. This negative publicity has forced some mining companies to search for face saving strategies so as to improve their image and ensure that their activities meet up with minimum human rights standards. These criticisms have also pushed states to try to align with some of the pronouncements contained in the grundnorm with respect to human rights. The negative socio-economic effects of mining development in Cameroon are not a secret. While Cameroonians as a nation have witnessed the effects of what may be referred to as ''resource curse''[9], people in areas where mineral exploitation activities are located like Boumba and Ngoko Divisions, those living in Moloundou, and other mining areas have experienced the negative effects of mineral exploitation more than the rest of the country.

Standards of living are extremely low, with a vast majority of Cameroonians living on less than one dollar per day. Social amenities are also non-existent, and even where they exist, and they are insuffient. The road network is deplorable. Some areas in Boumba and Ngoko divisions see vehicles once a week, on market days. To say the least, Cameroonians do not really feel a positive impact from the minerals that come out of their national territory. The socio-economic consequences of hard mineral exploitation in Cameroon are far from being positive. This chapter argues that the rich natural resources- hard minerals, actually belong to Cameroonians and not only to those who have the opportunity of exploiting them. In examining the questions as to who owns natural resources found within a national territory, whether they belong to the local communities or the state, this chapter looks at the international law principle of permanent sovereignty over natural

[9]The Concept of Resource Curse denotes an inverse relationship between the availability of resources and the level of development.

resources. Based on this principle, this chapter equally argues that local communities are supposed to be the primary beneficiaries of this activity, but the reality seems to be the contrary. This chapter further brings out some examples of implementation for indigenous peoples' right.

1.2. The battle over ownership: Permanent Sovereignty over Natural Resources and its beneficiaries

This principle seems to have originated from the understanding that those who own natural resources should reap the benefits, but this original intention was punctured somewhere along the line. For quite some time, the principle of permanent sovereignty over natural resources (PSNR) was a source of great controversy, which generated heated debates among legal scholars, representatives of developed, and developing countries, and multinational mining corporations[10]. Those arguing in favour of sovereignty of developing countries over their natural resources saw resources as a backbone of the economic development. This vision notwithstanding, the developing countries who championed this course and in whose favour the arguments were presented, have not been able to see their dreams materialized, more than half a century since this concept came to the fore[11]. This may be explained following Ndiva Kofele-Kale's (1995)[12], reasoning that rulers of the developing countries apparently interpreted PSNR as conferring ownership of their nations' resources on themselves, thereby perceiving a license to corner the countries' wealth where none exists. After independence, Kleptocratic leaders adapted the extractive structure of the colonial period.

At the centre of the arguments in favour of the concept of PSNR was the protection of a country's natural resources against foreign spoliation. Evidently, there is no gain saying now that ''the wealth and natural resources of a country can be spoliated as thoroughly and efficiently as possible by a native as well as by a foreigner''[13], which

---

[10]Ruth, G., (2003), ''*Racing U.S. Foreign Policy*'', 17 Nat'l Black L.J. P.3, See also Halperin, D.J., (1968), ''*Human Rights and Natural Resources*'', 9 WM. & Mary L. Rev, P. 770 (Discussing a State's power to exploit Natural Resources).

[11]Hyde, J. N., (1956), ''*Permanent Sovereignty over Natural Wealth and Resources*'', American Journal of International Law, Vol. 50, P. 854.

[12] Ndiva Kofele-Kale, (1995), ''*Patrimonicide: The International Economic Crime of indigenous Spoliation*'', Vand Journal of Transnational Law, Vol. 28, P. 57. (He indicates that for those Countries ''that have been victims of looking on a massive scale, indigenous spoliation has become the single most important obstacle to economic development'').

[13]Reisman, W.M., (1990), ''*Sovereignty and Human Rights in Contemporary International Law*'', American Journal of International Law, Vol. 84, P. 866.

deserves even a higher level of condemnation that foreign spoliators deserved. This is evidenced by the resource curse concept. To turn the hand of the clock on the current state of affairs means that a proper interpretation of instruments has to be made in relation to the question of who owns natural resources between the government and the citizens[14]. In line with this, this chapter asserts that the right to permanent sovereignty over natural resources is vested in peoples, not states, and that the term ''peoples'' should be used to mean the owners of natural resources. Consequently, government which should play a sovereign role should be considered as a mere trustee. However, this may not be the solution because holding that the resources belong to the people is one thing and ensuring that the government acts as a faithful trustees and competent managers of these resources is an entirely different and much more a difficult matter to handle.

To date, no legal definition of the term natural resources has been agreed upon. Depending on the field of expertise, it's possible to identify several methods. For example, a geological scientist will define natural resources as any material phenomena of nature freely given to man and his activities, the elements of land, air and sea associated with such, as well as their means of use for human beings, and an economist will depart from similar elements, however focusing on their economic value for man[15]. Other scholars choose to create categories, differentiating between natural resources (as stemming from nature), manmade resources (created by mankind), and induced resources (the result of natural resources used by mankind in example agriculture)[16].

A wide understanding of the term can include climate, population, cultural, intellectual, technological and economic resources as well as non-extractive industries. However, from a practical point of view and drawing from international treaties which contain definitions of resources within their scope of application, natural resources in general consist of natural occurrences of nature, such as oil, gas, minerals, fresh water, oceans, seas, air, forest, soils, genetic material and other biotic components of ecosystem with actual or potential use or value for humanity[17]. Furthermore, as the principle of PSNR is based upon

---

[14]Infra, discussion on PSNR, State or People Centred.

[15]Ginsburg, N., (1957), ''*Natural Resources and Economic Development*'', Annals of the Association of American Geographers, Vol. 47, N°. 3, P. 204; Skinner, B.J., (1979), ''*Earth Resources*'', Proceedings of the National Academy of Sciences of the United States of America, Vol. 76. N°. 9, P. 4213.

[16]Husch, B., (1987), ''*Guidelines for Forest Policy Formulation*'', FAO Forestry Paper N°. 81, P. 51.

[17]Art.2, Convention on Biological Diversity, June 5, 1992, 1992, 1760 UNTS 79; Art 77(4), United Nations Convention on the Law of the Sea, December 10, 1982, 1988 UNTS 3.

territorial Sovereignty, it can be assumed that the term includes natural resources found not only on the surface of the earth or on the sea bed but also located below and above it[18].

Nevertheless, due to the vastness of activities and divers management issues connected therewith, the regulation of natural resources is fragmented by location, exploitation methods and overall aim. Thus, no exhaustive definition of natural resources is listed within one instrument.

Historical genesis and evolution of PSNR

The concept of PSNR entered the international legal lexicon close to fifty years ago. Its genesis has been traced to General Assembly Resolution 626 (VII) of December 21, 1952 entitled, Right to Exploit Freely Natural Wealth and Resources.[19] However, the most significant expression of the principle is contained in General Assembly Resolution 1803 (XVII) of 1962 which declares that both people and nations have a right to exercise sovereignty over natural resources.[20]Indeed, the controversy over the legal status of PSNR dates as far back as the negotiation stages of earlier resolutions on the subject. [21] One very important question which the landmark Resolution 1803 did not address was the issue of who actually has the right over natural resources, the people or the State. This led to doubts being cast on the legal validity of the concept of PSNR. Kofele-Kale[22] advanced that the reason for doubting the validity of the concept as a legal principle was the difficulty of ascertaining who or what the concept relates to. This was definitely so because, quite an important notion – peoples – which is used in the concept, gives room to a variety of definitions. A

---

[18]Commission on Human Rights: ''Prevention of Discrimination and Protection of Indigenous Peoples, Indigenous Peoples' Permanent Sovereignty over Natural Resources, Final report of the Special Rapporteur, Erica-Irene A. Daes, July 12, 2004, Annex 11, P. 11 Para. 11, UN Doc. E/CN.4/Sub.2/2004/301/Add.1

[19] G.A. Res. 626 (VII), U.N. Doc.A/2361 (Dec. 21, 1952); See also Ian Brownlie, (2003), Principles of Public International Law, 6th ed., P. 30.

[20]G.A. Res. 1803 (XVII), U.N. Doc.A/5217 (Dec. 14, 1962). For an excellent discussion of the origins of the Resolution, see Karol N. G.,(1964), "Permanent Sovereignty Over Natural Resources: An Analytical Review of the United Nations Declaration and Its Genesis", 13 ICLQ, P. 398. Shortly after its passing, the Resolution was described as "the capstone of more than ten years of consideration of the subject by the General Assembly, the Human Rights Commission, the Economic and Social Council and a special Commission on Permanent Sovereignty over Natural Resources.", Stephen Schwebel, M., (1963), "The Story of the U.N.'s Declaration on Permanent Sovereignty over Natural Resources", Vol. 49, A.B.A.J, P. 463. Resolution 1803 was adopted with the objective of "determining the nature of the right of permanent sovereignty over natural resources, the manner in which the right should be exercised and what measures should be taken into account in accordance with international law." Lorne Clark, M., (1977) , "International Law and Natural Resources", Vol. 4, Syracuse J. Int'l L. & Com. P. 377.

[21]O'Keefe, P.J., (1974), "*The United Nations and Permanent Sovereignty Over Natural Resources*", Vol. 8, J. World Trade L. P.56.

[22] Kofele-Kale, (1964), Op.Cit., P.40.

definition of "peoples" is necessary to provide some understanding. In doing so, the dominant theories of treaty interpretation will be used so as to demonstrate that the right to PSNR is a peoples'/ Local Communities right, and that the definition of peoples contemplated in relevant international texts is one that encompasses all of the population.

1.3 Interpreting ambiguity: methodologies for deciphering PSNR

The concept of PSNR is mentioned in resolutions of the UN General Assembly,[23] and also in international conventions or treaties.[24] What is common to these United Nations resolutions and international conventions is the fact that all of the provisions are susceptible to a variety of interpretations.[25] For the purpose of this chapter, the intentions of the drafters of these various provisions have to be clarified so as to get rid of any vagueness or ambiguity that characterizes the instruments.

Over the years, a number of rules for the interpretation of treaties have emerged, prominent[26] among them is the Vienna Convention on the Law of Treaties (Vienna Convention).[27] This convention is believed

[23]UN General Assembly Resolutions on Permanent Sovereignty over Natural Resources (PSNR) in addition to those already mentioned include: Charter of Economic Rights and Duties of States, G.A. Res. 3281 (XXIX), art. 2, U.N. Doc. A/9631 (Dec. 12, 1974) ("Every State has and shall freely exercise fully Permanent Sovereignty, including possession, use and disposal, over all its wealth, Natural Resources and Economic Activity."); Declaration on the Establishment of a New Economic Order, G.A. Res. 3201 (S-VI), P 4(e), U.N. Doc. A/9559 (May 1, 1974) (providing for "full Permanent Sovereignty of every State over its Natural Resources and all economic activities"); Permanent Sovereignty over Natural Resources, G.A. Res 3171 (XXVIII), U.N. Doc.A/9030 (Dec. 17, 1973).

[24]Example, European Energy Charter Conference, Energy Charter Treaty, Dec. 17, 1994, 34 I.L.M. 360, 394 (1995); United Nations Convention on the Law of the Sea arts. 56, 93, Nov. 16, 1994, 1833 U.N.T.S. 397 (announcing that "in the exclusive economic zone, the coastal State has Sovereign rights for the purposes of exploring and exploiting, conserving and managing the natural resources" and providing for the "sovereign right of States to exploit their natural resources"); United Nations Framework Convention on Climate Change, Mar. 21, 1994, 1771 U.N.T.S. 107; United Nations Convention on Biological Diversity, June 5, 1992, 31 I.L.M. 818; Vienna Convention on Succession of States in Respect of State Property, Archives, and Debts art.38.2, U.N. Doc. A/CONF.117/14 (Apr. 7, 1983), reprinted in 22 I.L.M. 306 (1983); Organization of African Unity: Banjul Charter on Human and Peoples' Rights, OAU Doc. CAB/LEG/67/3 rev. 5, (Jan. 7-19, 1981), reprinted in 21 I.L.M. 58 (1982); Vienna Convention on Succession of States in Respect of Treaties art. 13, U.N. Doc A/CONF.80/31 (Aug. 22, 1978), reprinted in 17 I.L.M. 1488 (1978) (affirming permanent sovereignty over natural wealth and resources); International Covenant on Civil and Political Rights, G.A. Res. 2200 (XXI), arts.1(2), 47, U.N. Doc. A/6316 (Dec. 19, 1966), reprinted in 6 I.L.M. 368 (1967) (protecting people's right to utilze their natural wealth and resources to their fullest extent); International Covenant on Economic, Social and Cultural Rights, G.A. Res. 2200 (XXI), arts. 1(2), 11(2)(a), 25, U.N. Doc. A/6316 (Dec. 19, 1966), reprinted in 6 I.L.M. 360 (1967) (protecting people's right to dispose of their natural wealth and resources freely).

[25] Anghie, A., (1993), "*The Heart of My Home: Colonialism, Environmental Damage, and the Nauru Case", Vol. 34, Harv. Int'l L.J., P. 445.* (Noting the lack of clarity in the language of the instruments espousing the principle of PSNR, particularly the content of the right and the meaning of the term "Peoples," leaving them open to several conflicting interpretations).

[26]Mark Kadish, J., (1997),"*Article 36 of the Vienna Convention on Consular Relations: A Search for the Right to Consul"*, Vol. 18 Mich. J. Int'l L. P 565. (Stating that the Vienna Convention on the Law of Treaties governs the interpretation of Treaties).

[27] Vienna Convention on the Law of Treaties arts. 31-33, May 23, 1969, 1155 U.N.T.S. 331, 340.

by many to represent a codification of customary international law on treaty interpretation.[28] By virtue of the Vienna Convention, the most important way of determining meaning from a treaty provision is through a textual interpretation.[29] This method of interpretation could be justified on the ground that the drafters of the text may no longer be available to be interviewed or consulted. In this connection, it is necessary to examine the legislative history of the text. This is what may be referred to as the *travaux preparatoires*. The essence of this effort is to determine the intention of the treaty framer so as to avoid ambiguity. Some scholars have even gone further to suggest that the Vienna Convention does not necessarily require that an ambiguity be discovered before the preparatory texts are examined.[30] According to them, the *travaux preparatoires* or legislative history should be examined simultaneously with the corresponding text as well as other materials.[31] Laurence R. Helfer and Anne-Marie Slaughter (1997),[32] pointed out that it is common practice in international law to resolve potentially troublesome questions of textual interpretation by reference to a treaty's object and purpose. They say that:

> *Treaties should be interpreted in good faith and in accordance with the ordinary meaning of the terms in pertinent provisions, keeping in view the object, purpose, and the overall text of the treaty.*

Apart from the method of interpretation contained in the Vienna Convention, other interpretative methods are substantially similar. For example, Mark Villigier[33] identifies at least five methods of treaty interpretation whose origins long preceded the Vienna Convention and which were considered by the International Law Commission in drafting the Vienna Convention's interpretative scheme contained in Articles 31 and 32. The methods highlighted include: textual interpretation, which concentrates entirely on the text of the treaty;

---

[28]Some Scholars dispute the assertion that the Vienna Convention codifies customary international law on treaty interpretation. See e.g, Philip Nichols, M.,(l996), "*GATT Doctrine*", Vol., 36, Va. J. Int'l L., P. 379. (Stating that "whether the interpretive method suggested by the Vienna Convention has become customary is debatable" and citing to the conclusion of another scholar that Articles 31 and 32 of the Vienna Convention constitute an innovative scheme that does not represent a codification of custom).

[29]Vienna Convention on the Law of Treaties, Op,Cit, 1155 U.N.T.S. at 340, art. 31.

[30] Michael Straubel, S., (1994), "*Textualism, Contextualism and the Scientific Method in Treaty Interpretation: How Do We Find the Shared Intent of the Parties?*", Vol. 23, Wayne L. Rev. P. 1191.

[31] Ibid.

[32] (1997), "*Toward a Theory of Effective Supranational Adjudication*", Vol. 107, Yale L.J., P. 273. See also Pemmaraju Sreenivasa Rao, (2004), "Multiple International Judicial Forums: A Reflection of the Growing Strength of International Law or Its Fragmentation?", Vol. 25, Mich. J. Int'l L. P 929.

[33]Mark Villigier,(1985), "*Customary International Law and Treaties*", London, Blackwell Publishing, P. 327.

subjective interpretation, which often utilizes extrinsic material other than the travaux préparatoires; contextual interpretation, which seeks to locate the treaty text within a wider context; teleological interpretation, which goes beyond the text in order to achieve the treaty's goals; and logical interpretation, which utilizes reasoning and abstract legal principles.[34] It is important to bear in mind that in the interpretation of a treaty, one should consider not only the particular treaty's context, but also the wider context of conventional or customary international law.

With the foregoing in mind, this chapter now proceeds to interpret the provisions of international instruments on the PSNR with a view to determining the scope of the principles' application. This will assist in determining whether the hard minerals with which Cameroon is endowed, belongs to the State or to the people of Cameroon. The treaty interpretation shall be based on the text of the treaty and attention shall also be paid to the objective or purpose of the treaty.

1.4 The core contention: Is PSNR a right of the state or the people?

An omission which has already been pointed out in Resolution 1803 is the fact that it is not clear as to who possesses the right of permanent sovereignty over natural resources, as between the State and the people. Going by this resolution therefore, it is not clear whether hard mineral in Cameroon belongs to the State or to Cameroonians. This lacuna gives room for questioning the legal validity of the principle of PSNR. More important is how this omission affects full and proper enjoyment of PSNR. A threefold interpretation has emerged regarding the scope of the concept and the bearers of the right of permanent sovereignty over natural resources. The right to PSNR has been viewed alternatively as a right vested exclusively on peoples, solely in states (or nations), or jointly in peoples and states. Does the right to hard minerals belong to Cameroonians / Local Communities, to the State or jointly to Cameroonians/ Local Communities and the State?

Cameroon's national legislation[35] arrogates the right of natural resources generally to the State. However, this right is a right of sovereignty rather than a right of ownership *stricto senso*. This is in consonance with international law as evidenced by the hierarchy of norms provided for by Article 45 of the 1996 Constitution of Cameroon. The concept of ownership entails the right to enjoy, manage and dispose

[34]Philip Nichols, M., (1996) "*Corruption in the World Trade Organization: Discerning the Limits of the World Trade Organization's Authority*", Vol. 28 N.Y.U. J. Int'l & Pol., P. 711.

[35] See generally the preamble of the 1996 Constitution.

of property in a manner deemed necessary. Going by the methods of interpreting texts examined above, it is clear that this is not the intention of the legislator. Jurists and legal commentators sometimes speak of PSNR as a right of states. Schwebel notes with regard to the 1962 resolution that "much of the resolution consists of an affirmation of the permanent sovereignty of states over their natural wealth and resources".[36] Some observe that because the concept of PSNR emanated from relations between multinational resource extraction corporations and their host states, the right of the state to legislate for the common good in the area of natural resources and national economic activities has become the primary construction given to the principle of permanent sovereignty over natural resources. Judge Skubiszewski, in a dissenting opinion in the *East Timor case*,[37]adverted attention to the issue of each member of the UN respecting every other state's right to permanent sovereignty over natural resources. In the Liamco case, the sole arbitrator, noted that resolutions such as Resolution 1803, "if not a unanimous source of law, are evidence of the recent dominant trend of international opinion concerning the sovereign right of States over their natural resources."[38] As a matter of fact, a good number of international instruments dealing with the subject mention only the state with reference to the right.[39] Some scholars like James Crawford, are hesitant, but nevertheless lean toward the fact that the right is state oriented when he says that it is possible that:

> *The notion of permanent sovereignty ... is equivocal as between a right of peoples and a right of States at the moment, but also suspecting that the question of permanent sovereignty in relation to independent States is a right of States rather than peoples[40].*

Construing this right as vested in the state, is tantamount to saying that the state holds it exclusively and that only the government, as a

[36]Stephen Schwebel, M., (1963), "*The Story of the U.N.'s Declaration on Permanent Sovereignty over Natural Resources*", Vol. 49, A.B.A.J. P. 463. Resolution 1803 was adopted with the objective of "determining the nature of the right of Permanent Sovereignty over Natural Resources, the manner in which the right should be exercised and what measures should be taken into account in accordance with international law." See also Lorne Clark, S., (1977), "*International Law and Natural Resources*", Vol. 4, Syracuse J. Int'l L. & Com., P. 377.

[37]*East Timor (Port. v. Austl.)*, 1995 I.C.J. 90 (June 30).

[38]*Libyan American Oil Co. (LIAMCO) v. Libya*, reprinted in 20 I.L.M. 1, 53 (1981), See also *Klockner v. Cameroon*15 I.L.M. 2, 75 (1970).

[39]For example, the following Treaties consistently vest the right to Permanent Sovereignty in states only: United Nations Convention on Biological Diversity; United Nations Convention on the Law of the Sea, United Nations Framework Convention on Climate Change, and Energy Charter Treaty art. 18.1.

[40]Some Conclusions, in The Rights of Peoples 159, 171 (James Crawford ed., 1988).

representative of the state, can exercise it. It would also mean that the people would be unable to challenge natural resource policies and actions of the government at the national and international levels, even when such policies and actions work against their wishes and aspirations. What is more is that conceiving rights of this type as exclusive to the state implies as a practical matter that all the benefits arising from their exercise would accrue only to the elites while perpetuating socio-economic inequality in the country.[41]

Another way in which the right has been viewed is that it is jointly vested in the state and the peoples. Schrijver once observed that, "Resolution 1803 says that permanent sovereignty over natural resources is a right of nations and peoples."[42] This development is seen as evidence of the progression of international law in this area through the heavy influence of international human rights law. Some claim that the rights of permanent sovereignty and self-determination "can now be understood as being owed both to the state, and to peoples and groups within the state in different forms, notwithstanding that there may have been a time when self-determination and sovereignty over natural resources were seen as being owed exclusively to the state."[43]

The African Charter on Human and Peoples' Rights, a premier treaty on the recognition of peoples' rights,[44] can also be read as vesting rights concerning the exploitation and disposal of natural resources both in the state and the people.[45]A reading of the African Charter shows that the right to wealth and natural resources is guaranteed to both peoples and states. Commenting on this, R. M. D'Sa refers to Article 21 which proclaims that 'all peoples shall freely dispose of their wealth and natural resources.' He also asserts that this right is also given to African States themselves in Article 21(4).[46] Scholars have surmised from the various instruments on the subject that peoples and states, as opposed

[41] Stephen P., (1981), "*Marks, Emerging Human Rights: A New Generation for the 1980s?*", Vol.33, Rutgers L. Rev. P. 435

[42]Schrijver, N., (1997), *Sovereignty over Natural Resources: Balancing Rights and Duties*, United Kingdom, Cambridge University Press, P.311. See also Lorne Clark S., (1977), "*International Law and Natural Resources*", Vol. 4, Syracuse J. Int'L. & Com. P. 377 (Stating that the 1962 Declaration sought to "enshrine the rights of peoples and Nations to Permanent Sovereignty over their Natural Wealth and Resources").

[43] Margot Salomon E., & Ajun Sengupta, (2003), "*The Right to Development: Obligations of States and the Right of Minorities and Indigenous Peoples*", P. 35. Available at http:// www. Minority rights .org / admin / Download /pdf/IP_RTD_SalomonSengupta.pdf (accessed on June 23, 2013).

[44]Julia Swanson, (1991), "*The Emergence of New Rights in the African Charter", Vol. 12, N.Y.L. Sch. J. Int'l & Comp. L., P. 307.*

[45]Richard Kiwanuka N., (1998), *"The Meaning of "People" in the African Charter on Human and Peoples'* Rights", Vol.82, Am J. Int'l L., P. 95.

[46] "*The African Charter on Human and Peoples' Rights: Problems and Prospects for Regional Action*", (1983), Vol.10, Aust. Y.B. Int'l L. P. 118.

to states only, are the holders of this right. By dint of this reasoning therefore, Cameroonians and the state are holders of this right.

This joint vestiture seems to be justified on the basis of the interplay of internal and external factors in matters of economic self-determination. The state acts as an intermediary in dealings with external interests on behalf of the people in a way that is essentially impossible for the people to do themselves. However, Kiwanuka[47] points out the inherent danger in such fusion of rights in places where the interests of the state and the people diverge. He posits that equating states with "peoples" assumes that the interests of the people are adequately represented by their state, a rarity in most developing countries.[48] In consequence, equating peoples and states further strengthens the state and subjects the rights of the people to the whims of whoever controls the political process.

Some writers assume that there is really no difference between the rights of peoples and states' rights. Accordingly, they use the terms interchangeably or move from one to another with no qualms.[49] Professor Oji Umozurike, a former chairman of the African Commission on Human and Peoples' Rights, references the African Charter's recognition of the right of peoples to pursue their economic and social development and immediately adds the authority of state parties to freely dispose of their national wealth and resources for the purpose of strengthening African unity and solidarity.[50] Again, the difficulty with this situation is that it exposes the right of the people to a possible hijack by those in government, which is all too common, in many developing countries.

Some scholars argue, which position is adopted by this researcher, that the Declaration on Permanent Sovereignty over Natural Resources envisages that the right to sovereignty over natural resources belongs to the people or inhabitants of a given country.[51] Dufresne goes ahead to say that, because international law revolves around states, it is quite easier to lose sight of the fact that people hold the right over their natural

---

[47] Kiwanuka, R., (1998), Op.Cit., P. 95.

[48] Ibid. at P. 97.

[49] Example, Greta Gainer, (1983), "*Nationalization: The Dichotomy between Western and Third World Perspectives in International Law*", Vol. 26, How. L.J., P. 1560. ("States' rights to Permanent Sovereignty over Natural Resources emerged in the United Nations General Assembly resolutions. A 1952 resolution declared that 'the right of people freely to use and exploit their natural wealth is inherent in their sovereignty.").

[50] U.O. Umozurike, (1983), "*TheAfrican Charter on Human and Peoples' Rights*", Vol. 77, Am. J. Int'l L., P. 906.

[51] Robert Dufresne, (2004), "*The Opacity of Oil: Oil Corporations, Internal Violence, and International Law*", *Vol. 36, N.Y.U. J. Int'l L. & Pol., P. 356.*

resources. According to him, "this prerogative belongs to the people, not to the state, nor to its governmental authorities. Resolution 1803 and subsequent texts are consistent and clear in making such attribution."[52] The Human Rights Covenants provide additional support for this contention. Article 1(2) of both covenants states:

> *All peoples may, for their own ends, freely dispose of their natural wealth and resources without prejudice to any obligations arising out of international economic cooperation, based upon the principle of mutual benefit and international law. In no case may a people be deprived of its own means of subsistence.*[53]

Some scholars have interpreted the above provisions as vesting natural resources in peoples, not governments. Professor Antonio Cassese forcefully argues that Article 1(2) "is not merely a reaffirmation of the right of every state over its natural resources; it clearly provides that the right over natural wealth belongs to peoples."[54] Former Projects Director for Harvard's Human Rights Programme, Makau Wa Mutua also reads Article 1 of the Human Rights Covenants as making peoples the subjects of rights enumerated therein, viewing this development as "a departure from Western notions that human rights only attach to individuals."[55] Professor Theo van Boven notes that after an initial UN reluctance in the years immediately following World War II, driven by experiences stemming from that war, tovest in peoples the right to freely dispose of natural resources was a deliberate act.[56]

---

[52] Ibid.

[53] The Human Rights Covenants consists of (1) the International Covenant on Civil and Political Rights, G.A. Res. 2200 (XXI), at 52, U.N. Doc. A/6316 (Dec. 19, 1966); and (2) the International Covenant on Economic, Social and Cultural Rights, G.A. Res. 2200 (XXI), at 49, U.N. Doc.A/6316 (Dec. 19, 1966).

[54] Antonio Cassese, *The Self-Determination of Peoples, in The International Bill of Human Rights: The Covenant on Civil and Political Rights*, P. 103. (Louis Henkin ed., 1981) This view, however, has been disputed in the following terms:

> Although the right of free disposal over natural resources and of free determination of the internal political, economic, and social structure are sometimes categorized as peoples' rights (as in Art. 1 Para. 2 of the [Human Rights] Covenants of 1966), it is the state which is the subject of these rights. The concept of permanent sovereignty over natural resources and the non-interference rule, which functions as a correlate to the right to free determination of internal policies, do not enable a people to claim rights from states, but are claimed by states on behalf of peoples against other states.

Kunig, P., The Role of "*Peoples' Rights*" in the African Charter of Human and Peoples' Rights, in New Perspectives and Conceptions of International Law: An Afro-European Dialogue, P. 165, (K. Ginther & W. Benedek eds., 1983).

[55] Makau wa Mutua, (1995), "*The Banjul Charter and the African Cultural Fingerprint: An Evaluation of the Language of Duties", Vol. 35, Va. J. Int'l L. P. 376.*

[56] Ibid.

It can be argued on the basis of Article 21 of The African Charter on Human and Peoples' Rights as Oloka-Onyango[57] has done, that the right belongs to states as well as peoples and may also permit a more flexible reading that confers the right directly on the people without equating the people with states. A credible case may even be made in favour of the fact that the African Commission on Human and Peoples' Rights recently has implicitly adopted this more liberal interpretation.[58]

The people-centred interpretation of the right to PSNR has a strong historical background.[59] Article 1 of the Human Rights Covenants provides that: "The precedent for treating questions of permanent sovereignty over natural resources as rights of peoples, rather than as rights of States, is thus an established one."[60] Moreover, this interpretation is in consonance with the modern trend in international law away from focus on sovereign-state rights and towards an interest in the welfare of the nationals of these states.[61]

However, the views of critics are quite the contrary. Critics have argued first of all that, all relevant legal instruments do not clearly state that PSNR is vested in peoples.[62] The interpretation would have been more defensible if supported by the text of all the resolutions and conventions on PSNR or a considerable majority of them. Secondly, to them, some instruments appear to vest unambiguously the right in states with barely any reference to peoples.[63] In the same light, it could also be reasonably argued that by employing the word "sovereignty" these texts implicitly posit that control of natural resources is vested in states.[64] Also, as stated earlier, even a generous reading of some of the instruments would at best only argue that this is a right that is jointly vested in both states and peoples.

---

[57] Oloka-Onyango, J., (2003), "*Reinforcing Marginalized Rights in an Age of Globalization: International Mechanisms, Non-State Actors, and the Struggle for Peoples' Rights in Africa*", Vol. 18, Am. U. Int'l L. Rev., P. 890. ("Rather than privileging the interests of the State, it is possible to read the article as a direct boost to the rights and interests of peoples within the state, and of the responsibility of the state to those peoples."). Kunig presents a contrary view: For instance, Art.21 Para. 4 indicate clearly that the right to free disposal of wealth and natural resources is to be exercised by states. It is a right for the benefit of the people, and it has to be exercised on behalf of the people, but the only entity which can be the legally active subject is the state.

[58] Ibid. at P. 890.

[59] Crawford, at P. 170 (observing that the right to free disposal of wealth and natural resources "was originally treated as a right of peoples ....").

[60] Crawford, J.,The Rights of Peoples: 'Peoples' or 'Governments'? In The Rights of Peoples, Op.Cit., at P. 63.

[61] Claudio Grossman & Daniel Bradlow D.,(1993), "*Are We Being Propelled Towards a People-Centered Transnational Legal Order?", Vol. 9, Am. U. J. Int'l L & Pol'y, P.1* (Discussing transnational organizations that impinge upon traditional views of territorial sovereignty).

[62] Example, African Charter, (arguably vesting the right in states and peoples (though not peoples exclusively)); Charter of Economic Rights and Duties of States, (referring to states only in the context of PSNR).

[63] Example, The Energy Charter, Op.Cit., P. 232.

[64] Anupam Chander & Madhavi Sunder, (2004), *The Romance of the Public Domain, Vol. 92, Cal. L. Rev., P. 1366.*

There is no gainsaying the fact that some of the instruments speak of the right of peoples or a right of peoples and nations or even a right of states. At a minimum, therefore, the right to permanent sovereignty over natural resources could be viewed as a right belonging to peoples and others also (states). By analogy therefore, if governments are vested with a right, it is not necessary to also vest it in the people they represent. As Professor James Crawford has observed, "any insistence that peoples' rights are vested in governments disqualifies the right in question from being regarded as a peoples' right."[65]These arguments seem to erode completely the hopes of Cameroonians who may want to lay claims as having rights over the minerals found beneath their soil. Perhaps, a cursory look at the historical background of the principle of PSNR may revive the hopes of a people who seemingly see the presence of hard minerals on their land as a curse and its exploitation as a missed opportunity.

Historically, peoples and their wellbeing were at the centre of the formulation of the principle of PSNR. The concept of permanent sovereignty "was conceived as a right of peoples"[66] because the concept was viewed as "the economic corollary of the political and legal call for decolonization and self-determination."[67] There is therefore no denying the fact that the principal objective behind the emergence of PSNR was to prevent the weak or shortsighted leadership from adversely affecting the survival of the country through wide concessionary arrangements.[68] In the 1950s, during some of the earliest debates on sovereignty over natural resources, one state delegation (Saudi Arabia) emphasized that the intention behind including the phrase "means of subsistence" in the draft was to prevent a situation that occurred with much frequency in the 19th Century wherein a weak or penniless government would seriously jeopardize a country's future with its method of granting economic concessions.[69] Governments were therefore to be legally prevented from seriously disturbing the rights or destroying the interests of the people. Interpreting relevant instruments in any way that allows today's national leaders to spoliate their countries' resources with

---

[65]Crawford, (1988), Some Conclusions, Op.Cit., at P. 167, Cited in Philip Alston, Peoples' Rights: Their Rise and Fall, in Peoples' Rights, P. 290 (Philip Alston ed., 2001).

[66]Rudolf Dolzer, "*Permanent Sovereignty over Natural Resources and Economic Decolonization*", (1986), Vol. 7, Hum. Rts. L.J., P. 221.

[67] Ibid.

[68]James Hyde, N., (1956), "*Permanent Sovereignty over Natural Wealth and Resources*", Vol. 50, Am. J. Int'l L., P. 854.

[69] Ibid.

impunity, is tantamount to sinking the very foundation on which the principle of PSNR was laid.

It is apposite to posit that the principle of PSNR has two arms, namely, the sovereignty of states and the self-determination of peoples. Sovereignty is only one aspect of the origin of the principle. Therefore, while sovereignty covers one aspect of the origin, it in no way extinguishes the protection sought for peoples under the other arm of the principle. Furthermore, a state-centered interpretation of the right is sometimes understandable, given that the state can be seen as an exclusive medium through which the rights of the people could be effectively asserted against external interests and the international community.[70] Viewed from that perspective, the state is placed in the position of an agent, having authority to act on behalf of the principal, the entire population. Acting on behalf of the people includes making national policies on natural resource exploitation beneficial to all people. Where the governments act as agent, they act in a subsidiary capacity and not as holders of the right.[71] The government is in a fiduciary relationship vis-a-vis the people, and has to take into consideration all the duties incumbent on an agent in common law

In as much as the principal objective of the principle of PSNR was to deter national leaders from spoliating a country's wealth and resources, the situation apparently has not changed. Professor Nico Schrijver elaborates as follows:

> *This 'etatist' orientation in the evolution, interpretation and application of the principle of permanent sovereignty can well be understood as part of the economic and political emancipation process of developing countries, but equating peoples and States undoubtedly further strengthens the State and subordinates the rights of the people to the whims of those in power. However, a recent tendency can be discerned indicating that the . . . rights of peoples in a non-colonial context are receiving revived attention.... If this tendency is consolidated, the principle of permanent sovereignty will return to its two roots*

[70] Philip Alston, (1985) "*The Shortcomings of a "Garfield the Cat*" Approach to the Right to Development", Vol. 15, Cal. W. Int'l L.J., P. 512 (asserting in reference to the right to development that the state could serve "as the medium through which the rights of individuals are able to be effectively asserted vis-à-vis the international community").

[71] Crawford, (1988), Op.Cit., at P. 167.

[which] would certainly be a laudable development, as it implies that States should be instruments to serve the interests of peoples and not vice versa[72]

On the basis of the foregoing, the people of Cameroon have a right to the hard mineral being exploited from there, and the state is an instrument which has to serve the interest of the people. The need for a return to the original conception of permanent sovereignty cannot be overemphasized. It is simply imperative.

Having shown that the right to permanent sovereignty over natural resources is vested in the peoples of Cameroon, what remains unanswered is whether "peoples" here refers to those living in the areas hosting the hard mineral production activities or it refers to the whole nation. This worry calls for a definition of the concept of "peoples."

1.5 Defining the "people": who constitutes the rightful beneficiary?

No generally accepted definition of what constitutes a "people" exists,[73] though the term clearly has wide latitude and is also used in a wider number of legal instruments. In spite of this concern for peoples and peoples' rights, the term "people" has not been authoritatively defined in any of the instruments that employ it. Moreover, it is not used to convey identical meanings in all these instruments. The African Charter, one of the legal instruments in which the term is used, departs in very significant ways from contemporary multilateral human rights instruments. One of these is the dynamic entrenchment of the concept of "peoples" into international human rights theory, a concept, however, that had long enjoyed some currency in international law.[74] As early as 1790, the decree of the French Constituent Assembly referred to both the rights of man and the rights of peoples.[75] More recently, the term has been liberally invoked "in a number of international instruments on human rights, and General Assembly resolutions, more particularly those dealing with self-determination and permanent sovereignty over natural resources."[76] For example, the Charter of the United Nations was adopted in the name of "We the

---

[72] Schrijver N., (1997), Op.Cit., at P. 370.

[73]Theo van Boven, (1986), "*The Relations Between Peoples' Rights and Human Rights in the African Charter*", Vol. 7 , Hum. Rts. L.J., P. 191.

[74]Virally, (1983), '*Panorama du Droit International Contemporain: Cours Général de Droit International Public*'', 183 Recueil Des Cours , P. 57.

[75]Brownlie, (1985), "*The Rights of Peoples in Modern International Law*", Vol. 9, BULL. AUSTL. SOC'Y LEGAL PHIL., P. 107.

[76]Rembe, N.S., (1985), "*Africa and Regional Protection of Human Rights*" , Human Rights and Development in Africa (C. E. Welch & R. I. Meltzer eds., 1984), at P.122.

Peoples" and it recognized, in Article 1(2), the principle of "self-determination of peoples." Common Article 1 of the 1966 International Human Rights Covenants deals with the right of peoples to self-determination. In July 1976, a group of eminent individuals meeting in Algiers proposed to the world the Universal Declaration on the Rights of Peoples (Algiers Declaration),[77] in which a number of peoples' rights were elaborated. On its part, the Constitution of the Republic of Cameroon talks of "We the peoples".[78]

The intention of this section is to attempt to work out the meaning of the term "people" which national and international instruments deliberately leave undefined "so as not to end up in difficult discussions."[79] It will be argued that its meaning is not consistent in the various instruments, as it is always determined by the context of the particular rights referred to.

The definition and scope of the term "peoples" in international and national instruments leave fertile ground for questions and debates.[80] In the different contexts where "peoples" appear, at least four meanings are possible.[81] "Peoples" can refer to: (1) those under colonial occupation, (2) a portion of the population, especially indigenous peoples, (3) the whole of the population, or (4) a synonym for the state.[82] While each of these interpretations has merit and clearly applies in certain contexts, this chapter asserts that in relation to PSNR, "peoples" is used to encompass a country's whole population.

From the onset, the principle PSNR has always been considered to be a "peoples" right. The question which begs for an answer, is what specific meaning was contemplated at the time PSNR was formulated?

---

[77]For the text, IODC BULL., September 1976, at 47; R. FALK, Human Rights and State Sovereignty 225 (1981). For discussion of the declaration, see Pour un Droit des Peuples: Essais sur la Declaration D'Alger (A. Cassese & F. Jouve eds., 1981); Rigaux, The Algiers Declaration of the Rights of Peoples, in UN Law/Fundamental Rights : Two Topics in International Law 211 (A. Cassese ed. 1979); Falk, The Algiers Declaration of the Rights of People and the Struggle for Human Rights, in R. FALK, supra.

[78]Preamble of the 1996 Constitution of the Republic of Cameroon.

[79]Rapporteur's Report, OAU Doc. CM/1149 (XXXVII), Ann.1, at 4, Para. 13 (1981), *quoted in* N.S. REMBE, *supra* note 1, at 112. This is not the only instance where an international instrument intentionally eschews defining a crucial term. For example, the International Law Commission during its work on the draft Declaration on the Rights and Duties of States declined to define what a state was. The Commission did not believe that any useful purpose would be served by such a definition and preferred to allow the word to be interpreted according to international practice. *See* 1949 Y.B. INT'L L. COMM'N 289;Lachs, *Development and General Trends of International Law in Our Time,* 169 RECUEIL DES COURS 2, 29 (1980 IV).

[80] Daniel Turack, C., (1984), "*The African Charter on Human and Peoples' Rights: Some Preliminary Thoughts",* Vol. 17, Akron L. Rev., P. 379 (raising one such question shortly after the conclusion of the African Charter and indicating that it would spur academic discussions).

[81] See Kiwanuka, (1988), Op.Cit., at P. 80.

[82]Ibid. James Graff A., "Human Rights, Peoples, and the Right to Self-Determination, in Group Rights", P.186, (Judith Baker ed., 1994).

Emeka Duruigbo[83] points out that the term "peoples" was used during deliberations leading to the formulation of the principle to refer to peoples under colonial domination who could not fit into the definition of states or nations. He says that as those peoples acquired independence, it no longer became necessary to refer to peoples in discussing PSNR. According to him, "Peoples" cannot refer to the whole population under a colonial state for the following reasons: First, after 1962 many territories in the world remained under colonial rule such that alien subjugation and domination was still a major fact of life. Dispensing with the term "peoples" on the basis of some countries' independence would have been premature and cannot satisfactorily and conclusively explain the situation[84]. A contemporary interpretation of the term is that it encompasses a whole population (even though the colonial powers created "national" boundaries that had nothing to do with any classic understanding of nationhood) and there are indications that jurisprudence under the African Charter may toe this line.[85] Professor Cassese is emphatic that the term "peoples" contained in the Human Rights Covenants refers to all the inhabitants of a country or territory:

> *Literal as well as more comprehensive interpretation supports the conclusion that the words 'all peoples have the right . . .,' in Article 1 refer to any people irrespective of the international political status of the territory it inhabits. It applies, then, not only to the peoples of territories that have not yet attained political independence, but also to those of independent and sovereign states. This conclusion is borne out by the travaux preparatoires.*[86]

Alexander Kiss, writing about the International Covenant on

---

[83]*Permanent Sovereignty and Peoples Ownership of Natural Resources in International Law*,(2006), Vol. 38 Geo. Wash. Int'l L. Rev., Citing Schrijver, (1997), Op.Cit., at P. 9 (inferring that "the term 'Peoples' was originally meant to refer to those peoples which had not yet been able to exercise their right to political self-determination"). Some Scholars also believe that a more realistic interpretation of "peoples" for purposes of economic self-determination under the African Charter would show that the term is used in reference to exactly the same category of human beings that are entitled to political self-determination, which, in their opinion, are people under colonial rule or alien subjugation. Richard Gittleman, ,(1982), "*The African Charter on Human and Peoples' Rights: A Legal Analysis*", Vol. 22, Va. J. Int'l L.,P. 682.

[84] Ibid.

[85]Ibid. Citing Li-ann Thio, (2002), "Battling Balkanization: Regional Approaches Toward Minority Protection Beyond Europe", Vol. 43 Harv. Int'l L.J., P. 409 -464.(relaying the individual opinions of African Human and Peoples' Rights commissioners who favored the construction that "Peoples" under the African Charter refers to entire populations (or those) previously colonized by European States).

[86]Antonio Cassese, The Self-Determination of Peoples, in The International Bill of Human Rights: The Covenant on Civil and Political Rights, P.103, (Louis Henkin ed., 1981).

Economic, Social and Cultural Rights (ICESCR), states that "the economic resources of a country are to be used in the interest of the population" thereby construing the covenant's reference to "peoples" to apply to the entire population.[87] He adds that "this also includes that a people may not be spoliated of its own means of subsistence for the benefit of a layer of the population."[88]

That the term "peoples" in the context of PSNR refers to the entire population is also grounded in the fact that it is the most plausible, realistic and sustainable position once it is accepted that the right to PSNR is vested in peoples.[89]

As a synonym for states, "peoples" will lose its meaning, subsume the right of peoples in states, and work against the interest of the people. It is hard to argue that the right is vested in peoples while really meaning that it is vested in states. International texts would have stated that the right resides in states instead of making unnecessary circumlocutions.

In addition, there is evidence from the *travaux preparatoires* of the Human Rights Covenants that the use of "peoples" was not an automatic reference to states. In the course of drafting the International Covenant on Economic, Social and Cultural Rights and the International Covenant on Civil and Political Rights in 1955, the United Kingdom suggested that the word "people" necessarily meant sovereign state, but this argument was discountenanced. In contrast, the Chairman of the Working Party from El Salvador used two examples of "people" that did not constitute the sovereign state but were nevertheless intended to come under the Covenants' protection: a "tribe" in Tanganyika (now Tanzania) experiencing land deprivation and forced resettlement of the "people;" and the population of the Island of Nauru whose only source of natural wealth, its phosphates, was being unwisely overexploited

On the strength of the foregoing, it could be safely stated that the term "peoples" for the purpose of this work refers to the entire population of a country. Consequently, the right to PSNR is vested in the entire population of a country, which is the right-holder to the exclusion of all others. By the same strand of reasoning, the use of the term "peoples" in Cameroon refers to the entire population of

[87] Emeka Duruigbo, (1986), Op.Cit., citing Alexander Kiss, "*The Peoples' Right to Self-Determination*", Vol. 7, Hum. Rts. L.J., P. 171.
[88] Ibid.
[89] Ibid.

Cameroon, who therefore are the rightful owners of her hard minerals, entitled to the benefits accruing there from. This is in consonance with the preamble of the Constitution and the Mining Code which declares that the nation shall use its natural resources to improve the lives of its citizens. To operationalize the principle of PSNR, it may be appropriate to examine the ramifications of a people-centered interpretation of the principle for the Cameroon people.

1.6 Implications of a people centered interpretation of PSNR.

A people-centered construction of the principle of PSNR, gives rise to serious implications which call for a discussion. The first implication which apparently seems to be a negative one, is to the effect that a people-centered construction attracts controversy to the notion of peoples' rights.[90] The criticism of this construction coincides with that leveled against group rights to the effect that group rights have the tendency of overshadowing individual rights. The argument here is that peoples' rights pose a threat to individual rights because they are often claimed over or against individuals.[91] In this specific instance, a right of the entire Cameroon people to sovereignty over hard minerals could endanger individual rights by restricting the private property rights of individual landowners on whose land the minerals is found. It may be assumed that the alleged or real tension between individual rights and societal interests which lie at the heart of the ongoing discussion on peoples' rights and human rights finds a special manifestation in the area of natural resources. In many developing countries, the successful exploitation of natural resources is crucial for the development of the general economy; at the same time, it is also clear that the status of private property may directly and fundamentally be affected by rules governing natural resources.[92]

P. Sieghart cautioned as follows:

> *Abstract concepts have, in the past, only too often presented great dangers to the enjoyment by individuals of their human rights and fundamental freedoms. Some of the worst violations of those rights have been perpetrated in the service of some inspiring abstraction,*

[90]Marks, (1988), Op.Cit., at P. 448 ("The concept of rights of peoples is a highly controversial matter in international human rights today.").

[91]Jones P., (1999), "*Human Rights, Group Rights and Peoples' Rights*", Vol. 21 Hum. Rts. Q., P. 81. For further discussion of the concern that group rights can affect individual rights and interests, Douglas Sanders, (1991), "Collective Rights", Vol. 13 Hum. Rts. Q., P. 378.

[92]Rudolf Dolzer, (1986), "*Permanent Sovereignty over Natural Resources and Economic Decolonization*", Vol.7, Hum. Rts. L.J., P. 221.

such as 'the one true faith', 'the nation', 'the State' (including, as a recent example, 'das Reich'), 'the economy' (including 'a strong dollar (or pound)'), and indeed 'the masses'. A 'people' is no less an abstraction than any of these: it cannot in reality consist of anything more than the individuals who compose it. If any of the individual rights and freedoms protected by modern international human rights law ever came to be regarded as subservient to the rights of a 'people' . . . there would be a very real risk that legitimacy might yet again be claimed on such a ground for grave violations of the human rights of individuals.[93]

Professor Peter Jones[94] avers that one of the most common fears is that the rights of a group will be held against or over its own members so that, in ascribing rights to a group, we are simultaneously placing its individual members at the mercy of the group. He goes on to argue that this fear would be without basis, if these rights were viewed from a "collective conception" instead of a "corporate conception." Under the collective conception of group rights, individuals who constitute the group hold the right jointly and the group does not possess any standing separate from the standing of the individual members. Thus, morally, there is no group that has an existence independently of, and that can hold rights against, its own members. This is not necessarily the case under the corporate theory, which arguably makes credible the concern expressed by human rights theorists regarding group rights.[95]

This fear is not entirely baseless, when judged from the old adage which holds that unity is strength. The fear of the aforementioned consequences should not automatically invite an objection to the concept of peoples' rights where there is sufficient reason to believe that recognizing such rights would do more good than harm.[96] It is also contended that individual and people's rights are not necessarily in conflict and can support each other.[97] It can safely be submitted that

[93] The International Law of Human Rights, 1983, at 368

[94]Peter Jones, (1999), "*Human Rights, Group Rights and Peoples' Rights*", Vol.21, Hum. Rts. Q., P. 81. See also Douglas Sanders, (1991), "*Collective Rights*", Vol. 13 Hum. Rts. Q., P. 378.

[95]Ibid.See also Eugene Kamenka, "*Human Rights, Peoples' Rights, in The Rights of Peoples*", at 127, 131-34, ("The rights of peoples can become rights against one's own people. They regularly do. They should not.").

[96] Maleiha Malik, Communal Goods as Human Rights, in Understanding Human Rights, PP. 138 - 166. (Conor Gearty & Adam Tomkins eds., 1996), (expressing support for collective rights because they can be pursued in a manner that does not occasion the erosion of extant commitments to individual rights).

[97] Theo van Boven, (1995), "*Human Rights and Rights of Peoples*", Vol. 6, Eur. J. Int'l L., P. 470.

peoples' rights in general are complementary rather than conflicting. People have become increasingly aware of the fact that some major threats to human dignity are of a collective nature. Individual human rights no longer suffice; collective rights sometimes become a necessity.[98] There may be instances in which no specific individual right is adequate to protect the group interest in question. Here, it is arguable that a new group right must be constructed. In such cases, 'peoples' rights and individual rights are not only complementary but also interdependent[99]

Looking at the other side of the coin, a people-centered construction could forever change the way business is conducted in a country like Cameroon which is endowed with hard mineral resources. Antonio Cassese,[100] posits that this construction could be a tool of empowerment for peoples across the world to demand that the old order change and that their interests be given priority. He further submits that Article 1(2) of the Human Rights Covenants speaks of the rights of peoples to their natural resources, and consequently that sovereign governments are bound to utilize natural resources with the aim of benefiting the whole population.[101]Moreover, a people-centered construction gives the people the opportunity to assert themselves and challenge agreements entered into by the government and the mining companies where the provisions or the application of such contracts are an abuse to human understanding. For example, the Mining Convention between Cameroon and GEOVIC Cameroon PLC, had provisions which were couched in such a way as to override national laws[102]. Such obnoxious provisions could only be challenged by the collective effort of Cameroonians through civil society organizations.[103]

A people-centred construction would also mean, among other things, that mineral exploration and exploitation activities that severely endanger the environment, citizenry, or communities are open to possible censure. The natural consequence of this is that the people (civil society) will have a basis on which to question government action

---

[98]Peter R. Baehr & Koo Vander Wal, Introduction Item: Human Rights as Individual and as Collective Rights, in Human Rights in a Pluralist World: Individuals and Collectivities 33, 36 (Jan Berting et al. eds., 1990);

[99]Gillian Triggs, The Rights of 'Peoples' and Individual Rights: Conflict or Harmony?, in The Rights of Peoples, at P. 144 (discussing the concern that recognition of rights of peoples can trample or derogate from established individual rights).

[100]Antonio Cassese, The Self-Determination of Peoples, in The International Bill of Human Rights: The Covenant on Civil and Political Rights, P.103, (Louis Henkin ed., 1981).

[101] Ibid.

[102]Art.23 and 31 of the Convention.

[103] Dufresne, Op.Cit., at P. 360 – 62, laying the foundation for this reasoning.

in relation to the mining sector as well as the locus standi to confront recalcitrant mining companies. In the same light, Cameroonians will be able to monitor and question the rate at which minerals are exploited because future generations will also depend on it. The people will further be able to monitor and ensure that the government saves out of today's revenue in order to take care of the needs of the unborn.[104] This is to ensure that future generations are not deprived of the minerals through reckless exploitation since it is an exhaustible resource[105].

[104] The situation in Cameroon is not clear because of the Colonial Pact. It is the Colonial Pact that set up the common currency for the Francophone countries, the CFA franc, which demands that each of the fourteen CFA member countries must deposit 65% (plus another 20% for financial liabilities, making the dizziling total of 85%) of their foreign exchange reserves in an "operations Account at the French Treasury in Paris.... If they are in need of extra money, as they always are, they have to borrow from their own 65% in the French Treasury at commercial rates .... Amazingly, the final say on CFA arrangements belong to the French Treasury, which invests the African countries money in its own name on the Paris Bourse (the stock exchange). New African of February 2011, N^O^. 503 P. 13.

[105]The Supreme Court of the Phillipines has expounded the concept of intergenerational responsibility in relation to natural resource exploitation. See ***Oposa v. Sec'yof theDep't of Env't & NaturalRes.***, 33I.L.M. 173, 184 (1994).

CHAPTER TWO
JURISPRUDENTIAL PRECEDENTS: ASSERTING COMMUNITY RIGHTS IN PRACTICE

This case-study will determine how far the principle of PSNR and its corresponding rights have found reflection in practice. This case concern indigenous peoples and their entitlements to lands, territories, and natural resources in the republic of Suriname. It has recently been dealt with by human rights bodies, the committee on the Elimination of Racial Discrimination, the inter-American commission on Human Rights and the Inter-American Court of Human Rights. While the issue is pinding judgement, recommendations made by the other bodies are non-binding. However, the decisions are based on universally applicable standards and therefore can serve as precedents on a global level as well. This case study will serve as a possible method of claiming PSNR by indigenous/local communities, by enjoying a veto right with regard to activities having an effect on one's lands, territories and resources.

2.1 The Example of Suriname in Natural Resources Management

The Republic of Suriname, a Dutch colony until 1975, has a national economy which to a large degree is dependent on the natural resource extraction industry, i.e, mining and logging[106]. During the last 20 years, many concessions and exploration permits have been granted to foreign and national corporations, in most cases without informing, consulting with or participating local communities or tribal peoples. Moreover, their rights to lands and resources in general have received little legal recognition and guarantees[107], as Article 41 of 1987 constitution declares:

> *Natural riches and resources are property of the nation and shall be used to promote economic, social and cultural development. The nation shall have the inalienable right to take complete possession of the natural resources in order to apply them to the needs of*

[106]Committee on the Elimination of Racial Discrimination, concluding observations of the Committee on the elimination of Racial Discrimination- Suriname, May 4, 2004, P. 5.

[107]Free, Prior and Informed Consent: Two cases from Suriname, Forest Peoples Programme, March 2007, FPIC working papers, P. 2. Available at htt: //www. Forestpeoples.org/ documents/ law _hr /fpic_ suriname_ maro07_ eng.pdf. Accessed on August 1, 2014.

the Economic, Social and Cultural development of Suriname[108].

Thus, these circumstances have led to juridicial activities in two cases: firstly, concerning mining activities in the territory of the Kalinia and Lokono People, and secondly, concerning logging in the territory of the Saramaka People.

2.2 The example Kalina and Lokono People of West Suriname

Since 1997, Suriname has been issuing bauxite mining concessions in the territory of the Kalina and Lokono people of West Suriname without informing, consulting or undertaking to obtain their consent in advance. Thus endangering their culture and identities which are inherently linked to their close and spiritual relationship with their lands and resources[109]. While this case currently is still being dealt with at the Inter- American Commission on Human Rights, the committee on the Elimination of Rural Discrimination has issued several statements on the matter.

The committee has found that, firstly, Suriname has failed to respect the rights of local Communities concerned in all sectors of society with regard to employment, education, culture and participation, i.e, their rights to land and resources and their right to be consulted regarding mining concessions[110]. Secondly, Suriname has not adopted an adequate and effective legal framework guaranteeing the aforementioned rights of indigenous/local communities. Thirdly, the committee recognizing the right of the state to PSNR, however, stressed that this shall be exercised in accordance with the rights of indigenous people to:

Possess, develop, control and use their communal lands and to participate in the exploitation, management and conservation of the associated natural resources[111].

Finally, the informal consent of the affected indigenous peoples shall be obtained as far as possible, especially in situations in which the planned resource exploitation and associated activities pose substantial

[108]Art 41 Constitution of Suriname, 1987, with Reforms of 1992, Available at http://www.oas.org/juridico/MLa/en/sur/en_sur_Int-text-const.pdf. Accessed 1/08/2025.

[109]The Kalina and Lokono Peoples-Suriname (Admissibility), Inter-American Commission on Human Rights, Report No. 76/07, petition 198-07, paras, 3-4, 13, 22 (Oct. 15, 2003).

[110]Decision 3(62) Suriname, Committee on the Elimination of racial Discrimination, June 3, 2003, Para 3, UN Doc. CERD/C/62/Dec/3.

[111]Committee on the Elimination of Racial Discrimination, concluding observations on Suriname, Apr. 28, 2004, Para 11, UN doc. Cerd/C/64/Co/9.

threats to the affected indigenous communities[112]. This situation is similar to that of Peru[113]. Thus, the committee on the Elimination of Racial Discrimination has found with regard to information received from the Kalina and Lokono people that several essential rights have crystallized in International Law, which at minimum alter the freedom contained in the principle of PSNR for states by requiring it to be exercised in accordance with the interest of local indigenous peoples.

2.3 The example Twelve Saramaka Clans

After the government of the Republic of Suriname granted logging concessions to operate in the territory which the Saramaka people have traditionally inhabited, without informing, participating or consulting the affected communities in advance, they filed several complaints with the state government, without receiving an answer[114]. Thus, they brought an action to the inter-American commission on Human Rights and in 2006, the Commission adopted report 09/06, in which it found that the right of property, culture integrity and due process of the Saramaka people had been violated, and since no sufficient response was taken by the Suriname authorities, the case was submitted to the Inter-American Court of Human Rights[115].

The commission in particular held that the state, when granting the forestry and mining concessions in the affected territory neither consulted , nor obtained the free and informed consent of the Saramaka people, who as tribal people have a close and spiritual connection with the land, and furthermore are dependent on the woods for their survival[116]. Through substantial analysis the commission declared that the Saramaka people under International Law had a communal ownership right to their land, even if not recognized in legislative measures by the state.

---

[112]Decision 3(66) Suriname, Committee on the Elimination of Racial Discrimination, April 27, 2005, Para 2, UN Doc. CERD/C/DEC/SUR/1; Committee on the Elimination of Racial Discrimination, Concluding observations on Suriname, April 28, 2004, Para 13, UN Doc. CERD/c/64/CO/9; Decision 1/(67) on Suriname, Committee on the Elimination of Racial Discrimination, Nov. 1, 2005, Para.34 (b), UN Doc. CERD/C/DEC/SUR/4.

[113]Merino Jimenez, L., (2008), "*Community Right to Participate in Mining Policies with Reference to Tintaya and Rio Blanco Mining Conflict in Peru.*", Masters of Arts in Development Studies, Institute of Social Studies- the Netherlands, P.15.

[114]Free, Prior and informed Consent: Two cases from Suriname, Forest Peoples Programme, march 2007, FPIC working Papers, PP.7-8, Available at htt: // www. forestpeoples. org/ documents/ law_ hr/fpic_ surname_ Maro7_eng.pdf. Accessed 1//2024.

[115]Application of the Inter-American Court of Human Rights in the case of Twelve Saramaka clans against the republic of Suriname, inter-American Commission on Human Rights, case N° 12.338, Para.11, 69 (June 23, 2006).

[116]Application to the inter-American court of Human Rights in the case of Twelve Saramaka clans against the Republic of Suriname, Inter-American Commission on Human Rights, Case N^{O}. 12.338. Para. 83, 89, 107, 111, 136 (June 23, 2006).

Moreover, while recognizing the right of Suriname to development, the commission stated that such shall occur under the premises of ensuring that local indigenous people are appropriately consulted and consent obtained in cases of natural exploitation and further stated that:

> *In the light of the way international human rights legislation has evolved with respect to the rights of indigenous peoples, that the indigenous people's consent to natural resource exploitation activities on their traditional territories is always required by law*[117].

The Inter-American court of Human Rights passed its judgement on the case in 2007, confirming much of the commission's findings. Firstly, it held that the Saramaka people constitute a tribal people with distinct social, cultural and economic characteristics, and has a close link to their territories[118]. Secondly, it confirmed that Saramaka People possessed a right to their communal territories, and were entitled to its protection, requiring positive state action to ensure the respect for and control over the lands the local communities are entitled to[119].

Finally, the court declared that indigenous and tribal peoples ''have the right to own the natural resources they have traditionally used within their territory''. Necessary for the physical and cultural survival of such entities, the entitlement to ownership and control over natural resources guarantees their protection from extinction[120]. The court also reasoned that the mere right to lose and enjoy their territory would be rendered meaningless if they did not enjoy the same rights with regard to the natural resources located on and within the land.

However, at the time the court held that while it recognised that the granting of logging and mining concessions would affect the rights of the Saramaka people, restrictions of property rights are permissible in limited Circumstances, ie when previously established by law; necessary; proportional; with the aim of achieving a legitimate objective in a democratic society, and when it does not deny the survival of Saramaka people[121]. Furthermore, the court listed three safeguards,

---

[117]Ibid.

[118]Case of the Saramaka People v. Suriname (Prel.Obj., Merits, reparations, and costs), 2007 Inter-Am.ct. H.R., Para. 84-86 (Judgment, Nov. 28).

[119]Ibid. Paras. 96-115.

[120]Case of the Yakye Axa Indigenous Community V. Paraguay (merits, Raparations and Costs), 2005, Inter-American court of Human Rights, paras, 135-136 (judgment, June 17).

[121]Case of the Saramaka People v. Suriname (Prel.obj., Merits, Reparations and costs), 2007 Inter-American Court of Human Rights, Paras. 126-128 (Judgment, Nov. 28)

referring also to Article 32 of the United Nations Declaration on the Rights of Indigenous Peoples: affective participation of the people concerned; inclusion in the distribution of any benefits derived from the planned activity, prior environmental and social impact assessment[122]. Most importantly, the court came to the conclusion that in situations which are linked to:

> *Large-scale development or investment projects within Saramaka territory, the state has a duty, not only to consult with the Saramaka's but also to obtain their free prior and informed consent, according to their customs and traditions[123].*

To conclude, for the Saramaka People to effectively enjoy their rights over their lands and territories, it is necessary that they also are that right-bearers with regard to any natural resources located on and within their areas, and the state in principle is not permitted to interfere with their ownership rights. However, in limited circumstances, the state may claim an own entitlement to PSNR and use the resources for the aim of development. Especially in those instances where this touches upon the subsistence of the affected indigenous peoples though, activities may only be undertaken after obtaining their free, prior, and informed consent.

This judgment therefore carries the rights identified within the reports of the committee on the Elimination of racial Discrimination one step further, providing a future framework for the recognition of the Principle of PSNR not only applicable to states, but also to indigenous/local and tribal peoples and that thus, in decisions concerning natural resources which both entitles claim entitlement to a balancing process is required with both sides possessing a possible veto in instances where their subsistence should otherwise be endangered.

This chapter is by no means arguing that a people-centred construction of the principle of PSNR should erode or undermine state sovereignty. What it seeks to highlight is that, this construction should give people/local communities the opportunity to hold valid claims in international law against the government in relation to the control of

---

[122]See jane Hofbauer, A., (2009), ''*The Principle of Permanent Sovereignty over Natural Resources and its Modern Implications*'', Masters Thesis, University of Iceland, P. 81

[123]Case of the Saramaka People v. Suriname (Prel.Obj., Merits, reparations, and Costs), 2007 Inter-American court of Human Rights, Para. 134 (judgment, Nov. 28); See also Committee on the Elimination of Racial Discrimination, concluding observations of the committee on the Elimination of Racial Discrimination-Ecuador, June 2, 2003, PP. 3-4, Para. 16, UN Doc. CERD/C/62/co/2

mining the industry. It also affords the people a basis to make valid and sustainable claims under national law against mining companies. A pessimist may be tempted to argue that a people-centred construction will have disastrous consequences on the inflow of foreign investments and therefore thwart government's effort in trying to attract foreign capital which itself is a booster for economic development. However, this argument may not hold because in the current state-centred scenario, foreign investments are being attracted through very attractive laws[124], but the supposed economic development is not evident. Consequently, going by the equitable maxim ''he who seeks equity must do equity'', if the government expects development through the inflow of foreign investments and fears that a people –centred interpretation of peoples' rights will deter foreign investments, then she should give the people the expected development. Only then will she have ''equity'' because she has done ''equity''. The point that has been made here is that if the government acts for the benefit of the people, then it can make concessions to MNCS for the purpose of attracting them. It does mean though, that the kind of concessions the government can make will be constrained; but that is essential to the process.

The point which this chapter makes is that a people-centred construction should enable the people or local communities to have the opportunity to hold valid and sustainable claims in national and international law against mining companies and the government with respect to activities in the mining industry. Professor Crawford Commenting in relation to this said that:

> *The key criterion of a peoples' right in this respect must be whether the right avails as against decisions of the government of the territory in which the people live: that is to say, whether governmental decisions on the disposal of natural resources are subject to the principle of domestic jurisdiction, or whether they are on the contrary, subject to international security on the basis that particular decisions are abusive*[125].

Still in relation to this, but writing with reference to self-determination under the African charter, Professor, Li-Ann Thio raises

[124]For example Law N°. 99/013 of 22nd December 1999, Law N°. 2002/004 of 19th April 2002 and their Decrees of Application, etc.

[125]Crawford, J., (ed.,), (1988), *Some Conclusions, in the Rights of Peoples,* Cambridge, P. 171.

the following issue touching on the rights of peoples over their governments:

> *Peoples' could be understood to constitute all the persons within the state, an aggregate of different groups who assert a collect right against their state. The right of self-determination as a continuing right would freely entitle peoples to determine their political status and to pursue socio-economic development, thus empowering an oppressed people against an abusive governing elite by grounding legitimacy in popular will. Distinguishing the 'state' from 'peoples' conforms with a concept of popular sovereignty providing that the right to self-determination is violated where states do not legitimately represent their people, consisting of both majority and minority groups*[126].

Emeka Duruigbo[127] while citingNmehielle[128] rightly explains that although Thio's contention is in connection with the political aspect of self-determination, it seems reasonable to also apply this reasoning to economic self-determination, of which the principle of permanent sovereignty over natural resources is undoubtedly a component. Accordingly, actions not grounded in the 'peoples' interest taken by government, which involve natural resources could be open to challenge as violations of international law. Therefore, in line with Anthony Carty[129] whether the government acts without the consent of the People, or turns out not to have acted in the interest of the people, the principle makes the action of the government subject to subsequent scrutiny.

The equitable maxim which provides that ''where there is a right there is a remedy'' suggests that right holders must be capable of enforcing their rights. Consequently, arguing that Cameroonians have a right to sovereignty over hard mineral resources equally suggests that a duty is attached to some person or entity. In this connection, a cause of action will be both under international Law as well as under domestic legislation. Here, the government or mining companies, as moral

[126]Li-ann Thio, (2002), ''*Battling Balkanization: Regional Approaches Towards Minority Protection Beyond Europe*'', Harvard International Law Journal, Vol. 43, P. 406.

[127]Emeka Duruigbo, (2009), ''*The Global Energy Challenge and Nigeria's Emergence as a Major Gas Power: Promise, Peril or Paradox of Plenty*'', Georgetown International Environmental Law Review, Vol. 21, P. 395.

[128]Nmehielle orlu, O.V., (2001), "*The African Human Rights System. Its Laws, Practice and Institutions,*'' P. 147.

[129]Carty, A., (1992), (ed.), ''*The Third World claim to Economic self-determination: Economic Rights of Peoples: Theoretical Aspects, in the Right to Development in International Law*'' P. 44.

persons, are the bearers of that duty. Also, if people have a right to permanent sovereignty over hard mineral resources, they can equally have a right to development and a healthy environment. As shown by the case-study with regard to Suriname, this takes local communities/ indigenous peoples one step further in creating fair and equitable terms for their relationships with the state[130].

[130]Jane Hofbauer, A., (2009), Op. Cit., P. 84.

CHAPTER THREE
THE UNFULFILLED COVENANT: THE RIGHT TO DEVELOPMENT AND A HEALTHY ENVIRONMENT OF LOCAL COMMUNITIES

The right to development (RTD) and a Healthy Environment has been part of the international debate on human rights for close to forty years. The protection of minorities and indigenous peoples[131] rights have been the preoccupation of national and international bodies today.[132] However, this has not yet entered the practical realm of development planning and implementation in Cameroon. For example, Cameroon has tended to express rhetorical support for this right but neglected its basic precepts in development practice. The purpose of this chapter is to show that the RTD and healthy environment are the rights available to local communities in particular and Cameroonians in general as a result of hard mineral exploitation from their land, and how these rights are being violated. The consequence of the violation of these rights will lead to the absence of sustainable development[133].Economic and social rights, and consequently the right to development and the right to a healthy environment are justiciable rights. Therefore, local communities or any inhabitant of a local community can bring an action in court so as to enforce these rights.

3.1 The evolution of the right to development in international law

In the 1970s and 1980s, the RTD was introduced as one of the several rights belonging to a third ''generation'' of human

---

[131]Today, the term indigenous refers broadly to the living descendants of pre-invasion inhabitants to lands now dominated by others. Indigenous peoples, nations or communities are culturally distinctive group that find themselves engulfed by settler societies born of the forces of empire and conquest. These people are indigenous because their ancestral roots are embedded in the lands in which they live, or would like to live, much more deeply than the roots of more powerful sectors of society living on the same lands or in close proximity. Furthermore, these are peoples to the extent that they comprise distinct communities with a continuity of existence and identity that link them to the communities, tribes, or nations of their ancestral past.

Indigenous people have been deprived of vast land holdings and access to life-sustaining resources, and they have suffered historical forces that have actively suppressed their political and cultural institutions.

International Labour Organization Convention 169 on Indigenous and tribal Peoples of 1989 marked the first significant attempt towards the recognition of the rights of indigenous peoples, but was largely insufficient. This led to the signing of the U.N Declaration on the Rights of Indigenous Peoples (DRIP) of 2007.

[132]See the following; Donfack Sokeng, L., (2001), ''*Le Droit des Minorites et des Peuples Autochtones au Cameroun*'', Ph.D Thesis, Université de Nantes, Titanji Duga, E., (2010), ''*Justiciability of the Right of Indigenous Peoples in Municipal and International Law*'', Ph.D Thesis, University of Yaoundé II-Soa, PP. 1-2

[133]See generally; Nkongho, A.E., (2015), ''*Indigenous Rights in Cameroon and Sustainable Development in an Emerging Economy: A Critical Review*'', African Journal of Social Sciences, Vol. 6, N°. 3, PP. 81-92.

rights.[134]According to this, the first generation consisted of civil and political rights conceived as freedom from state abuse. The second generation consisted of economic, social and cultural rights, including claims made against exploiters and oppressors. The third generation consisted of solidarity rights belonging to peoples and covering global concerns like development, environment, humanitarian assistance, peace, communication and common heritage. The cataloguing of human rights into such neat generation is appealing in its simplicity. A general priority has been given to guaranteeing individual freedom in the eighteenth-century revolutionary struggles of Europe and North America, to advancing social justice in the nineteenth and twentieth century struggles against economic exploitation and to assigning rights and obligations to the principal agents able to advance global public goods in the late twentieth century.[135]

The right to development can be traced back to the 1944 Declaration of Philadelphia, which was incorporated into the ILO constitution of 1946.[136] That Declaration affirmed the following principles: ''All Human beings, irrespective of race, need or sex have the right to pursue both their material well-being and their spiritual development in conditions of freedom and dignity of economic security and equal opportunity. The U.N Charter requires members of the United Nations to promote, as an ensemble, ''higher standards of living full employment and conditions of economic and social progress and development''[137]. The Universal Declaration of Human Rights gives this idea another twist by providing that everyone is entitled to realization, through national effort and international co-operation and in accordance with the organization and resources of each state, of the economic, social and cultural rights indispensable for his dignity and the free development of his personality.'' The Universal Declaration adds: ''everyone is entitled to a social and international order in which the rights and freedoms set forth in the Declaration can be fully realized.'' The right to development also has been connected with the right to life. The argument is that because everyone is entitled to a ''decent life'' and not merely to the right to exist, the realization of

---

[134]Marks, S.P., (1981), ''*Emerging Human Rights: A New generation for the 1980?*'', Rutgers Law review, Vol. 33, P. 52.

[135]Marks, S.P., (2004), ''*The Right to Development: Between Rhetoric and Reality*'', Harvard Human Rights Journal, Vol. 35, P. 137.

[136]International Labour Organization Constitution Annex II (a), at P. 24 (1969). See 9m. Hudson, International Legislation 124 (1950).

[137]UN.Chater.Art 55, Para. a.

economic, social and cultural rights must be essential to an individual's physical and intellectual well-being. As early as 1968, the International Conference on Human Rights pointed out in the Teheran declaration that ''the achievement of lasting progress in the achievement of human rights is dependent upon sound and effective national and international policies of social and economic development.''[138]

The special importance of the right to development was first brought to the consciousness of governments and scholars by Judge Keba M'Baye who was Chief Justice of the Supreme Court of Senegal, and an active member of the UN Commission on Human Right,[139] and later Vice-President of ICJ. In his many writings and speeches since 1972, Judge M'Baye strongly advocated the recognition of the right to development as human right. The right to development he argued, must be a human right, because it is essential to the exercise of other human rights. Due to his influence, UNESCO'S 1978 Declaration on Race and Racial prejudice[140] included the following broad definition of the right to development: ''the right of equal access to the means of personal and collective advancement and fulfilment in a climate of respect for the values of civilizations and cultures, both national and world-wide. After the formal articulation of the RTD in the form of texts using the Human rights terminology in the late twentieth century by Judge M'baye, the UN General Assembly Proclaimed development as a human right in its 1986 Declaration on the right to development.

The 1993 Vienna Declaration and programme of Action called the RTD ''a Universal and inalienable right and an integral part of fundamental human rights''. The RTD has also been given prominence in the mandate of the High Commissioner for Human Rights,[141] and the General Assembly required the High Commissioner to establish ''a new branch whose primary responsibilities would include the promotion and protection of the right to development.'' The right is regularly mentioned in declarations of International conferences and summits and in the annual resolutions of the General Assembly and the Commission on Human Rights.

---

[138] 23 UN GAOR Supp (N^{O}. 41) at.14, 16 (Resolution XVII and XXI) UN Doc. A/Conf. 32/41, (1968)

[139] Judge Keba M'baye, ''*Le Droit au Développement Comme un Droit de L'Homme*'' (The Right to Development as a Human Right), Leçon Inaugurale de la Troisieme session d'enseignement de l'Institut International des Droits de L'Homme (Inaugural Address to the Third Teaching Session of the International Institute of Human Rights) (July 3, 1972), Revue Des Droits De L'Homme (Human Rights Journal, J03, (1972)

[140] Adopted Nov.27. 1978, by the General Conference of the United Nations Educational, Scientific and Cultural organization at its 20th Session, Section 111. C.1.

[141] G.A. Res. 48/141, UN. GAOR, 48th Sess, Supp. N° 49, at 261, UN Doc. A/48/141 (1993).

The United States opposed and was reluctant to recognise the right to development as an international Human Right and voted against its adoption. However, other countries on their part, had a strong basis for decrying the failure of half-century of decolonization and development cooperation to eliminate poverty and achieve the objectives of numerous development strategies. They took the position ''that developing countries continued to face difficulties in participating in the globalization process and that many risked being marginalized and effectively excluded from its benefits.''[142] They therefore stressed the impact of the international trade, access to technology, debt burden and the like on the enjoyment of the RTD.[143] In consequence therefore, developing countries had a breakthrough on April 22, 1998, when the UN, Commission on Human Rights adopted by Consensus, a resolution on the RTD,[144] recommending to the Economic and social Council, the establishment of a follow-up mechanism consisting of an open-ended working group, (OEWG) and an independent Expert. The purpose of the working Group was to monitor and review the progress of the Independent Expert and report back to the Commission.

The independent Expert was to ''present to the working group at each of its sessions, a study on the current state of progress in the implementation of the right to development as a basis for a focussed discussion, taking inter alia, the deliberations and suggestions of the working group''. Dr. Arjun Sengupta, a prominent Indian economist, was appointed independent expert and by 2004 had produced eight reports, while the OEWG had held five sessions. The Independent Expert was replaced by a High-Level Task Force (HLTF) on the implementation of the RTD, which was installed in pursuance of the Commission on Human Rights resolution 2004/7 within the framework of the OEWG under the chairperson of Professor Stephen Marks,[145] the objective of the HLTF is to provide expert support to the OEWG in fulfilling its mandate. The task force is composed of representatives from identified trade, finance and development institutions or organizations and additionally, of five experts from diverse

[142]G.A. Res. 56/150, UN, GAOR, 56th Sess. Supp. N°.49, at 341, UN Doc.A/56/150 (2001).

[143]Ibid.

[144]Commission on Human Rights Res. 72, Un. ESCOR. 44thSes., Supp. N°. 3, at 229, U.N. Doc. E/CN.4/1998/177 (1998).

[145]Professor Stephen Marks is a Francois-Xavier professor of Health and Human Rights at Harvard School of Public Health.

backgrounds with practical experience related to the implementation of the RTD.[146]

The RTD has evolved through various resolutions to the current United Nations Commission on Human Rights resolution 63/179 of 18 December 2008, which was adopted with a striking majority in favour of the right and envisaged the elaboration of a convention envisaged in this resolution, brings to minds the content of the right to development which will be discussed in the section that follows.

3.2 Core components and defining the right to development

The Declaration on the Right to Development (DRTD) is not a very clear document and as a result, the content of the right to development has been the subject of many interpretations. The following components seem to constitute the core content of the right. Most provisions are consistent with current development thinking.

3.3 The phenomenon of Comprehensive Development

The DRTD places the human person at the centre of development. Development is not defined solely in terms of economic growth, but as a ''comprehensive'' and multi-faceted ''process'', with social, cultural and political as well as economic elements.[147]

3.3.1 Ensuring the respect for all Human Rights

The development process should be respectful of all human rights and fundamental freedoms, and helps the realization of rights for all.[148] Failure to observe rights constitutes an obstacle to development. The realisation of the right to development cannot justify violations of human rights.[149]

The DRTD affirms that human rights are indivisible and interdependent. This entails that equal attention should be given to economic, social and cultural rights as to civil and political rights, and that human rights should be addressed in an integrated manner, and not through the separate realization of individual rights. This is consistent with the general affirmation of the equal status to be given to all human rights at the 1993 Vienna World Conference on Human Right which followed the end of the Cold War.

---

[146]Report of the OEWG on the RTD on its fifth session, 18 March 2004, UN Doc. E/CN.4/2004/23, P.16. By virtue of resolution 9/3, of September 2008, the HLTF and the OEWG have a mandate until 2010.

[147]Art. 2(1), 4(2), and 8(1) DRTD.

[148]Art. 1 and 6 DRTD.

[149]Vienna Declaration and Programme of Action (VDPA): ''while development facilitates the enjoyment of all human rights, the lack of development may not be invoked to justify the abridgement of internationally recognised human rights.'' Para 10.

3.3.2 The situation of Participation

The DRTD requires that states and the International Community Formulate appropriate development policies. As the human person is at the centre of development, the processes through which such policies are developed should be participative.[150] The right of women to participate, and the duty of the state to ensure their participation is emphasised[151]

3.3.3The necessity of Social Justice

The DRTD also requires that the development process promote social justice, including the ''fair distribution of the benefits'' of development for individuals[152] and ''equality of opportunity for all'' in access to basic resources and services, and the eradication of all social injustice.[153]

3.3.4 The element of International Co-operation

The realization of the right to development requires not only appropriate national policies but also suitable international conditions for development, with appropriate international policies and co-operation[154]. This requirement also includes the creation of a new International Economic Order[155]as well as International Peace and Security, including disarmament.[156] The nature of the duty to formulate appropriate international development policies and the provision of ''effective International Co-operation'' is one of the most controversial elements of the Declaration on the Right to Development.

3.3.5The Position of Self-Determination

The DRTD establishes that development ''implies the full realisation of the right of peoples to self-determination''.[157] The provision on self-determination have been interpreted by some not just to refer to a reaffirmation of the independence and equality of nations, but also strengthen the rights of persons belonging to minorities and indigenous groups to determine for themselves the processes and forms

---

[150]DRTD Art. 2(3): ''...that aim at the constant improvement of the well-being of the entire population and of all individuals, on the basis of their active, free and meaningful participation in development...'', Art. 1(1): right to individuals and peoples to ''participate in, contribute to and enjoy'' development; the human person as an ''active participant and beneficiary'' of right to development; Article 8(2) encourage ''popular participation''.

[151]DRTD.Art.8: ''Effective measures should be undertaken to ensure that women have an active role in the development process.''.

[152]*Ibid* Art 2(3).

[153]*Ibid*. Art. 8(1).

[154]*Ibid*. Art. 3 and 4.

[155]*Ibid*. Art. 3(3).

[156]I*bid*. Art. 7.

[157]*Ibid*. Art. 1(2).

of development that are appropriate for their cultures and circumstances.[158] Self-determination here means that as a minimum, minorities must enjoy the right to participate in the design and implementation of a genuine sustainable development policy.

From the foregoing, it would be realised that the right to development is more or less a melting-pot of all human rights. But if the core content of the right to development is relatively straight forward, clarifying the nature of the right is more problematic as much as how it relates to the rights of local communities/indigenous peoples.

3.4 Legal standing: from soft law aspiration to justiciable right

International Commitment by governments does not necessarily translate into a legally binding right. The RTD itself is not yet a legally binding concept, but draws its legal foundation from binding human rights Covenants and National Instruments. From a legal point of view, the RTD can be described as ''soft Law'',[159] accepted but not binding. The right to development has been recognised in the international, regional and national legal instruments.

The right to development is guaranteed to local communities based on the UN General Resolution 41/128 of 4th December 1986, on the DRTD that was used as the basis for discussion. Article 1 of the DRTD states:

> 1. *"The right to development is an inalienable human right by virtue of which every human person and all people are entitled to participate in, contribute to, and enjoy economic, social, cultural and political development, in which all human rights and fundamental freedoms can be fully realised.*
> 2. *The human right to development also implies the full realisation of the right of people's self-determination, which includes, subject to relevant provisions of both international conventions on Human Rights to full*

[158]Art.5 states that, as precondition for the right to development, ''states shall take resolute steps to eliminate the massive and flagrant violations of the human rights of peoples and human beings effected by situations such as those resulting from... refusal to recognise the fundamental rights of people to self-determination''. More recently, the 2001 General Assembly Resolution stated: ''Special attention should be given to persons belong to minorities'', A/RES/56/50, Paragraph 16.

[159]This term denotes a group of human rights which have been generally accepted by the world community and reaffirmed in declaration and resolutions by the members of many states, but which have not reached the status of law in those countries.

sovereignty over all other natural wealth and resources".

The Declaration on the Rights of indigenous peoples (DRIP) recognises the right to development as an indigenous People's right. The DRIP states in its preamble that the General Assembly is ''concerned that indigenous Peoples have suffered from historic injustices as a result of inter alia, their colonisation and dispossession of their lands, territories and resources, thus preventing them from exercising, in particular their right to development in accordance with their own needs and interests.''

Article 23 of the DRIP elaborates ''indigenous people have the right to determine and develop priorities and strategies for exercising their right to development. In particular, indigenous people have the right to be actively involved in developing and determining health, housing and other economic and social programmes affecting them and as far as possible, to administer such programmes through their own institutions.''

Even here too, the DRIP jumbles civil and political rights with economic, social and cultural rights.[160] The direct consequence is that it has become increasingly difficult to determine the scope of the right of indigenous/local communities to development as was the case with their right to education.

While the DRIP allows for participation in development, it has often been abused as a way to exploit the natural resources of local/indigenous people in ways that often threaten rather than enhance their survival. This happens to be an ongoing problem facing local/indigenous people. This dilemma is highlighted by the words of Ted Moses, Grand Chief of the Crees when he declared in January 1990:[161]

> *I appeared here in Geneva as an expert with regards to the Global Consultation in the Realisation of the Right to Development as a Human Right. At that time, I said:*

---

[160] Art. 20.

1. Indigenous Peoples/Local Communities have the right to maintain and develop their political, economic and social systems or institutions to be secure in the enjoyment of their own means of subsistence and development, and to engage freely in all their traditional and other economic activities. And Article 21
2. Indigenous peoples/Local Communities have the right without discrimination to the improvement of their economic and social conditions, including, inter alia, in the areas of education, employment, vocational training and retraining, housing, sanitation, health and social security.

[161] Statement to Working Group on the Right to Development; Available at http://www.unpo.org/content/view/214/236/, Para 6 , Accessed 19/08/2024.

I am not against development, but would like you to know that indigenous people know development primarily as victims of development. Our history, particularly the history of indigenous peoples in the western Hemisphere since Columbus, is characterised by the extermination of indigenous People as a direct result of development...Indigenous human rights, the right to life, the right to our own means of subsistence, have historically been denied to us because of development in our lands; forced development that ignored our needs, our economies, our very existence. That is the history of indigenous peoples in the Americas. But it is also contemporary history- it is still going on.

According to some theorist, the impact of globalisation and the actions of trans-national corporations (TNCS) have tended to further exacerbate the problems of indigenous peoples and it has been noted that the TNCS mostly acted in their own solely for profit-motivated interest. Concrete examples of human rights abuses and displacement of indigenous peoples/local communities to make way for development programmes from which they have not benefited can be cited from all round the globe. These are often government- facilitated projects and in several instances are enforced by police or locally hired paramilitaries.

The local communities/indigenous people's caucus made local the following statement with reference to TNCS:

The history of corporate ''development'' in indigenous lands has mostly been of expropriation, destruction and abuses; thus building a legacy of mistrust towards corporations. Acknowledgement of this history and acceptance of responsibility for past actions is a first step towards the recognition and respect for indigenous people by corporations and investors. Corporations are increasingly prepared to endorse voluntary codes of conduct, which are too general to be monitored and lack sanctions. But these same companies have campaigned and worked tirelessly to weaken laws and liberalize regulations protecting indigenous rights and too often avoid their responsibility in actual projects.[162]

The difficulty with the right to development of local communities/ indigenous peoples is best highlighted by the following statements of Ted Moses to the UN working Group on the Right to Development that the right to development should also mean the right to say no to ''development'' He stated:

> *As far as my people are concerned, the debate regarding our right as indigenous/local peoples to control development on our lands is concluded. Those days are over; we are the owners of the land and its resources. We will control development on our lands. And we will consider and judge any denial of our right to development to be ill-founded and defective in law. We will act accordingly.*

One may therefore state that, the right of indigenous /local communities to development is invariably linked to their right to choose the type of development convenient to them and more especially to their right to own and exploit their indigenous lands which as has been demonstrated is the nerve-centre of the existence of the local/indigenous peoples.

With respect to the legal basis or recognition of the right to development in treaty law, several international, regional as well as national instruments have been highlighted as referring directly or indirectly to the right, or even to an element of it.

3.4.1 Recognition in multilateral treaty law.

The 1966 International Convention on Civil and Political Rights (ICCPR),[163] and the 1966 International Covenant on Economic, Social and Cultural Rights (ICESCR),[164] were adopted as an elaboration of the Universal Declaration of Human Rights (UDHR) in two legally binding human rights instruments. In as much as express reference on the right to development is not found in these covenants, implicit reference is found in their common Article 1, which provides in relation to the right to self-determination, that all peoples shall freely pursue their economic, social and cultural development.[165] The Article further

---

[162]*Ibid* at Para 9.

[163]Adopted in New York, 16 December 1996, entry into force 23 March 1976.

[164]ICESCR, adopted in New York, 16 December 1966, entry into force 3 January 1976.

[165]Article 1(1) ICCPR, ICESCR.

provides that "in no case, may a people be deprived of its own means of subsistence". Equally, implicit recognition of the right to development is most glaring in Article 2 and 11 of the ICESCR, dealing with international Cooperation. Article 2(1) provides that:

> *Each state party to the present covenant undertakes to take steps, individually and through international assistance and co-operation, especially economic and technical, to the maximum of its available resources, with a view to achieving progressively the full realization of the rights recognised in the present covenant by all appropriate means, including particularly the adoption of legislative measures.*

On its part, Article 11 on the right to an adequate standard of living provides for the duty "to continuous improvement of the living conditions; as well as recognizing to this effect, the essential importance of international cooperation based on free consent". This clearly shows similarities with the right to development in terms of the gradual character of the provision as well as the importance of international cooperation.

Traces of the right to development are also found in the 1981 convention on the elimination of all forms of Discrimination Against women,[166] the 1989 convention on the Rights of the child,[167] and the 2006 convention on the Rights of persons with Disabilities.

3.4.2. Regional affirmation particularly the African charter.

The concept of the right to development finds implicit recognition in regional instruments like the 1969 American Convention on Human Rights and the 1988 Additional Protocol on economic, social and cultural rights (protocol of San Salvador),[168] and the 1961 European Social Charter.[169] However, the only regional hard law guarantee of the right to development which exist in the realm of international human rights law, is the African Charter on Human and Peoples' Rights[170].

---

[166]Adopted in New York 18 December 1979, entry into force 3 September 1981.

[167]Adopted in New York, 20 November 1989, entry into force 2 September 1990.

[168]Adopted in San Jose, 22 November 1969, entry into force 18 July 1978; Protocol of San Salvador, adopted on 17 November 1988, entry into force 16 November 1999.

[169]Adopted in Turin, 18 October 1961, entry into force, 26 February 1965, revised in Strasbourg, 3 May 1996, entry into force, 1 July 1999.

[170]Adopted in Banjul 1989, entry into force, 21 October 1986. Article 22 of this Charter provides that: (1) All People shall have a right to their economic, social and cultural development with due regard to their freedom and identity and in the equal enjoyment of the common heritage of mankind. (2) States shall have the duty, individually or collectively to ensure the exercise of the right to development.

The express recognition of the right to development by the African charter in Article 22, read in conjunction with Article 21, is a plus for this work which argues that the local communities of Cameroon deserve to have an enhancement in the quality of their lives as a result of the flourishing mining industry.

By recognizing the right to development as belonging to all peoples and encompassing economic, social and cultural aspects and because states have a duty to ensure the exercise of the right to development, it may be said that all peoples have a right to a general satisfactory environment favourable to their development. Although the African charter does not define what development is, the United Nations Development Programme offered a sufficient working definition. It considers development in terms of human development and in turn views and concerns the notion of human development as the creation of ''an environment in which people can develop their full potential and lead productive, creative lives in accordance with their needs and interests''. By analogy therefore, the right to development entails the creation of the stated kind of environment.

3.4.3 Constitutional and legislative guarantees in Cameroon

Under the Cameroon grundnorm, the state resolves to harness all it natural resources in order to ensure the well-being of its citizens and to do it without discrimination of any kind. If these provisions were to be applied to the letter, then the state will not only cater for the well-being of everyone but also raise their living standards. This takes us back to the idea of intra-generational equity, which as we have demonstrated earlier, is one of the cornerstones of sustainable development.

The Cameroonian Constitution[171] has guaranteed the right of access to natural resources for the well-being of every citizen, the raising of living standards and the right to development. This therefore implies that the local communities' right to development is constitutional also and therefore, it can be justiciable.

The Cameroonian mining code in its Article 1(1) also recognises the right of the local communities to development. According to this code, the exploration and exploitation of mineral resources shall have as objective the economic and social development as well as poverty alleviation of the citizens.

[171] 1996 Constitution in its Preambular Paragraph 3.

The development of the local communities has become an obligation on the mining companies operating in Cameroon today. This is due to the fact that mining agreements signed between the state of Cameroon and the mining companies as the case may be, do contain provision imposing obligations on these companies to develop the local communities wherein they are operating. In this light, Article 9 of the mining convention between the state of Cameroon and GEOVIC Cameroon PLC provides that ''within the framework of its mining, GEOVIC shall undertake to build appropriate housing, medical, educational, sports and recreational facilities''. Article 10 (2) of the mining Convention between the state of Cameroon and C& K Mining Inc. is to the effect that; ''C & K mining Inc. Shall provide and finance local communities development program as stipulated under the Environmental and Social management plan geared at ameliorating social and economic conditions of the local communities. This programme shall be discussed upon and executed between C & K mining Inc. and the local population concerned.'' The mining convention between the state of Cameroon and CAM IRON S.A in its Article 29.5(a) states that; "Cam Iron shall implement a specific planning and development program for the East Regions of Cameroon ("South and East Regions Plan'') with the view to managing the social and environmental impact resulting from the project. Although it is primarily the state's responsibility, the implementation of the South and East Regions plan call for the involvement of Cam Iron, as a corporate citizen.

The right to development therefore has been recognised internationally, regionally and nationally. As a result of this, the local communities are entitled to this right as of merit. Our main worry is whether this right to development has been respected by the mining companies in Cameroon? And also are the local communities wherein mineral exploration and exploitation are taking place being develop?

CHAPTER FOUR
THE DEVELOPMENT DEFICIT: MINING'S FAILURE TO FULFILLE ITS PROMISE IN CAMEROON

The Declaration on the right to Development in Article 1 defines such a right as an inalienable human right by virtue of which every human person and all peoples are entitled to participate in, contribute to and enjoy economic, social, cultural and political development in which all human rights and fundamental freedoms can be fully realized. A Development Right therefore is the right that is due to someone to advocate his personality as well as his environment. This is a meaningful right that enhances the achievement of one's purpose in life or a right that ensures ones development. Prof Pat Cahplan[172] defines development to mean: health and wellbeing of all, Education for all, fair rewards for labour and improvement not only of the standard of living but the quality of life. John Shishi is of the opinion that Democracy and Development rights have linked especially in Nigeria.[173] These rights includes full sovereignty over natural resources, self-determination, sovereignty over natural resources, self-determination, popular participation in development, equality of opportunity and the creation of favourable conditions for the enjoyment of other civil, political, social, economic and cultural rights.[174]

The exploitation of the hard mineral creates the illusion of a changed life without work or a life for free. This seems to have been the expectations of local communities but the reality is quite different.

Local communities in particular and Cameroonians in general still live in abject poverty despite mineral resources exploited from their lands. The country still remains with a poor social indicator. A household survey conducted in 2001 showed that 40.2% of the population lived below the poverty line. Mortality rate was also shown to stand at 75.8% per 1000 live births. Road infrastructure is deplorable. For example, the localities of Mobilong, Mbalam, Lomie, Moloundu, Long, Mang and Long of the Eastern Region of Cameroon which is endowed with enormous mineral resources, the roads are near

[172]Prof. Pat Chaplan, ''*The meaning of Development: The example of Mafia Island*''; Lecture given at the New Lizu Hotel Kihndon Mafia Island Tanzania on 11th August 1994, Retrieved from Google on 1/12.2024.

[173]Shishi, J.M., (2012), ''*The Link Between Democracy and Development Right in Nigeria*'', Benue state University Law Journal, Vol. 4, N^{O}. 1, Bellan Press, Makurdi, P. 89.

[174] Morin, J-Y, (1997), *Les Droits Fondamentaux,* Bruylant .Bruxelles, P. 59.

impassable in some seasons. Even if the road net work itself in these localities are bad, the heavy duty trucks of the Mining companies carrying exploitation in these localities contribute to worsen the situation.[175]

An issue worth investigating is whether the mineral industry was not making any contribution to the government budget. The result of the investigation was that the industry makes a huge contribution. For example, in 2011 CIMENCAM paid 250.84457.25 being its usual taxes, ROCAGLIA that same year paid 2.779208 also to the state treasury. Figuil council was expected to receive 41.900757.3FCFA between 2009 and 2011, while the local committees were expected to receive 27.933838.2FCFA as their share of the extraction paid by the two extraction companies operating in Figuil. But it cannot be ascertained that these amounts reached the local councils or the local communities. Following the CelPro Correspondence to the Ministers for Finance, Minister of mines and the minister of Environment on the 13th of March 2012 raising the issue of non transfer of royalties, no response from the competent authorities was received.[176] This simply shows that the government receives taxes from these companies and does not use it for the benefit of the local communities and again 10% and 15% destine for the benefit of local Communities and local council respectively is not respected by the government. The consequence of this is that the local communities will remain undeveloped since they do not have the means.[177] We also gathered from our investigation that C & K mining Inc. for the year 2013 paid to the state treasury as it usual taxes the sum of 72881 187.5FCFA. so if the local Communities wherein mining companies are located does not feel the positive impact of these companies when development is concerned, the reason is simply lack of political commitment of the government and not that these companies do not pay in their taxes to the state coffers.[178] It is important to point out that the mineral industry is directly under the

---

[175]My observation during field study in these localities.

[176]Bissou, M., Bamenjo, J., and Koagne, A., (2014), *Sub National payments and transfer from Quarry exploitation in the locality of Figuil,* RELUFA and Natural Resource Governance Institute, P. 45.

[177]Pursuant to Article 89 of the Cameroon Mining code, Municipal Councils and Communities affected by mining projects have a right to compensation paid out of the ad valorem tax or tax on extraction of quarry mines. In accordance with Article 137(1) of Decree N°. 2002/848/PM of 26 March 2002 laying down detailed rules for the application of law N° 001 of 16 April 2001 on the mining code, 25% of the Ad Valorem tax or tax on extraction is allocated to local councils and local communities where the mining project is located.

[178]Nguiffo, S., and Bamenjo, J., (2014), *Monitoring Local content and Fiscal obligations of Mining Companies in Cameroon: Case of the Diamond Mining project of Cameroon and Korea Mining Incorporation – Mobilong, East Cameroon*, RELUFA and CED, P. 33.

control of the ministry of mines. In this connection, for any company to be allowed to exploit hard minerals in Cameroon, such a company must set up a subsidiary in the country and give 20% of its shares to the government of Cameroon. According to an official of one of the mining companies in Cameroon, [179] if Cameroonians did not benefit from mineral money, it was as a result of the mismanagement. In answer to the question on the contribution of the mineral industry in the enhancement of the standard of living of Cameroonians, the official pointed out that the industry was ''doing a lot; we are trying for example, in the East-region, to have a programme on renovating schools, granting scholarships and providing healthcare.''[180] The official also pointed out that a cooperation project was launched in 2011 referred to as ''*Developpement Durable des Zones riveraines des sites d'exploitation minieres*'' (Sustainable Development in Zones Neighbouring to mineral extraction activities)[181] the project members were: the ministry of Mines, Industry and Technological Development, Ministry of Finance and the Ministry of Territorial Administration and Decentralisation. The aim of this project was to enhance an enjoyment of the right to development. The official was however, unable to access the current status of the project.

From the foregoing, it could be attested that companies exploiting hard mineral resources in Cameroon at least make a contribution to the national treasury, sufficient enough to stimulate an enhancement of the RTD. However, if the benefits do not trickle down to the owners of the mineral resources, then it is as a result of poor governance. Priority is given to other projects. This situation is different from what is obtained in Mali wherein the gold sector contributes a lot to the development of the local communities.[182] The development of the local community can be better achieved by mining companies wherein they operate.[183]

Although the government has the primary responsibility to develop its local communities, mining companies operating in these communities have to make their presence felt positively by the inhabitants of communities wherein they are operating. The reality on

[179]Informal interview of a top official who claimed anonymity in Yaoundé on May 15, 2025. The choice of C & K Mining Inc. was chosen because of its long experience of Mining in Cameroon.

[180]*Ibid.*

[181]*Ibid.*

[182]Mainguy, C., (2010), ''*Natural Resources and Development: The Gold Sector in Mali*'', Journal of Resources Policy, Vol. 36, Elsevier Ltd, P. 131.

[183]Kemp, D., (2010), ''*Mining and Community Development: Problems and Possibilities of local-level Practice*'', Community Development Journal, Vol. 45, N^{O}. 2, Oxford University Press. P. 218

the field is that mining companies in Cameroon do not contribute to local development.[184] During our field study in Kongo village wherein GEOVIC is exploiting Nickel, Cobalt and Manganese, we did discover that the village is still enclaved and the dreams of the villagers shattered. In an interview with the chief of the village in his palace, he was bitter in expressing his disappointment with GEOVIC; ''we do not have electricity, drinking water, and schools. This people (referring to GEOVIC) came here and made promises to us and since then nothing has been realised''. [185] Another inhabitant of Kongo village wherein GEOVIC is exploiting confirmed the disappointment of the chief of the village when he said angrily; ''we were very happy when GEOVIC came here. They did promise us water, electricity and schools and since then nobody is saying anything. The presence of this company has instead worsened situation to us.''[186] According to Adjao Marie; ''GEOVIC look at us as villagers, they do not care about our needs. But however, I remained hopeful and maybe one day things shall change for the better even if we are dead, our children shall benefit from GEOVIC''.[187]

The Baka in this community feel frustrated also with the presence of GEOVIC in their community. This can be affirmed in an interview with Nicolas Yana, an indigene of Baka when he cried out to the researcher that; "When these people (referring to GEOVIC) came here they brought us hats and distributed to us. Our request for the construction of a village school and a health centre were turned down. Our children move for about 2 to 3 km to Moloundou everyday to attend school. We need to go to Moloundou for treatment, sometimes because of the distance; our children and wife die on the way before reaching the hospital. "Nous Sommes [188]abandonnés à nous – meme"(We are abandoned to ourselves)"[189]. Paved roads, improved healthcare facilities, schools, electricity and communication services, agriculture

---

[184] Kouokam, R., ''*Mines et Développement: Vers la Contribution Effective Du Secteur Minier au Développement Local''*, A Paper Presented at the Conference Organized by the Ministry of Mines, Industry and Technological Development and Ametrade on ''Developing Central Africa's Sustainable Mining Sector'', Held at Yaounde Conference Centre, 27-29 May 2015, Bamenjo, J., ''*Mining and Local Development in Cameroon''*, A Paper Presented at the Conference Organized by the Centre of Environment and Development on ''Governance des Ressources Naturelles et droits des Communautés au Cameroun de 1994 à 2014: Bilan et Perspectives!, held at Hôtel Mont Fébé, Yaoundé; 13 to 16 April 2015.

[185] Interview, Djoam Cyprien, Chief of Kongo village, 15/10/2024.

[186] Interview, Gbamine Jacques, Farmer, Kongo village, 15/10/2024.

[187] Interview, Adjao Marie, Farmer, Kongo village, 15/10/2024

[188] My observation on the field, 15 October 2024.

[189] Interview, Nicolas Yana, Kongo Village, 15 October 2024.

and husbandry education and portable water are lacking need to be brought to these people.

The situation is not different in Lolabé village wherein Sinosteel Cam is exploiting Iron Ore on Mount Mamelles. In an interview with the third class chief on whether the company has brought development, he responded as follow; "They have done nothing (referring to Sinosteel Cam), we do not have electricity, we do not have drinking water,… we need these and a pharmacy…"[190].

From the foregoing we can affirm that the right to development in Cameroon has been derived by both the government and mining operators despite the fact that this right is being accorded to local communities by international, regional and national instruments and hence it can be justiciable. One of the key rights of local communities is that to a healthy environment.

4.1 The right to a healthy environment: a prerequite for life and dignity

An era that has witnessed and is witnessing environmental destruction as a result of activities related to mineral exploitation calls for more attention on the right to a healthy environment. That all other human rights depend on this right is not an overstatement, if we consider the fact that the highest right accorded a person-the right to life[191] could become meaningless if the environment in which the person is living has so degraded that the right to life is threatened. The question whether there should be a recognised international human right to a ''healthy environment'', becomes relevant or do people posses only state-created ''environmental rights, which however important, fall short of a standard that is both universal and fundamental in nature as human rights are understood to be? Is it even necessary that a universal right to a healthy environment should exits or are the environmental rights expressed in national laws or found as components of other recognized human rights sufficient? If a human right to a healthy environment exists, what does the phrase ''healthy environment'' encompass? How does it compare to other established international human rights such as freedom from torture or the right to life?[192] Or even the RTD just discussed?

---

[190]Interview, Third class Chief of Lolabé, at Lolabé – Kribi, Tuesday 22 November 2024.

[191]Preamble of the Cameroon Constitution of 1996 as amended by Law N° 2008/001 of 14/4/2008.

[192]These and other fundamental right are contained in example Art.3 and 5 of the Universal Declaration on Human Rights, G.A. Res. 217A, U.N Doc.A/810, at 71 (1948), and Art.6 and Art. 7 of the International Covenant on civil and political Rights, 999 U.N.T.S. (1966).

From 1990, and especially in conjunction with the 1992 UN Conference on Environment and Development, [193] much ink has flowed regarding the acceptance of a right to a healthy environment as a recognised principle of International human rights law.[194]But the universal question was to know when an environmental violation becomes human rights violation. John Lee,[195]proposes that an environmental violation becomes significant enough to become a human right violation when, as a result of a specific way of state action, a degraded environment occurs with either serious health consequences for a specific group of people or a disruption of a people's way of life while agreeing with Lee, this researcher thinks that the definition is not wide enough to cause all those whose actions are capable of causing a degraded environment. He fails to recognised that non state actors like multinational corporations have a potential of carrying out activities capable of degrading the environment. He also fails to recognize the fact that the violation could affect only an individual. According to this research therefore, an environmental violation will be considered to have risen to the status of a human right violation if as a specific course of state or non-state actor's action, a degraded environment occurs with either serious health consequences for an individual or a specific group of people, or a disruption of an individual or peoples way of life.

This section of the work sets out first of all to establish the existence of the right and secondly to demonstrate that individuals have a private right of action. Before developing this argument, it is necessary to have an overview of this right.

4.2. The emergence of an environmental right in international discourse

The environmental movement which began in the late 1960s evolved into the adoption of the Stockholm Declaration on the Human Environment in 1972.[196] While it is not a binding instrument, it

[193]This conference was held in Rio de Janeiro from June 3-14, 1992, and was attended by 178 nations and 100 heads of states. Out of this conference came the Rio Declaration on Environment and Development, U.N. Doc. A/CONF:151/5/rev.1 (1992) [hereinafter Rio Declaration]; the framework Convention on Biological Diversity; U.N.E.P. Doc. Bio. Div. IN7-INCS/4(1992), entered into force December 29, 1993; and Agenda 21, U.N. Doc. A/CONF. 151/26/Rev. 1(1992).

[194]Dinah, S., (1991), ''*Human Right, Environmental Rights, and the Right to Environment,*'' Stan. J. Int'l.L. Vol. 28, P. 103, Hodkova, I; (1991), ''*Is there a right to a Healthy Environment in the International Legal Order?*'', Conn. J. Int'l. L, Vol.7, P. 65.

[195]Lee, J; (2000), ''*The underlying Legal Theory to support a well- defined human right to a healthy Environment as a Principle of Customary International Law.*'', Columbia Journal of Environmental Law, Vol. 25, P. 283.

[196]Declaration of the United Nations Conference on the Human Environment, Preamble U.N. doc. A/CONF. 48/14 (1972), reprinted in 11 I.l.M. 1416 [hereinafter Stockholm Declaration].

references some form of ''environmental right'' in principle 1.[197] The Preamble of the Stockholm Declaration recognized the intimate relationship between environmental protection and the enjoyment of human rights and indeed noted that a healthy environment is necessary for the enjoyment of human rights.[198] Despite this recognition in 1972, the progress towards accepting a human right to a healthy environment has been slow.

The Stockholm Declaration adopted in 1972 recognised the link between environmental protection and human right in several of its provisions. The preamble, for example, states that the natural and man-made environment are essential to his (man's) well-being and to the enjoyment of basic human rights-even the right to life itself.''[199] This is clear recognition of the fact that, to enjoy human rights, a healthy natural and man-made environment is essential, although the formulation does not refer to a healthy or clean environment.[200]

Principle 1 of the Declaration also embodies similar language, although it is generally thought of as falling short of recognizing a right to a clean environment; nor does it embody the right language employed in UN Human Rights Instruments.[201] According to Principle 1:

> *Man has the fundamental right to freedom, equality and adequate conditions of life, in an environment of a quality that permits a life of dignity and well-being and he bears a solemn responsibility to protect and improve the environment for the present and future generations.*[202]

This formulation recognizes the fundamental right of man to freedom, equality and adequate conditions of life and not a right to a healthy environment per se.[203] In other words; it recognizes that an environment of a particular quality is necessary for man to enjoy his fundamental right to freedom, equality and adequate conditions of life. This is different from recognizing an independent right to a clean environment, because it refers also to a political and social environment. This formulation falls within the second distinction made above, namely a healthy environment being necessary to enjoying other

[197]*Ibid* at 1417.
[198]*Ibid.* at 1416.
[199]*Ibid* at 1416.
[200]*Ibid.* at 1416.
[201]*Ibid.* at 1416.
[202]*Ibid.* at 1416.
[203]The use of the word ''man'' here instead of ''person'' has been interpreted as using non right language.

basic human rights. Therefore, the Stockholm Declaration falls short of recognizing an independent fundamental right to a clean environment.

At the time of the Stockholm conference, the United States, which vehemently opposed the inclusion of a similar right twenty years later in the Rio Declaration, proposed the inclusion of a specific right to a clean environment in the Stockholm Declaration.[204] The formulation proposed by the United States reads as follows: "every human being has a right to a healthful and safe environment, including air, water and earth, and to food and other material necessities, all of which should be sufficiently free of contamination and other elements which detract from the health or well-being of man".[205] The conference participants, particularly those from developing countries, however, preferred the indirect formulation in Principle 1. Therefore, the American formulation was rejected.

The next milestone in the evolution of International Environmental Law was the world charter for nature adopted in 1982.[206] This instrument is unique in that it is the first and so far the only of its kind which recognised the rights of nature, distinct from the rights of human beings.[207] Most other instruments recognise the need for environmental protection because of its utility to man, not because it needs protection in its own right. In other words, most instruments approach environmental protection in an anthropocentric manner, while the world charter for nature was the first instrument, albeit non-binding, to adopt an ecocentric approach.[208] As such, it does not embody the right of man in human right parlance. On the contrary, it endorses the right of every form of life "warranting respect regardless of it's worth to man".[209]

Additionally, the world charter for nature embodies certain environmental rights: it provides for the right of all persons to participate in the decision-making process and to "have access to... redress when their environment has suffered damage."[210] It also provides for the Environmental Impact Assessment (EIA) process, which provides access to information and the right to participate in the decision-making process.

[204]Dinah, S; (1992), "*What happened at Rio to Human Rights?,* Y.B. Int'l. L. J, Vol. 75, P. 77.
[205]*Ibid*.
[206]G.A. Res. 37/7, U.N.GAOR, 37th Sess., U.N.Doc.A./RES/37/7 (1982), reprinted in 22 I.L.M. 455.
[207]*Ibid*.At 457.
[208]*Ibid*.
[209]*Ibid* at 456.
[210]*Ibid* at 460.

Next, came the World Commission on Environmental and Development (WCED) which coined the now famous phrase ''sustainable development'' in a bid to reconcile the increasing polarized debate on environmental protection and economic development.[211] There is no doubt that sustainable development is anthropocentric in nature and provides for the rights of present and future generations to develop in a sustainable manner. The draft principle on sustainable development appealed to the report contained a provision on human rights; it provides that ''all human beings have the fundamental right to an environment adequate for their health and well-being.''[212] This formulation is clearly drafted in ''right language'', although the language itself is rather ambiguous and too open. The Report of the legal Expert accepts this when it says that, although this formulation is better than the Stockholm formulation for several reasons, ''the requirement that the environment must be 'adequate for human health and well-being' is extremely vague".[213] It simply provides in principle 1 that ''human beings are at the centre of concerns for sustainable development. They are entitled to a healthy and productive life in harmony with nature.''[214] This formulation was heavily criticized for its manifestly anthropocentric nature,[215] which does not recognize a human right to the healthy environment, even though policy-makers had ample opportunity to do so at the conference. Instead, the Rio Declaration places human beings at the centre of development, and while sustainable development underlies the entire Declaration, there is further recognition of a fundamental right to a clean environment. The debate at the conference suggests that the omission was deliberate and not a mere oversight. Marc Pallemaerts, comparing the Stockholm Declaration with the Rio Declaration states: ''by contrast, the first principle of the Rio Declaration, where it clamors that 'human beings are at the centre of the concerns for sustainable development,' sound like the triumph of a delirious anthropocentrism''.

---

[211]World Commission on Environmental and Development, (1989), ''*Our Common Future;* PP. 4 -5.

[212]Experts Group on Environmental Law of the World Commission and Development, Environmental Protection and Sustainable Development, Legal principles and Recommendations, (R.D. Munro & J.G. Lammers eds., 1987) .

[213] U.N. Conference on Environment and Development: Rio Declaration on Environment and Development, U.N. Doc.A/CONF.151/5/Rev.1 (1992), reprinted in 31 I.L.M. 874.

[214]Ibid.At 876.

[215]Pallemaerts, M., (1996), "*The Future of Environmental Regulation: International Environmental Law in the Age of Sustainable Development: A Critical Assessment of the UNCED* ", Journal of Law and Commence, Vol. 15, P. 642.

4.3. Formal recognition in international, national and regional law

Several International Instruments and judicial decisions recognize the right to a healthy environment as a customary norm.[216] This further illustrates the readiness of the international community to accept an explicit human right to a healthy environment.

4.3.1 International Acknowledgement of the Right to healthy environment

The Stockholm Declaration and the Rio Declaration recognizes the principle of Environmental Protection. Principle 1 of the Stockholm convention holds that a ''a man has the fundamental right to... adequate conditions of life, in an environment of a quality that permits a life of dignity and well-being, and he bears a solemn responsibility to protect and improve the environment for present and future generations.''[217] The Rio Declaration was also an effort to reflect growing international consensus of the importance of environmental protection and exposes the need for state involvement in achieving sustainable development.[218] Although these Declarations are non-binding Law, they may establish a growing opinion Juris towards environmental protection which if coupled with widespread states practice of environmental protection can lead to the development of a new customary international norm. For now, these Declarations simply establish growing principles of environmental protection and states obligation that can be later incorporated into treaties.

Conventions on International humanitarian Law lead to the development of historical norms which recognize the fundamental nature of environmental protection.[219]Protocol 1 of the General Convention bans ''methods or means of warfare which are intended or maybe expected to cause widespread, long-term and severe damage to the natural environment.''[220] A similar provision is mirrored in the 1977 Convention on the prohibition of military or any other hostile use of environmental modification techniques, which prohibit each state from engaging in such techniques ''having widespread, long-lasting or

[216]Berat, L., (1993), ''*Defending the Right to a healthy Environment: Towards a Crime of Genocide in International Law*'' B.U. International Law Journal, Vol. 11, P. 338.

[217]United Nations Conferences on Human Environment, June 3-14, 1972, Stockholm Declaration, P 1, U.N. Doc. A/. CONF.48/14/Rev.1(June 5-16, 1972).

[218]United Nations Conference on Environment and Development, June 3-14 1992, Rio Declaration on Environment and Development, P 7, U.N. Doc. A/CONF. 151/26 (Aug 12 1992).

[219]Hunler, D., (2007), *International Environmental Law and Policy, 3rd* Edition, P. 316.

[220]Protocol Additional to the Geneva Convention relating to the Protection of Victims of International Armed Conflicts (Protocol 1),Art. 35(3), Dec. 12, 1977, 1125 U.N.T.S. 3.

severe effects as the means of destruction, damage or injury to any other state party.''[221] In addition, the 1980 Convention on prohibitations or restrictions on the use of certain conventional weapons which may be deemed to be excessively injurious or to have indiscriminate effect prohibits incendiary attacks on forest and plant cover unless the forest is part of a military objective or the military requires use of natural elements to cover, conceal, or camouflage combatants.[222]

4.3.2 National Appreciation of the Right to a Healthy Environment

National Legislation and Constitution also show Universal Consensus in environmental rights. The Angolan constitution holds that ''All citizens shall have the right to live in a healthy and unpolluted environment,''[223] and the Argentinian Constitution holds that ''All residents enjoy the right to a healthy, balanced environment which is fit for human development...''.[224] Brazil's Constitution holds that ''everyone has the right to an ecological balanced environment, which is a public good for the peoples use and is essential for a healthy life''.[225] Turkey and Portugal have similar provisions for environmental health.[226] South Africa more poignantly established that ''everyone has the right to an environment that is not harmful to their health or well-being.''[227] In Juan Antonio Oposa v. factoran[228], the Philippine Supreme court held that the right to a healthy environment is a basic human right and Lawmakers need not write in the constitution and the fact that it is codified, underscores its importance and requirement of state compliance.[229] In the Cameroonian context, questions relating to the protection of the environment have also taken the form of human right to a healthy environment. This was incorporated into the revised constitution of 1996 and maintained in that of 2008 in the following words: ''every person shall have a right to a healthy environment. The protection of the environment shall be the duty of every citizen. The state shall ensure the protection and improvement of the

---

[221]Convention on the Prohibition of Military or any other hostile use of Environmental modification techniques, art.1.1, Dec. 19, 1976, 31 U.N.S.T. 333, 1108 U.N.T.S. 152.

[222]Convention on Prohibition of Restrictions on the use of certain Conventional Weapons which may be deemed to be excessively injurious or to have indiscriminate effects, art 2 (4), Oct. 10, 1980, 1342 U.N.T.S. 137.

[223]Angolan Constitution [Angl] art.24(1).

[224]Constitucion Argentina [Const.Arg.][Constitution] art. 41.

[225]Constitucao Federal [C.F.] [Constitution] art.225 (Braz.).

[226]Constitution of Turkey [Turk] art.56 provides:"*Everyone has the right to live in a Healthy, balance environment.* ''Id. Constitution of the Portuguese Republic art. 66 provides: ''*Everyone has the right to a healthy and ecological balanced human environment and the duty to defend it.*

[227]South Africa Constitution 1996 CL. 24 (a).

[228] Reprint in 2011 , M.I,53, 1981.

[229]Ibid.

environment.''[230] A question which deserves attention at this juncture is whether the Cameroonian constitution creates an enforceable right or whether the right needs to be embodied in another legislation or decree before providing a right enforceable by Cameroonians against each other and against the state or non-state actors? It is important to point out that the preamble of the constitution of Cameroon is not merely a declaration of aspirations but it is also an integral part of the constitution which creates enforceable rights.

The right to a healthy environment owed to the local communities wherein mineral resources are being exploited has been recognized under the Cameroonian mining code and various mining conventions or agreements entered into between the states and mining companies. The Cameroonian mining code makes it an obligation on the mining companies in Cameroon to respect the laws and regulations relating to environmental protection and management. In this light, the mining companies are called upon to ensure the safety of its workers[231] and local population by using adapted techniques and methods during their operation so as to protect the environment.[232] The mining agreement entered into between the state of Cameroon and GEOVIC provides in its Article 6.1; ''GEOVIC in the course of exercising its activity shall enable to protect the environment and that of the population''. Article 11(4) of the mining agreement between the state of Cameroon and C & K mining Inc. is to the effect that; C & K mining Inc. during the period of exploitation of diamond shall respect the laws and regulations governing environmental protection in Cameroon. The Mbalam Convention on the exploitation of iron ore is not left out when the guarantee of the right of healthy environment to the Cameroonians in general and local population in particular is concerned. In this light, Article 29.1(a) of this convention provides that: ''the parties acknowledge that the protection of the Environment and the issues of safety, health and protection of living beings and local communities are the key elements of the project.''

4.3.3 Regional Link between Human Rights and the Environment

Regional human rights treaties also recognise the right of the local communities to a healthy environment wherein the mining companies

[230]Paragraph 26 of the Preamble of the Constitution.

[231] Ndukong Nforkwe, M., (2015), "*The Protection of the Employer's interest under Cameroonian Labour Legislation*", Masters Thesis, University of Dschang.

[232]Article 85 (New) et seq. of the M.C. See also, Ndukong Nforkwe, M., (2015), OP. Cit., P. 46.

are operating. The first regional instrument to do so was the African charter on Human and Peoples Rights in 1981, which recognized the right of all people to a ''satisfactory environment favourable to their development.''[233] In 1988, the additional Protocol to the American Convention on Human Rights in the area of Economics, social and Cultural Rights, created by the Organization of American states, initiated a right to a healthy environment through the following provision: ''(1) everyone shall have the right to live in a healthy environment and to have access to basic public service and (2) the state parties shall promote the protection, preservation and improvement of the environment.''[234] The protocol also includes states action guidelines, such as requiring states to cooperate at international level and adopt all necessary measure to protect environmental rights, depending on the available resources and degree of development of the state.[235] Moreover, the organization of Economic Cooperation and Development (''OECD) propounded that the right to a healthy environment is a fundamental human right.

Furthermore, regional human rights bodies have successfully filed suits for inadequate environmental conditions[236] although there is no explicit right to a healthy environment in the European Convention on Human Right, the European Court recognizes environmental right under other rights made explicit by the convention, namely the right to life and property.[237]Besides Lopez Ostra v. Spain,[238] the European Court of Human Rights presided over numerous Human Right cases involving environmental harm. For example, in Guerra v. Italy,[239] the European court held that Italy violated the applicant's right to privacy and family life under Article 8 of the European Convention on Human Rights, when Italy failed to protect applicants from the severe environmental pollution imposed upon the town of Manfredonia by the Enichem Agricultural Factory. The court found that the toxic emissions

---

[233]African Charter on Human and Peoples Rights art.24, June 27, 1981, 21 I.L.M. 58.See also; Otto Duclaux, C.M., (2013) ,*Exploitation Forestière et Droits des Populations en Afrique Centrale,* L'Harmattan, Paris, P. 148 .

[234]Additional Protocol to the American Convention on Human Rights in the Area of Economic, Social and Cultural Rights ''Protocol of San Salvador'', art.11, Nov. 17, 1988, O.A.S.T.S. No 69, reprinted in Basic Documents Pertaining to Human Rights in the Inter-American system 79 (San Jose, Costa Rica Secretariat of the Inter-American Court of Human Rights 2003), available at http://www.oas.org/juridico/English/treaties/a-52.html.

[235]Ibid. Art. 1.

[236]Osofstry, H.m., (2005), ''*Learning from Environmental Justice: A New Model for International Environmental Rights*'', Stan. Envtl.L.J. Vol. 24. P.109.

[237]Jennifer, C., (2007),''*Enforcing Environmental Human Rights: Selected Strategies of US N*GOs'', NW.U.J.Int'l Hum.Rts.Vol.6, P. 126.

[238] (1993), ECHR, case no. 41/1993/436/515.

[239]Guerra v. Italy, 26 Eur.Ct.H.R. 211, 228 (1998).

affected the individual's well-being and prevented them from enjoining their manfredonia homes, thereby affecting their private and family lives and giving a private cause of action.

Similarly, the African Commission on Human and Peoples Rights in Social and Economic Rights Action Centre (SERAC) and the Centre for Economic and Social Rights (CESR) v. Nigeria,[240] relying upon inter alia Article 24 of the African Charter on Human and People's Rights, found Nigeria in violation of the right to a satisfactory environment by permitting SHELL corporation to disregard the health and environment of communities when exploiting minerals in Ogoni land. The commission held that the Nigerian government condoned the violation of international environmental standards by (1) providing military support to mineral industry; (2) failing to provide environmental impact studies; and (3) refusing an independent assessment of environmental harm.[241] Although the commission only made non-binding recommendations, the newly enacted African Court on Human and peoples' Rights is authorised to give advisory opinions, order payment of compensation, and can hear cases brought directly by individuals.

In Maya Indigenous Communities of the Toledo District v. Belize,[242] the Inter-American Court of Human Right found that Belize violated the rights of the mayan communities when it permitted the exploitation of natural resources within Mayan lands without the community's informed consent,[243] and permitted mineral exploitation that caused irreversible environmental harm to the land received upon for subsistence by the Mayan communities. While recognizing the states concern for economic growth, the commission held that development activities must be accompanied by appropriate and effective measures to ensure that they do not proceed at the expense of the fundamental rights of persons, who may be particularly and negatively affected, including indigenous communities and the environment upon which they depend for their physical, cultural and

---

[240]Justice C. Nwobike The African Commission on Human and People Rights and the Demystification of Second and Third Generation Rights under the African Charter: Social and Economic Rights Action Centre (SERAC) and the Centre for Economic and social Rights (CESR) v. Nigeria, 1 Afr. Legal stud. 129, 137-38 (2005).

[241]Ibid .

[242]Maya Indigenous Cmtys of the Toledo Dist. V. Belize, case 12.053, Inter-Am. C.H.R., report No40/04, OE/Ser.L/V/II.122, doc. 5 rev. P. 153 (2004), available at htt://www.cidh.org/annualrep/2004 eng/Belize.12053 eng.htm. Accessed on May 6th 2024.

[243]Baker, S.H., (2012), "*Why the IFC's Free, Prior, and Informed Consent policy does not matter (yet) to Indigenous Communities affected by Development Projects*", Wisconsin International Law Journal, Vol. 30, P. 38.

spiritual well-being.[244] The court through this decision indicated its recognition of the connection between human rights and the environment. This same situation is similar to the one faced by the local communities living around the Argentine Andes Mining sites who have been suffering from serious environmental degradation but seems not to know where to find solution.[245]

4.4 Theoretical underpinning: linking environmental health to human right

The right to a healthy environment is a prerequisite for other International human rights, such as the rights to life and health, thereby requiring environmental protection as part of the protection of human rights. In 2001, Klaus Toepfer expressed this notion in his statement to the 57th session of the Commission on Human Rights:

> *Environmental conditions clearly help to determine the extent to which people enjoy basic right to life, health, adequate food and housing and traditional livelihood and culture. It is time to recognize that those who pollute or destroy the natural environment are not just committing a crime against nature, but are violating human rights as well. This, a healthy environment is a precondition for the protection of other inherent rights.*[246]

Various adjudicative bodies affirm the link between environmental harm and the right to life. For example, the United Nations Human Rights Committee recognized this connection in Port Hope Environmental group v. Canada,[247]stating that environmental harm may also violate the right to life in Article 6(1) of the ICCPR. In his opinion in the Gabcikovo-Nagymaros case, judge Weeramantry stated that:

> *The protection of the environment is...a vital part of contemporary human rights doctrine for it is a sine qua non for numerous human rights such as the right to health and the right to life itself. Damage to the*

[244]Ibid.

[245]Wilmarth, C.M., (2012), ''*Mining Megaliths in the Argentine Andes: Where will victims of Environmental Degradation find Justice?*'', William and Mary Environment Law and Policy Review, Vol. 36, PP. 1-30.

[246]Klaus Toepfer is the Former Executive Director of the United Nations Environmental Program. His statement is quoted in press release, United Nations Environment Programme, living in a pollution-free world, a Basic Human Right (Apr. 27, 2001), available at http://www.unep.org/documents , Accessed 6 of May, 2025.

[247]Port Hope Envtl. Group v. Canada, Communication N°. 67/1980, 2nd selected decision of the Human Rights Committee under the optional Protocol 22, UN. Doc.ccpr/c/op/2; U.N Sales N°.E.89.XIV.1(1990).

environment can impair and undermine all the human Rights spoken of in the Universal Declaration and other human Rights instruments[248].

It was said in that case that actual death is not necessary to present a right to life claim in international law. One needs only to show that the environmental present is a grave risk to human life. The Human Rights Committee (''Committee'') in Port-Hope acknowledged that he plaintiff was able to argue a right to life claim based on the threat to life created by toxic waste.

The ideal human right to a healthy environment should be both universal (as a human right it is possessed by all people) and useful (it should be of benefit to those who possess the right),[249] providing a remedy for an environmental violation that is also a human right violation. The right can be useful either indirectly (defined broadly in an idealized form and used solely as a basis or catalyst for national laws which address the environmental situation) or directly (defined as invocable by individual holder of the right).

It has been suggested earlier on at the beginning of this work that an environmental violation is also a human rights violation when ''as a result of a specific course of action, a degraded environment occurs with either serious health consequences for a specific group of people or a disruption of a peoples' way of life. This suggestion can now be seen to finally support the manner in which a right to a healthy environment is developing as a principle of customary international law.

Principle 1 of the Rio Declaration which has set the standard for a pattern of consistent and widespread state practice, provides that ''human beings...are entitled to a healthy and productive life in harmony with nature''. Considering principle 1 in conjunction with the contextual development of a right to a healthy environment, a right to a sustainable and the right of future generations, it follows that effects on health and a continuation of an established way of life are integral component of any right to a healthy environment.

A right that is directly useful in the sense used here must be justiciable. There are four general components as expressed by the European court of human rights that can be used to determine the

[248] Gabakovo – Nagymaros Project (Hug. V. Slovk), 1997.I.C.J.7, 92(Sept.25) (Separate opinion of the Vice President Weeramantry).

[249]For the Universality see the U.D.H.R.

justiciability of a right. These components are of a sufficiently broad nature, so that they should apply to nearly every judicial system of appropriate jurisdiction and therefore provide a common standard of justiciability. In the absence of a multilateral treaty or convention regarding a right to a healthy environment, the development of a right as a principle of customary law can be compared against this standard to judge the direct usefulness of the right.

4.4.1 The Right and individual Recognition

Human rights are not only universal but also individual rights; even in a group context, the individual is the beneficiary of the right. In the context of a right to a healthy environment, the fact that the right benefits individuals is reflected in Principle 1 of the Rio Declaration andmany national constitutions, as well as inseveral national and international court cases.

While all individuals are beneficiaries of the right, determining who among this group can benefit from the right in a particular environmental situation invokes the concept of 'standing'. The concept of standing provides that the individual must show that the challenged conduct has caused him individual "injury in fact."[250] This principle of standing is reflected in *Balmer-Schafroth and Others v. Switzerland,*[251] a European Court of Human Rights case in which the Court stated that applicants had failed to show that the operation of the power station at issue exposed them "personally to a danger that was not only serious but also specific and, above all, imminent."

An important analogy can also be drawn from the concept of "direct effects," as used in the law of the European Union. A provision of Community law is "directly effective" if it creates rights for individuals, and not merely obligations for states, without any legislative action on the part of the states required.[252] A key requirement for a directly effective provision is that of precise definition.[253] While

---

[250] Black's Law Dictionary 590 (Pocket ed. 1996).

[251] *Balmer-Schafroth v. Switzerland* (Application N°. 22110/93) (1998) 25 E.H.R.R. 598, August 26, 1997, Applicants requested that a nuclear power station be closed down because it did not satisfy the applicable technical and safety requirements and was a threat to the region's environment.

[252] Case 26/62, *Van Gend en Loos v. Nederlandse Administratie der Belastingen*, E.C.R. 1 (1963). This landmark decision by the European Court of Justice, described direct effects as "an obligation, ... not qualified by any reservation on the part of states which would make its implementation conditional upon a positive legislative measure enacted under national law."

[253] Case 41/74, *Van Duyn v. Home Office*, E.C.R. 1337 (1974).The Court of Justice, in a case concerning whether art. 48 of the European Economic Community Treaty was directly effective, stated at p. 6, "These provisions impose upon Member States a precise obligation which does not require the adoption of any further measure on the part either of the Community institutions or of the Member States and which leaves them, in relation to its implementation, no discretionary power."

the rights are granted to all individuals in a Member State, the individual must be "individually concerned" by a violation of that right in order to state a claim.[254] This requirement was recently addressed in the context of environmental rights in *Stichting Greenpeace Council (Greenpeace International) and Others v. EC Commission.*[255] In this ECJ case, Greenpeace appealed from a decision by the Court of First Instance declaring Greenpeace's action inadmissible because it was not individually concerned in the controversy.[256] In the appeal, Greenpeace alleged that the Court of First Instance did not take into account the specific nature and character of the "environmental legal interest."[257] Greenpeace argued that because its interest in environmental protection was shared by all Community citizens, requiring that an act which can harm an individual, will effectively bar individuals from challenging Community measures that affect their environmental interests.[258] The construction project was commenced before an environmental impact assessment had been obtained, in violation of Directive 85/337, which had been determined by the Court of Justice to be "of a clear and unconditional nature, thus producing direct effects in the domestic legal order."[259]

The Court in its decision stated that while "environmental protection is one of the fundamental objectives of the Community," this recognition does not confer on a natural or legal person a right or legal interest that is automatically enforceable. It said that this is true regardless of the specific nature of the legal interest in environment protection or the modern developments in international law concerning environmental protection, as exemplified by the Rio Declaration and Agenda 21.

While the Stitching case was concerned with a procedural matter, it is applicable to the issue of justifiability for a right to a healthy environment. A well-defined human right to a healthy environment as a principle of customary international law provides the human right in

[254]Treaty of European Union at art., P.4, "Any natural or legal person may, under the same conditions, institute proceedings against a decision addressed to that person or against a decision which, although... addressed to another person, is of direct or individual concern to the former."

[255]Case C-321/95P, *Stichting Greenpeace Council (Greenpeace International) and Others v E.C. Commission,* 3 C.M.L.R. 1 (1998).

[256]Ibid. at P 1. (Greenpeace brought an action seeking annulment under art. 173 of the TEC, of the decision taken by the Commission to disburse to the Spanish government funds in reimbursement of expenses incurred in the construction of the two power stations on the Canary Islands.).

[257]*Ibid.* at P. 23.

[258]*Ibid.* at P. 24.

[259]*Ibid.*at PP.20- 21.

a universal manner to all people, in essence making it directly effective. But to be useful, the right must also be justiciable. The concepts of standing and "individual concern" are similar in nature, and are linked as a general principle of law with regard to the procedural requirements concerning the justiciability of a right. As illustrated by *Balmer-Schafroth* and *Greenpeace,* the recognized individuals (or group of similarly situated individuals) whose rights have been violated must claim the beneficial remedy, as they alone have suffered the violation. Similarly, the affected group must be limited and definable in order for the right to sustainable development and the rights of future generations to be recognized

4.4.2 The Right and the burden of duty on Recognised group.

At common law, a duty can arise in tort or in contract.[260] For a universal human right to a healthy environment, the duties must arise in tort, as a tort is a breach of a duty the law imposes universally.[261] The duty established by a human right to a healthy environment is narrower than that established by a tort, as the former is limited by the applicability of international and human rights law.[262] Despite its relative narrowness, there is a duty imposed by law to provide a healthy environment. In general, for every duty there is a corresponding right.

In a tort situation, a duty is a legal relationship arising from a standard of care, the violation of which subjects the responsible party to liability.[263] The legal relationship, in the absence of a multilateral treaty or convention, is supplied by customary international law, which binds the states to uphold a right to a healthy environment as a principle of customary law. But there is also a secondary legal relationship between the state and the individual, who would be the possessor of any right to a healthy environment. Under human rights law, the state accepts an obligation to ensure the protection of the rights of the individuals[264] and becomes the "responsible party" or "recognized

---

[260] Garner, B.A., (1999), Op.Cit., P. 455. (a contract is defined as "any legal duty not imposed by the law of tort; esp. a duty created by decree or declaration of a court."). See also Trietel, *The Law of Contract,* 10thEd. London: Sweet and Maxwell, 1999, at P. 1.

[261] Ibid.

[262] In general, international law imposes duties between states, while human rights law imposes a duty upon the state to protect the rights of individuals under its jurisdiction. These duties are not imposed upon individuals.

[263] Ibid.

[264] Donna Gomien et al., Law and Practice of the European Convention for Human Rights and the European Social Charter 17 (1996) (describing the relationship between the State and individual in human rights law).

group" upon whom the duty is imposed.[265] But a secondary party, such as a transnational corporation, could also be a responsible party.[266]

4.4.3. The Link between the Duties and the Right for a Healthy Environment

This component involves a standard of care, the violation of which subjects the responsible party to liability. A case has been made here that the standard for a human right to a healthy environment should be: As a result of a specific course of action; a degraded environment occurs, with either serious health consequences for a specific group of people or a disruption of a people's way of life. The nature of this violation includes causation and liability.

The state or a party (such as a TNC) acting within a legal relationship with the state, should be subject to liability. It is thus proposed that acts of commission and only certain acts of omission by the responsible party should satisfy the causation requirement.

There are two ways an "environmental violation of such serious magnitude so as to be also a breach of one's fundamental human rights" could occur. There can either be a violation on the part of a state of an international obligation, or an internationally lawful activity that acts as the cause of the violation.[267] In general, a state is responsible for any violation of its obligations under international law resulting from action or inaction by the government of the state or any political subdivisions of the state. This responsibility occurs only for official acts, or official inaction when there was a duty to act. A state's duties are the obligations imposed upon it by international law as well as by its own constitution. In general, inaction results when the state fails to carry out

[265]For example, the duty of the state to protect the environment is explicitly recognized in 61 national constitutions. It is also recognized in the European Court of Justice Case *Diego Cali & Figli Srl v. Servizi Ecologici Porto Di Genova SpA (SEPG)*. The court used this case, which involved the competition rules of the TEC, to clarify to what extent protection of the environment constitutes a state responsibility. It stated that based on an analysis of the TEC, as well as princs. 4, 7 and 11 of the Rio Declaration, and Agenda 21, "protection of the environment, particularly when based on prevention, constitutes a public authority activity".

[266]Lugano Convention, June 21, 1993, Europ. T.S. No. 150, ch. III, arts. art. 8, which exempts liability if the responsible party was acting on specific orders of a public authority.

[267]Catherine Tinker, State Responsibility and the Precautionary Principle, in The Precautionary Principle and International Law 58-60, 66-67 (David Freestone et al. eds., 1996). A distinction has been drawn in the Brundtland Report (World Commission on Environment and Development, Our Common Future (1986)) and by the International Law Commission (Report of the International Law Commission on the Work of its Twenty-eighth Session, (1976) 2 Yearbook of the International Law Commission, U.N. Doc.A/CN.4/Ser.A/1976/Add.1 (pt. 2)) for purposes of state responsibility, between violations of international law and acts that are not unlawful under international law. In a comment to art. 21, the Brundtland Report states "The notion of state responsibility must not be confused with the notion of strict liability under international law... While the rules and principles of international law regarding state responsibility ... deal with the occurrence and consequences of internationally wrongful acts, ... strict liability involves the financial accountability of States under international law for the harmful consequences of acts which are not unlawful under international law."

an international obligation to act imposed by agreement or customary law. Similarly, customary international human rights law is violated only if the violation is practiced, encouraged or condoned by the state as official state policy.

A state, therefore, violates an obligation either through commission or omission. Defined as either a neglect of a duty or a failure to do something, omissions can take various forms.[268] One form of omission results when there is a deliberate inaction as a matter of state policy. As seen above, this triggers state responsibility for the inaction. Next, an omission can result due to a measure of uncertainty as to the risk of a violation. Here, while there has been no violation of the obligation, it remains a possibility. Finally, there may be an unintentional omission. This omission results when economic or cultural factors infringe upon a state's ability to address an environmental situation. Both the second and third types of omission may include lawful activity which is responsible for the environmental situation.

The precautionary principle, and its relationship to state responsibility and human rights law, sheds light on the second and third types of omissions. The precautionary principle is an anticipatory response used in situations of uncertainty where a violation has not yet occurred and no harm has been done, but where a strong risk of such a violation exists.[269] A remedy is provided in anticipation of a violation. In human rights situations, the precautionary principle is followed where there is uncertainty in the face of imminent, serious and irreparable harm.[270]

There are two problems with the use of the precautionary principle in a human rights context. First, no one has yet suffered a violation of his or her human rights. However, this absence is not a serious obstacle to the justiciability of a right. The requirement for standing can still be satisfied, as there exist a well-defined group of individuals, who risk a violation of their rights.

Of greater concern is the relationship between the precautionary principle and state or mining responsibility. Before the precautionary principle is used to trigger state and mining responsibility, there must

[268] Garner, B.A., (1999), Op.Cit., P. 455.

[269] Kamminga M, T., The Precautionary Approach in International Human Rights Law: How It Can Benefit the Environment, in The Precautionary Principle and International Law (David Freestone et al., eds., 1996).

[270] Ibid. at 181, 184 (The Human Rights Committee requires the risk to be imminent.).

be a clearly defined legal obligation that the state or mining company has a duty to uphold. Additionally, a question has been asked as to whether there exists a legal obligation to follow the precautionary principle in an environmental context.[271]

Despite these uncertainties, it remains well-established that a well-defined human right to a healthy environment as a principle of customary law is necessary to set a clear standard for state conduct. Acts or omissions that, as a matter of state policy, violate a clearly defined right to a healthy environment would trigger state responsibility. In an uncertain case, only those state omissions that risk imminent and serious violation of the well-defined standard would invoke the precautionary principle and state responsibility. A similar result is obtained in the unintentional omission case, thereby eliminating cases of general inaction due to economic or cultural factors; though general inaction could create an imminent and serious risk. Through this standard, the linkage between the state duties and the right exists.

4.4.4. The Duties Must Be of a Kind that the Court Can Recognize and Enforce.

Duties of the state that have been well-defined through a clear standard, which will eventually constitute part of the right to a healthy environment, should be enforceable in any court of proper jurisdiction as a recognized principle of customary international law.

After discussing the underlying legal support for the right of the local communities to a healthy environment, the question which demand answer is whether a rigorous and narrow definition of this right, to make it useful and justiciable is necessary for Cameroon?

[271]Tinker, C., (1966), Op.Cit., P.67. ("If the first step of establishing the existence of a legal obligation or duty to observe the precautionary principle fails, then it is difficult, if not impossible, to imagine moving to the second step of the state responsibility analysis, that of demonstrating a breach of a legal duty or obligation; ... At this stage the failure of a state to follow the precautionary principle is not an 'internationally-wrongful' act triggering state responsibility for its breach.").

CHAPTER FIVE
PATHWAYS TO REDRESS: THE JUSTICIABILITY OF ECONOMIC, SOCIAL, AND ENVIRONMENTAL RIGHTS

According to Collier J. and Lowe V.,[272] justiciability refers to the focusing of a disagreement or clash of interests into a concrete dispute, capable of resolution by a judicial process on the basis of the law. A dispute will therefore be justiciable if a specific disagreement exists of a kind which can be resolved by the application of rules of law by a judicial process. This section examines justiciability of the rights of local communities to development and to a healthy environment. If such rights are not justiciable, then even the most credible judiciary system will have nothing to offer in that respect. On the other hand, if such rights are justiciable, then focus will be on the credibility, predictability and reliability of the judiciary system in dealing with them. This section argues that economic and social rights, and consequently the right to development and the right to a healthy environment are justiciable rights.

5.1 Legal Preconditions for Adjudicating Rights

For the concept of justiciability to be invoked, certain rules must operate. They include the doctrine of locus standi, the exhaustion of domestic remedies, political questions and the lack of sufficient interest in the subject matter.

5.1.1 The Locus Standi

This refers to the personal element in the adjudication of disputes. It implies that the litigant must have a legal interest in the subject matter of the dispute, which interest must be real and not merely illusory, and that substantial harm has been suffered. This doctrine was clearly articulated by Justice Brandeis in the following words:

> *The court will not pass upon the validity of a statute upon complaint of one who fails to show that he is injured by its operations.... Among the many applications of this rule, none is more striking than the*

---

[272] Collier J, and Lowe., (1999),*The Settlement of Disputes in International Law: Institutions and Procedures,* Oxford University Press, P. 10.

denial of the right to one who lacks a personal or property rights.[273]

The issue of locus standi was raised and discussed in the *Bakweri Lands Claims Committee – BLCC v. Cameroon*[274] where the BLCC filed a complaint under Articles 55, 56 and 58 of the African Charter of Human and Peoples' Rights concerning the violation of the land rights of the Bakweri people. In answer to the complaint, the State of Cameroon argued that the matter be thrown out on grounds inter alia that the BLCC had no locus standi to bring an action on behalf of Bakweri people. The Commission, however, ruled that the BLCC had the locus standi to file the complaint in view of the fact that the council and BLCC had been authorized by a resolution of an assembly of chiefs to do so.

5.1.2 The Exhaustion of Local Remedies

With respect to the admissibility of complaints in international law, the complainant, as a rule, has to exhaust all local remedies available to him before seeking adjudication by an international court or tribunal. This rule according to Brownlie[275] is justified by practical and political considerations and not by any logical necessity flowing from international law. Thus, where a complaint is brought against a State for transgressing the rights of her citizens, the said state ought to be given an opportunity by the complainant to provide redress under her own legal system. If the State is unable to provide the relief sought, then the complaint may then be brought before an international tribunal or court. In *BLCC v . Cameroon,*[276] a complaint was brought directly before the African Commission on Human and Peoples' Rights in disregard of the exhaustion of local remedies rule. The Commission threw the matter out on the ground that Cameroon had not been given the opportunity to provide local remedies. However, the exhaustion of local remedies rule would be said to have been satisfied if the proceedings were unduly and unreasonably delayed.[277] Where a case had been pending on appeal for over five years, it was held by the

---

[273] *Ashwander V. TVA*, 297 U.S. 288 (1936).

[274] The African Commission on Human and Peoples Rights in Communication N°.260/2002.It should be noted that complainants were seeking a declaration from the Government of Cameroon that lands registered in the Imperial German land registers (*Grundbuch*), occupied by CDC since 1947, and defined as Private Property under Cameroon's 1974 Land Law belong to the Bakweri.

[275] Brownlie, (2005), *Principles of Public International Law*, 6th Edition, Oxford University Press, P. 473.

[276] Communication N°. 287/2004.

[277] Ibid.

Commission that it was unduly delayed and consequently, the complainant will not be required to exhaust local remedies.[278]

5.1.3 The situation of a Political Questions Doctrine

This doctrine limits the range of issues that the court can entertain. It frees the political branches from judicial review in respect of certain matters.[279] It is not just a question about the precise circumstances in which the courts act, but it represents a judgment that with respect to certain issues, the government will function best if the political branches operate without any judicial control at all.[280] In many cases, the political question doctrine is merely a confusing and unnecessary way to express the obvious point that the courts should not invent constraints on the political branches where the constitution does not impose any.[281] For a dispute to be justiciable, it must be susceptible of a decision on the basis of law. This means that the dispute must be a legal dispute, to which the court can apply the principle of law. Consequently, purely political questions cannot be justiciable.

5.1.4 Lack of Satisfactory Awareness in the Subject Matter

Where the claimant has no interest or no sufficient interest in the subject matter of the claim, the dispute will be inadmissible. A complainant may lack sufficient interest with respect to locus standi. In the ***Barcelona Traction Case***,[282] Belgium's claim was thrown out on the grounds that she lacked sufficient interest in the subject matter of the dispute. The fact that a majority of shareholders were Belgians, did not give Belgium the locus standi to bring an action on behalf of a company which was incorporated in Canada.

If the rights to a healthy environment and to development are to be enforced through adjudication, the complainant should first and foremost make sure that the complaint is justiciable on the basis of the foregoing discussion. Having highlighted the meaning of justiciability, it may now be necessary to examine the controversy surrounding this concept, so as to be able to determine whether local communities in particular and Cameroonians in general can be able to enforce the rights mentioned herein above, by bringing actions before the courts.

---

[278] Ibid.

[279] Siegel, J., (1989) "*A Theory of Justiciability*", *Texas Law Review,* Vol. 86, P. 74.

[280] Titanji Duga, E., (2010), Op.Cit., P. 192- 3.

[281] Henkin, L., (1976), "*Is there a Political Question Doctrine?*", Yale Law Journal, Vol. 85,P. 622.

[282] *Belgium v. Spain*, Second Phase, ICJ Report, 3.

5.2. Navigating the Debate: From Philosophical Objection to Legal Enforcement

The potential of Economic and Social Rights (ESR) as a tool to ensure the inherent dignity[283] of all has been, to use a popular phrase, "detained for questioning."[284] Over the last sixty years, debate has centered on arguments denying the justiciability and judicial enforcement of Economic and Social Rights. However, the former UN High Commissioner on Human Rights, Louise Arbour, recently stated that "it is now widely recognized that there is nothing inherently non-justiciable about economic, social and cultural rights."[285] The enactment of an Optional Protocol on Economic, Social and Cultural Rights, detailing an international "communications procedure" for violations of ESR supports Ms Arbour's contention.[286] However, scholars, nation-states, and courts themselves still argue against the idea that ESR are justiciable rights capable of being adjudicated by the courts of law. Even where objections to ESR's justiciability are overcome, arguments are still made in favour of limiting the scope of judicial oversight, oft-times by the courts themselves.

The assertion that an elected government only, and not the courts, has the absolute and exclusive legitimacy to decide on questions of resource allocation is a sham. Traditional arguments against the justiciability of ESR are rooted in the concept of *democratic deficit*; traditional arguments in favour of ESR are made in terms of a comparative analysis to civil and political rights (CPR). This is based in the concept of the indivisibility of rights. ESR are instruments providing for certain social outcomes. To this extent, they are normative, and are rooted in the presumption of achieving human dignity through every individual's right to minimum levels of certain, interlinked goods, such as food, water, healthcare, education, healthy environment, good roads, and the like. These are to be provided through a combination of the state's direct action and the state putting in place

---

[283] International Covenant on Economic, Social and Cultural Rights (henceforth ICESCR), Preamble, 16 (December 1966).

[284] Deval, D,(2010), "*Courting Legitimacy :Democratic Agency and the Justiciability of Economic and Social Rights", Interdisciplinary Journal of HumanRights Law,* Vol. 30, P. 35.

[285] High Commissioner backs work on mechanism to consider complaints of breaches of economic, social and cultural rights, United Nations Press Release, 16 July 2007, at www.unhchr. ch/huricane/ huricane.nsf/ view01/BAB7C795CD5D6F23C125731B004C4E7B? Open document, Accessed 10 September 2025.

[286] United Nations Department of Public Information, Third Committee Recommends General Assembly Adoption of Optional Protocol to International Convention on Economic, Social and Cultural Rights Press Release GA/SHC/3938 (18 Nov. 2008), www.un.org/News/Press/docs/2008/gashc3938.doc.htm. Accessed 10, September 2025.

conditions that enable each individual to gain access to the same. Because these social outcomes have some distributive implications, it follows that they impact the social order, and, further, as rights, they exist in law. Michelman asserted that:

> *When a legal inquiry will identify ECS Rights as one of those norms to which anyone who aims to be law-abiding should, for that very reason, normally feel a substantial if not decisive pressure to adhere. To get a norm into law is to produce a state of public affairs in which that sort of pressure can be expected to impinge on whoever is supposed to bear obligations attendant upon the norm.*[287]

This argument suggests that there is an expectation upon all arms of the state that they will develop and execute policies in order that, or, more generally, to ensure that social outcomes desired by the citizenry are achieved. The fact that this obligation exists upon the legislative and executive branches is uncontroversial. However, the involvement of the judicial branch has led the intellectual debate onto a more rugged, contested terrain. Indeed, such a line of argumentation comes from those who are extremely positive about civil and political rights (CPR). Aryeh Neier, a notable "believer in very strong civil and political rights," posited in relation to ESR's justiciability as follows:

> *...ESR are unmanageable through the judicial process and that intrudes fundamentally into an area where the democratic process ought to prevail.... The purpose of the democratic process is essentially to deal with two questions: public safety and the development and allocation of a society's resources.... Economic and security matters ought to be questions of public debate. To withdraw either of them from the democratic process is to carve the heart out of that process.... A court is not the place where it is possible to engage in the necessary sort of negotiation and compromise.*[288]

These arguments against justiciability lean on the issue of resource distribution and legitimacy and suggest that a court cannot and should not decide on issues of resource distribution because arguably,

[287]Frank I. M., (2008), "*Socio Economic Rights in Constitutional Law: Explaining America Away*", INT'L J. CONST. L., Vol. 76, P. 667.

[288]Aryeh , N., (2006), "*Social and Economic Rights: A Critique*", HUM. RTS. BRIEF, Vol. 13, PP. 1-2.

it is not set up to do so nor does it have the mandate to do it. This appears to be the dominant situation in Cameroon drawing from the fact that this research did not come across any cases in that light in the East and South Regions of Cameroon despite the violation of these rights of the local communities by the mining companies located there. To argue against justiciability is to presuppose that the court is an inappropriate forum to decide questions of public resource-allocation and people's material well-being, which in turn, is to presuppose that the moral and rational approach of a court is *deontological*, while that of the government is *utilitarian*. This implies that the government, with its utilitarian approach, is best placed to deal with public funds as they are limited, and thus a utility-maximizing approach is preferred.

This traditional deontological/utilitarian distinction between the approaches of the court and legislature means that courts were inherently incapable of allocating resources; however, recent studies show that there is no inherent difference between the possible allocative logics of the court and legislature when dealing with ESR. The courts' decision making, in fact, takes into account a host of factors in the same way that the legislature's does, including popular demands, infrastructural issues, governmental priorities, resource allocation.[289] If the court is in fact capable of executing such an approach, objections to justiciability then fall into two categories: practical and normative. The former set of objections contends that the court lacks sufficient practical capacity to engage in questions of resource allocation. The latter set contends that the judiciary is not competent to rule on ESR matters as they involve budgetary allocation and the running of programmes, which only the legislature and executive are competent to carry out. The implication is that it would not be legitimate for the judiciary to carry out a costing exercise when democratically elected rulers should do so. In this view, the judiciary's role is at best one of oversight. This is the democratic deficit argument. If ESR were to be considered justiciable:

> *...courts would stray too far from their legitimate role in a constitutional democracy if they adjudicated these kinds of rights ... ESR are too vague, costly, and institutionally complex for the judiciary to implement. In order to enforce a housing guarantee in the face of government neglect, for example, courts might have to*

[289] Varun Gauri & Daniel M. Brinks, Introduction: The Elements of Legalization and the Triangular Shape of Social and Economic Rights, in Varun Gauri & Daniel M. Brinks (eds.), Courting Social Justice 1, 5 (2008).

design housing programs, require money be spent to implement them, and perhaps even take over their administration. Thus, it is argued, that courts cannot enforce ESR without usurping the role of the legislative and/or administrative branches of government ... Yet, even those who argue for a robust judicial role in the enforcement of ESR admit that their full implementation threatens to strain judicial capacities and push boundaries of judicial legitimacy.[290]

Historically, it has been argued and traditionally accepted that socio-economic rights are non-justiciable.[291] Advocates of this position asserted that, while these rights have value as moral statements of a nation's ideals, they should not be viewed as a legal declaration of enforceable rights.[292] Adjudication of such rights requires an assessment of fundamental social values that can only be carried out legitimately by the political branches of government, and the proper enforcement of socio-economic rights requires significant government resources that can only be adequately assessed and balanced by the legislature. Judges and courts therefore, lack the political legitimacy and institutional competence to decide such matters. The argument goes on to assert that economic, social and cultural rights are "aspirational" or "abstract"; they cannot be the subject of either affirmative state obligation or immediate realization and enforcement.

This notwithstanding, if we go by the current UN doctrine which proclaims that all human rights are, "universal, indivisible, interdependent and interrelated,"[293] they must all be accorded equivalent enforcement mechanisms. The heart of this argument, however, lies in the contention that state compliance with economic, social, and cultural rights must be "justiciable", subject to the possibility of formal third-party adjudication, with remedies for findings of noncompliance. Also, both the Indian and South African courts have effectively rejected this non-justiciability argument.[294] To

[290] Alana, K., (2008), "*Judging as Nudging: New Governance Approaches for the Enforcement of Constitutional Social and Economic Rights*", Colum. Hum. Rts. L. Rev. Vol. 39, P. 354.

[291] Christiansen, E.C., (2007), "*Adjudicating Non-Justiciable Rights: Socio-Economic Rights and the South African Constitutional Court*", Columbia HumanRights Law Review, Vol., 56, P. 457.

[292] Ibid.

[293] Vienna Declaration and Programme of Action, pt.I, Para. 5,UN Doc. A/CONF.157/23 (1993), 32 ILM 1661 (1993)(adopted at the 1993 World Conference on Human Rights)

[294] Remarks of former Indian Chief Justice Bhagwati on Public Interest Litigation (PIL) as a necessary tool to foster the enforcement of economic and social rights in the case of People's Union v. Union of India [1983] 1 S.C.R 456, 469.

make economic and social rights resonate for the vast majority of the human population for whom these rights are critical, this thesis agrees with the South African Constitutional Court which adopts the "affordability"[295] argument by stating that:

> *It is true that the inclusion of socio-economic rights may result in courts making orders that have direct implications for budgetary matters. However, even when a court enforces civil and political rights such as equality, freedom of speech and the right to a fair trial, the order it makes will often have such implications. A court may require the provision of legal aid, or the extension of state beneficiaries of such benefits. In our view, it cannot be said that by including socio-economic rights within a bill of rights, a task is conferred upon them by a bill of rights that it can result in a breach of the separation of powers.*[296]

Indeed, Shadrack Gutto[297] opined that the incorporation of justiciable rights in the Bill of Rights of a constitutional democracy that respects the Rule of Law, under conditions of social inequalities, "... means that such rights and processes of their justiciability are open to all - rich and poor, the advantaged and disadvantaged."[298] According to him, the rich and advantaged are entitled to use the rights to defend their position, while the poor and disadvantaged are entitled to do so in pursuit of their interests to enter the camp of the rich and advantaged and to improve their life conditions."[299] Although Gutto argues that the social actions of all social classes tend to "balance out", the more important issue is that social and economic rights are not obscure entitlements. Such rights can, indeed, be the subject of rights discourse and enforcement at the domestic level. The judgment of the South African court goes to a considerable distance in clarifying what has traditionally been an extremely murky terrain.[300]

---

[295] This argument provides that the enforcement of social and economic rights must be dependent on the capacity of a state to afford the cost entailed.

[296] Certification Judgment of the South African Constitutional Court, (10) BCLR P 77. See also Shadrack Gutto, (1998), "*Beyond Justiciability: Challenges of Implementing/Enforcing Socio-Economic Rights in South Africa*", Buff. Hum. Rts. L. Rev., Vol., 79, P. 91.

[297] Shadrack Gutto, (1998), "*Beyond Justiciability: Challenges of Implementing/Enforcing Socio-Economic Rights in South Africa*", Buff. Hum. Rts. L. Rev., Vol., 79, P. 91.

[298] Ibid. at P. 92.

[299] Ibid.

[300] This can also be illustrated by the Indian examples where the process of Social Action Litigation (SAL) has considerably expanded the parameters of the judicial enforcement of human rights. See P.N. Bhagwati, Liberty

The African Charter on Human and Peoples Rights has been extolled,[301] particularly with respect to the recognition of economic, social, and cultural rights.[302] In this connection, the Charter in its Preamble stipulates that it is "henceforth essential" to pay particular attention to the right to development.[303] In the same vein, it asserts that civil and political rights "cannot be dissociated" from economic, social and cultural rights in conception as well as in universality.[304] The preamble concludes, with an affirmation that "... the satisfaction of economic, social and cultural rights is a guarantee for the enjoyment of civil and political rights."[305]Thus, civil and political rights could therefore not be fully justiciable while social and economic rights are non-justiciable.

Some scholars have argued that all that the African Charter accomplishes is to place economic, social and cultural rights and group ("third generation") rights on the same footing as civil and political rights.[306] Therefore, the Charter has conceptually shifted the emphasis from the traditional focus on civil and political rights alone, to one including economic and social rights.

The justiciability of economic and social rights suggests that an action could be individual or collective. The institution of an individual action poses fewer difficulties than will the institution of a collective action. The institution of a collective action will raise issues of locus standi or standing to sue. An understanding of the issues involved here necessitates an examination of the concept of public law litigation.

5.2.1 Public Interest Litigation as a Mechanism for Enforcement

The phrase "public law litigation" is used to refer to the practice of American lawyers seeking to achieve social change through adjudication.[307] The emergence of this kind of litigation in the United States of America is linked to the case of *Brown v. Board of Education*

---

and Security of the Person in India, with a particular emphasis on Access to Courts, in Developing Human Rights Jurisprudence 203-216 (Commonwealth Secretariat/Inter-rights ed. 1998).

[301] Rose D'sa, (1985), *"Human and Peoples' Rights: Distinctive Features of the African Charter"*, J. Afr. Law, Vol. 29, P. 81.

[302] Nana Busia, K.A., & Bibiane Mbaye, (1996), "*Filing Communications on Economic and Social Rights under the African Charter on Human and Peoples' Rights (The Banjul Charter)*", E. Afr. J. Peace & Hum. Rts., Vol., 3, P. 193.

[303]Preamble of the Charter. See also Jean-Marie B., (1997), "*International Instruments Relating to Human Rights*", Hum. Rts. L. J., Vol. 18, P. 79.

[304] Ibid.

[305] Ibid.

[306] Ibid.

[307]Chayes, A., (1976), "*The role of the judge in Public Law Litigation*", Harvard Law Review, P. 1281.

of Topeka.[308] In that case, the U.S. Supreme Court declared unconstitutional state segregation of pupils on the basis of race. The procedural features of this case now form part of public law litigation. In that case, the defendant was a public institution; the claimants were a self-constituted group whose membership changed over time; relief was prospective, seeking to reform future action by government agents; and the judge played a major role.[309] These features clearly show the difference between public interest litigation and the ordinary classical litigation where there is a private bipolar dispute marked by individual participation and the imposition of retrospective relief involving a tight fit between right and remedy.[310]

Public Interest Litigation, which is synonymous with Public Interest Law, is therefore the process whereby organizations or individuals use litigation in the courts to enforce collective rights or to influence social change.[311] There is typically either a single plaintiff who seeks to create a precedent, or a class action of people "similarly situated" as described under the US Federal Rules of Civil Procedure. The class may act as a collective matter, but there is always a clearly identifiable plaintiff, or class of plaintiffs, with classic standing. What makes it public interest is that in a way-but only in a way-the success of the suit is more important to those prosecuting the case than the success of the particular plaintiff. A clear picture of the purpose of Public Interest Litigation was painted by the former Chief Justice of India, P.N Bhagwati in Peoples Union for Democratic Rights and Others in the following terms:[312]

> *Public Interest Litigation as brought before the court is not for the purpose of enforcing the right of an individual against another as happens in the case of ordinary litigation, but is intended to promote and vindicate public interest which demands that violations of constitutional or legal rights of large numbers of people who are poor, ignorant or in a socially or economically backward position should not go unnoticed or unredressed.*

---

308 (1954), 347 US 483.

309 Herskoff, H.,(2000), "*Public Interest Litigation: Selected Issues and Examples*", Available at http://wwwl.worldbank.org/publicsector/legal/access.htm#public. Last accessed on 12 March ,2025.

310 Fuller, L., (1978), "*The Forms and Limits of Adjudication*", *Harvard Law Review, P.* 353.

311 Odhiambo, C. R., (2003), The University of Nairobi Law Journal, Vol.1, P. 256.

312 All India Report, 1982 SC 1473.

Public Interest Litigation therefore is the lawyer's response to the violations of the right to development as indicated in the Declaration on the Right to Development, as well as the violation of the right to a healthy environment. It is a form of civil litigation which must be filed and prosecuted in a prescribed form. Such actions take the form of representative suits or class actions. Lord Shand in the case of **Duke of *Bedford v. Ellis***[313] pointed out that:

> *The rule has been framed and adopted for a useful and important object - the saving of the multiplication of actions with the attendant costs, in cases where one action would serve to determine the rights of persons in question with another party called a defendant. A series of different actions one after another by different plaintiffs are to be no longer necessary in cases where numerous persons have same interest in one cause or matter for, in such cases, one or more of such persons may sue on behalf of or for the benefit of all persons so interested.*

The legal difficulties that must be overcome for one to successfully carry out a public interest litigation are the existence of a cause of action and the issue of locus standi.[314]

5.2.1.1 Cause of Action

It is a well settled and established rule of procedure that a court of law will not entertain an action which does not clearly outline a cause of action. In this connection, cause of action has been defined as:

> *An act or excision of one party in violation of the legal right or rights of the other, and its essential elements are legal right of the plaintiff, correlative obligation of the defendant and act or omission of the defendant in violation of the said legal right.*[315]

The Philippine Supreme Court in the case of *Oposa v. Factoran & Others,*[316] dealt with the issue of cause of action. It not only recognized that the Philippine constitution guarantees the right of citizens to a balanced, ecologically healthy environment, but also that the petitioners in the suit had a valid cause of action to claim under the

---

[313] 1901, AC 1.
[314] Titanji, Duga. E, (2010), Op.Cit., PP. 216 – 218.
[315] *Madrona V. Rosal*, 204 SCRA 1 [1991] (Philopmer).
[316] Reported in Judicial Decisions/National Decisions, Vol. 1, P. 22 – 33.

head of inter-generational responsibility and justice for generations to come. This ruling implies that a court which is seized of a matter may extend its jurisdiction to cover causes of action which prima facie do not expose an immediate cause of action especially in relation to novel collective rights like the RTD and the right to a healthy environment.

5.2.1.2 Legal Capacity in Bringing an Action

The issue which merits attention here is: who has the standing to sue in relation to class actions. All members of the class must have standing or be deemed to have it. Capacity to sue is a matter of law and fact and not a mere matter of discretion. For one to have the standing to bring a public interest litigation suit there must exist a special relationship between the plaintiff and the person sued. Such a relationship can be as general as one being a citizen of a country. On the other hand, there does not need to be a similarity of circumstances among the members of the class. However, the issue of standing to sue, especially in relation to class actions may be extended to all interested persons, representatives of groups and also to non-governmental organizations. Khamoni J.[317] pointed out that:

> *In law, each of the parties ... is a legal person just as each one of the parties in the Notice of Motion before me is. As such, each legal person is capable of suing and being sued in a court of law independently of all the rest ....*

On the strength of the foregoing discussions, it is logical that economic and social rights so long as they are collective or group rights, could be enforced through adjudication either by an individual or group of individuals, and either in a domestic or international tribunal. This research was unable to find any local cases brought in Cameroon against Mining multinationals, for violating human rights. Although Mining multinationals in Cameroon have been shown to violate human rights, not even a single law suit has been instituted against any of them. The activities of CAMINCO[318] in Bétaré – Oya is capable of generating litigation. This is because of the constant pollution of River Mari and marshland flooding. It should be noted that River Mari acts as a source of income to about five thousands (5000) inhabitants that make up the Community. This is because this river is used for artisanal fishing

[317] *Kenyan case of R v. Minister for Information & Broadcasting & Ahmed Jibril ex Parte EATN.*

[318] CAMINCO Mining Company is located in Bétaré – Oya and its activities involve the exploitation of Gold and associated Minerals.

activities and other uses. Unfortunately, no litigation has been brought against this company as the result of these violations. In an attempt at finding out whether those who are affected by that are losing their means of livelihood;if they were aware that they could bring an action, this researcher caught up with a fisherman who identified himself as Mana Soua.[319] In a discussion with him, he started by pointing out that River Mari to him was his 'alpha and omega' (by this he meant that everything of his depended on that river). He was by this saying that his livelihood depends on water. When the researcher sought to find out the magnitude and consequences of the pollution, he simply shook his head and while laughing said "I almost lost my wife because I went out of business". When he was asked whether he was aware of any remedy available to him at the time, he quickly retorted by saying that the only remedy was to look for an alternative so as to keep his family together. He actually pointed to a small provision store which he said he used his savings to setup at that time. This researcher drew the conclusion that this man was not even aware of the fact that his rights and by extension those of his entire community had been violated. It could also be inferred from this conversation that even if he was aware of the violation, he was not aware of any remedy available to him. Attempts to get the CAMINCO authorities to talk on the pollution met with a lot of bureaucracy which ended up discouraging the researcher.

While discussing with a staff of the legal department of CAMINCO, who claimed anonymity, he intimated that he had been working in that department for three years but had never seen a complaint from any community or members thereof, trying to enforce their rights. He however said he was not aware of the kind of violations I was talking about.

The local communities living wherein mineral resources are being exploited have the right to claim for development and to a healthy environment from both the government and the mining company doing the exploitation. It is no longer any gain saying that these natural resources belong to the indigenous peoples 'and as a result they need to feel the positive impact of such exploitation. The case today is the degradation of their environment by these MNCs mining companies. The right of the local communities to development and to a healthy environment are fundamental rights which have been recognised at the

[319] Discussion took place on the 15 of August 2025, in Bétaré - Oya, East Region of Cameroon.

international, regional and national level. Despite the recognition of these rights, the reality on the field as we gathered is that local communities inhabiting the mining companies are still extremely undeveloped and the environment in which they live degrades everyday as the result of the activities of these MNCs mining companies. Economic and Social Rights, and consequently the right to development and the right to a healthy environment are justiciable rights. Cameroonians in general and local communities in particular have the possibility of instituting actions in court so as to enforce these rights. But these rights are constantly being violated by mining companies. A glaring example is the situation in Kongo village as seen above wherein GEOVIC is exploiting Nickel, Colbalt and manganese, Lolabé village hosting SINOSTEEL CAM Mining Company and the activities of CAMINCO in Bétaré - Oya. The local Communities in this part of the country have never made their voices heard. The reason is that they are not even aware of these rights.

CHAPTER SIX
THE DUALITY OF EXTRACTION: SOCIO-ECONOMIC AND ENVIRONMENTAL IMPACTS OF MINING

When a country is involved in a very beneficial process like mining activities, be it artisanal or industrial, it is in a bid to see how it can help improve on the livelihood of its citizen and to enhance growth and environmental development. However, instead of propelling the social-economic development of a nation, many developing countries with abundant resources like Cameroon are confronted with the issue of ''resource curse''.[320] The ''so called development'' brought by mining exploitation always comes with its effects. The effects of mining activities can both be positive and negative as is the case with our discussion.

The environmental and social effects can to a larger extent change the dynamics of community living and can make the lives of its residents better or worse. The way these effects are managed by the communities and the mining companies involved can either further worsen or make lives better for the said communities. This calls for drastic attention being paid to issues of corporate social responsibility where mining companies afford in honouring their social obligations to the communities of operation.

6.1 The Promise of Progress: Alleged Positive Effects and Benefits

The discovery, extraction and processing of mineral resources is widely regarded as a ''blessing'' to the host country in general and the catchment communities in particular. This is because Mining operations present a lot of benefits for communities where such mining takes place and the country at large.

[320]This theory postulates that existence of mineral resources in many third world countries have turned out to be curses rather than blessings, as many companies, governments and other actors siphon away their wealth leaving the sources of the wealth battling with plethoria of economic hurdles which sometimes lead to social unrest and conflicts. The ''resource curse'' thesis further suggest that natural resources abundance generate a series of economic and political distortions which ultimately undermines the contributions of the extractive industry to development. It is also argued under the same hypothesis that mining is associated with poor growth performance. Bebbington, A., et al; (2008), ''*Contention and Ambiguity: Mining and possibilities of development*'', Journal of Development and Change, Vol. 39. N°. 6, Blackwell Publishing, P. 914.

6.1.1 Education and Health Care Enhancement

Educational opportunities have increased with increase in mining activities. Some of the mining companies in Cameroon have been supporting the local communities through the provision of school materials and free health consultation to the local population. In Lolabé where SINOSTEEL CAM PLC is exploiting Iron Ore from Mount Mamelles in the South Region, the researcher was informed that the company distributed 35 school bags, books, balls, pens to the pupils of that community and didactic school materials handed to the Headmistress of Government Primary School Lolabé. In addition, mobile free consultation has always been provided by the company to the local communities.[321] Also, the increase in mining revenues have tended to improve educational facilities in the catchment communities in Cameroon. This is as a result of the distribution of these revenues between the state and the local communities. The end result is the boost in educational and healthcare improvement. Cameroon mining code has also laid a lot of emphasis on safety and health care of miners and as such protecting the miners thus leading to high productivity in the sector. The mining code is specific on regulation to protect miners from all forms of work which seems dangerous, unhealthy and obnoxious to the miners.[322]

6.1.2 Mining and Poverty Lessening

Mining activities in Cameroon particularly artisanal and small-scale mining for now is both poverty driven and poverty alleviating for the local communities. The improvement and the legal regulation put in place is a booster to miners and in this way leading to poverty alleviation. In the TNS area, at least 3,510 people (517 miners and their dependants) almost a quarter of the area's population depend upon mining income from the artisanal and small-scale mining carried out. Over 70% of the miners attain primary school level or no education at all. Besides, mining is the main activity for about 79% of the active population of Cameroons in the areas where gold and diamond have been discovered and agriculture and timber exploitation only follow.[323] The miners are not very organised so most of the minerals mined are either sold directly to individual buyers or possibly to state agent or organizations created to facilitate, assist and promote small-scale

[321]Interview, Jean Hubert Bessala, Sub-Divisional Officer of Kribi, Monday 21 February 2025

[322]Art. 109 of the Mining Code.

[323]This is particular in the localities of Mobilong, Ampaya, Mboy I and II and Mparo, all in the East Region.

mining. This however helps the local miners to sell their products at very encouraging prices, giving them enough money to provide for their daily needs. The prices of diamond turns to fluctuate greatly and are being calculated as unit prices as the miners posses no method or tool to analyses weight or quality to determine the real value, it makes the organization to shove away the clandestine buyers who use to buy at very low prices and thereby making the local miners to remain poor.

This organization is an encouragement to most miners and drive toward the Millennium development gold. The annual net income from gold and diamond after reduction of cost for production, materials, labour and transport were 575338 CFA and 812644 CFA respectively in Cameroon giving about 1,130 and 15% U.S$ a day, they still look low. Nevertheless, mining activities continue to expand as the average miner can make up to three times a higher income than others in the same area or locality, who practice a combination of forming, hunting and gathering forest products. Mining income pays for important basic needs such as food (although alcoholic drinks represent about 20% of the food cost), education, cloths, medicines, construction of houses and consumer goods.

6.1.3 The notion of Mining and Employment

Mining activity is an attractive employment option for many in rural areas: barriers to entry are minimal. Activity levels are dynamic as precious minerals are often inversely correlated with economic opportunity and periods of economic crisis. The diamond industry provides livelihoods for thousands of people in Cameroon and into millions around the globe. For example, employment figures in a few African countries includes; DRC (75000), Zimbabwe (35000), Tanzania (600000). With the implementation of CAPAM, about 60.000 autonomous artisanal miners from the base are constantly being employed; in addition, C & K is currently employing 23 from the village of Mboy II.[324] SINOSTEEL CAM is currently employing youths of the localities of Lolabé and Kribi to supply them unskilled labour in the company.[325] These employment opportunities allow thousands of Cameroonians to make a salary, obtain proper health care from the higher income gotten from the mining sector, create better home environment and set the families living standards high and also

[324]Interview, Chief of Mboy II, 14/10/2025.
[325]Interview, Youth leader, Lolabé, 22/10/2024.

encourage grounds, increase of infrastructure into the forest environment.[326]

However, two types of miners are usually observed in mining activities in Cameroon particularly on artisanal. We have diggers who dig small pits and drivers who scoop sand and soil from the River. Although from diverse ethnic groups, the majority (95% from Cameroon and 87% from CAR) of miners are permanently based in the local towns or villages. For example, the mining in the East Region which is mostly locally carried out by villagers and some companies who use just the local machines for the digging of the soil to extract gold. The mining code however, insists on mechanised form of artisanal mining which should be done with the use of an excavator and other local machines. Thereafter is washed in the local river or streams to extract the minerals from the ground, before it is sent for further cleaning. Particularly with individuals or companies who use mechanized forms, they may use other mechanized form of separating the minerals from the soil. On the other hand, industrial mining activities are carried with the use of high technological plants around the area of exploitation. The ages of most miners in Cameroon vary from 17 to 75 with an average of about 37 years in Cameroon as against 36 years. It indicates that the average age of a miner can be about 9.5 years. In CAR, no woman has been seen to be a leader in the mining activities whereas in Cameroon 13% of miners are women. However, in both countries, particularly Cameroon, research showed that most of the people involved in local mining are married and mostly mining activities are characterised and supported by family labour, involving married women and their children. The Cameroon government is doing everything possible to make sure that mining activities create job opportunities to her citizens, and by making it an obligation to recruit Cameroonians as part of the mining agreement signed between the state of Cameroon and any prospective mining investor. It is estimated that when full exploitation of all the country's natural resources will start, about 4000 Cameroonians shall be employed.

6. 1.4 Improvement on Livelihoods of persons

Africa produces more than 60 metals and products and is a major producer of several of the world's most important minerals and metals including Gold and diamonds. Although under explored, Africa has

[326]Observation, Mboy II and Lolabé.

about 30% of the planets mineral resources, including 40% of Gold, 60% Cobalt and 90% of the World's precious gains mineral reserves. In terms of contribution to livelihoods and income of Africans, the revenue generated from gold and Diamond mining has transformed and continues to transform the lives of many people. The revenue generated does not only increase the overall standard of living, but also find essential government services such as health, education, and development programs. Countries such as Namibia and South Africa offer on-going proof that Diamond revenue can create sizeable benefits to the economy in countries where they are discovered.

Apart from cash income to local and national economies, small scale mining is labour intensive and could form a measure purveyor of employment, thus reducing rural employment rates besides socio-economic contributions. Artisanal mining often precedes large scale mining because the former provides the indicator of industrial prospecting of significant deposit. This opens a window for conflict in a social context if the small and the large-scale miners have to operate at the same side. The 2010 mining code differentiates between large scale and small-scale mining but at the centre gives provision for the two to operate at the same side. The reason includes the fact that small scale mines cannot go beyond 30m depth, while the industrial can go even beyond 400m as in South Africa. Another reason is that the code recognises the fact that miners were born or have been residing in the area for decades with several families dependent on the activity for livelihood.

The researcher sort to investigate, on the activities of some of the giant mining Companies in Cameroon, on the catchment communities. We took C&K mining incorporation harbouring communities like Mussiembo, Mang, Long, and Batouri. A significantly large number of the respondents stated that the mine has provided some form of vocational training for the youths. In contrast, a relatively small number were of the view that no vocational training was being conducted for the youths. Interviews conducted indicated that vocational training covering masonry, mobile phone repairing, carpentry etc was ongoing at the time of the study. This affirms that C&K mining incorporation has shown some level of commitment in providing vocational training for persons without trade.[327]

[327]Reunion or Focus Group Discussion, Mobilong, 5/11/2024.

As to whether the communities were satisfied with the livelihood empowerment programmes or not, most of the inhabitants of these localities indicated that they were satisfied with the kind of livelihood empowerment programmes that have been implemented by the C & K mining incorporation. This means that the majority of the people were content with the livelihood empowerment programme. Comparatively, the effects of C & K mining Inc on the livelihood of its catchment communities is similar to that of Golden star wassa Limited on its catchment communities in Ghana.[328]

6.1.5 The situation of Mining and Income Distribution

Whether industrial, artisanal or small-scale mining, mining activities increase the level of income distribution. This can be evident by the fact that minerals such as diamond and gold mostly mined are very expensive and thereby influences the spending nature of the miners who turn to use the income to purchase their basic needs sending the mining income back into the economy. This boosts the financial sector as against those who keep money on themselves without spending nor saving which cripples the economy instead. This can be further buttressed by an explanation made by the Divisional delegate of Mines in the Boumba and Ngoko Division in the Eastern Region of Cameroon. He affirmed that the sector is socially very important for the livelihoods of the local miners to meet daily needs. He reiterated that the major drawback to miners capitalizing the economic value of their revenue from mining is that they do not have a saving culture; most local miners spend over 40% of their income on alcoholic drinks and spirits. Stories of resulting violence and abuses caused by over consumption associated the miners thereby redistributing the money into other sectors.[329] Be it as it may, mining activities play a significant role on income distribution in local communities in Cameroon especially in the Easter Region where mining activity is on an increase.

6.1.6 The National Economic Upshot

The creation of sustainable future for Africa in general and Cameroon in particular may lie in its ability to develop and maximise its natural resources. Mining activities can therefore contribute both nationally and locally to the economic development of a State.[330] In

---

[328]Boateng Owusu D., (2012), ''*The Impact of Golden Star Wassa Limited (G S W L) Operations on its Catchment Communities''*, Commonwealth Executive Masters thesis of public Administration, Kwame Nkrumah University of Science and Technology, Ghana, PP. 55-6.

[329]Discussion with the Divisional Delegate of Mines, Youkadouma, 22/11/2015.

[330]Barber, E., (2005), *Natural Resources and Economic Development,* Cambridge University Press, P. 402.

Cameroon for example, solid mines in 1997/1998 fiscal year contributed to 4.8 billion to the G D P of the country. In CAR, diamond mining was the country's leading industry in top expert commodity in 2002. Mining counted for about 4% of GDP and 40-50% of export earnings. Diamond accounts for 76% of Botswana's revenue, 45% of the government revenue and 43% of the GDP approximately 3 billion US dollars. Since the discovery of diamond in 1966 the GDP annual growth rate has average 7%. Botswana has one of the fastest growing economies in the world due to diamond.[331]

At the local level, a mining activity contributes a lot to the local communities by creating wealth, providing jobs and stimulating business ventures for community members.[332]

6.1.7 Mining encourage Foreign Direct Investments

In the face of inadequate resources to finance long term development in Africa in general and Cameroon in particular, and with poverty reduction and other millennium development goals looking forward to achieve by 2035, attracting foreign direct investment has assumed a prominent place in the strategies of economic renewal being advocated by policy markets at the national, regional and international levels. The experience with a small number of countries in Africa and recently Cameroon with its 2035 emerging economy vision has strengthened the belief that attracting FDI is key to bridging the resource gap of other low income countries avoiding further building up of debt while directly tackling the cause of poverty. On the other hand, calls for an accelerated pace of opening up to FDI have intensified on the assumption that this will bring not only more stable capital inflow but also greater technological know-how, higher paying jobs, entrepreneurial and workplace skills and new expert opportunities.

This is not an altogether new direction in development policy thinking in the African and the Cameroonian contexts. Immediately following the independence, policy makers in the country hoped that attracting FDI often with the bait of higher tariff protection and generous incentive packages would provide the catalyst for a late industrialization drive. And following the debt crisis the early 1980s, the architects of the structural adjustment also saw increased FDI as key to sustain economy recovery, this time in conformity with market fundamentals. From this prospective, the pursuit of responsible

[331]Diamond Facts Book, 2010.
[332]Deanna, K., (2009), Op.Cit., P. 218.

macroeconomic policy combined with an accelerating pace of liberalization, deregulation and above all privatization were expected to attract FDI to Cameroon.

Despite the efforts of the Cameroon government to comply with this policy advice, the records of the past two decades with respect to reducing poverty and attracting FDI have been disappointing at best but for the mining industry with an open market system of small scale and artisanal mining that attracts FDI. In response to the disappointment, a second generation of reforms introduced in the 1990s also sought to address short comings in programmes design and implementation by placing much greater emphasis on poverty reduction, combined with policy ownership, credibility and transparency. Moreover, the promise of getting government right has also lead to greater flow of FDI which has gone a long way to improve on the investment climate.[333]

Mining activities in Cameroon have spurred economic growth and reduced poverty and will more than ever before be an avoidable area of foreign direct investment in the country. Indeed, while the mining activities continue, it will always attract foreign investors to invest in the sector. Also, with the increase in awareness of the mining potentials of Cameroon, the average annual FDI flow of Cameroon is increasing so rapidly now than ever before. Cameroon can be looked upon as a new mining destination in Africa. In fact, the FDI has doubled now than it was in the 1970s and 1980s. On a per capita basis, this translates into a more than fourfold increase compared to the 1980s; nevertheless, a casual comparison of this with the flow to other developing countries is likened to a simple story about Cameroon.

6.1.8 The Mining Sector in the encouragement of Research

The Cameroon mining code is an incentive and very friendly to both Cameroon and foreigners who want to invest in the sector. The World Bank becomes increasingly involved in the conceptualization and introduction of Institutional reforms in the 1990s. This was done from the perspective of financial institutions, privileging strategies favouring short fiscal redress and incentives to attract potential investors.

The present-day mining activity has also increased the level of further research and the opening of new school programmes to ensure the efficient study on new methods and the most mechanized forms of

[333] Ibi Ajayi, S., (2006), Op. Cit, P. 23.

carrying out mining activities for the benefit of all and at a very low cost. Education and research in the sector has also increased because the sector is able to produce enough income that can be used to train specialist in the mining sector and provision that permit companies to go for a relentless search to see if there exist other minerals that are yet to be discovered and which if done will be an upload to the national treasury and will also provide more jobs to the growing population of Cameroon. In this light, some schools and courses specialise in mining have been created throughout the country so as to better boost research in the sector. For example, the school of Geology and Mining at Meiganga. This school which is attached to the University of Ngaoundéré, trains mining engineers and other experts in the domain of mining. Also the department of Geology, Faculty of Science of the University of Dschang, offers courses in mining such as Mining legislation, mines and petrol all geared at contributing to the growth of the mining industry in Cameroon. In addition, some higher private institutions do offer some programmes in mining. For example, the recent creation of the department of mining at the Gulf-Field Higher Institute of Petroleum Management and control at Limbe, South West Region of Cameroon. All these go to support the fact that, mining encourages research.

6.1.9 Ensuring Capacity Building through the Mining Sector

Capacity building or capacity development is ''the process by which individuals, groups, organizations, institutions and societies increase their abilities to perform functions, solve problems and achieve objectives; to understand and deal with their development needs in a broader context and in a sustainable manner''[334] developmental objectives notably through a redistributive measures in order to ensure greater social cohesion or regulatory to monitor the use of non-renewable resources and ensure the protection of the environment, were to be placed very much in a secondary position as compared to the emphasis on policies to attract foreign investment and promote export. As detailed in a study devoted to gold mining in the East Region of Cameroon, the mining sector has received priority attention under the country's economic recovery program initiated as the sector is now considered as the key to the country's economic recovery. In fact, this

[334]Lusthaus, C., (1999), ''*Capacity Development: Definitions, Issues and Implication for Planning, Monitoring and Evaluation.* ''Available at http://www.universalia.com/files/occas35.pdf.Accessed 11/04/2025.

sector has received a tremendous boost with policy changes dynamically initiated since the 1990s.

Mining activities particularly with artisanal and small scale mining has come in to diversify the primary activity of the people. Normally, it is an understanding principle that the main economic activity of an African man is agriculture and mostly subsistence agriculture in which the man and his family do just for the purpose of feeding their family and the surplus for sales only to realize other needs that cannot be cultivated. The second is the agro pastoralism which is usually carried by means of cultivation during the rainy season and by the dry season the agro pastoralist carry their flock to the valley where fresh pastures are available. Now with the birth, growth and continuity of mining activities in Cameroon, it is a remarkable issue that mining has now diversified agriculture since not everybody can go to the farm for agricultural production particularly on large scales but those who do agriculture on large scale in order to sell to those who are employed in the mining fields, and those in the mining activities can also buy in a very encouraging manner that will further encourage the farmers to increase production. This diversification as well lead to an increase of the socio-economic life of the farmers and also increase the GDP of the country and active circulation of the currency.

Furthermore, the high level of the indigenous people in the East region of Cameroon particularly in Bertoua, Puma, Yokadoma where most of the mines are found, involvement in hunting has also reduced because many people who were actively involved in hunting as their main economic activity are now involved in mining from which they receive better payment.[335] Mining therefore has not only diversified the economic activity of hunting but has also lead to the respect of the forestry laws on pouching or illegal hunting since many of the hunters are now involved into mining activities.

6.1.10 An improvement of Infrastructural Development

The revenue generated from mineral exploitation helps to build many countries where they exist mining in general now than ever before is at a stage where many infrastructural developments are needed either for the transportation of the minerals already tapped or plans at the sides. These ancillary facilities include ports, access and haulage roads, railways and the development of mining towns.

[335] Divisional Officer of Boumba and Ngoko Division, (2008), *Mot d'ouverture de monsieur le préfet du département de la Boumba et Ngoko, Atelier de lancement de LLS dans le TNS Youkadouma*, P. 4.

6.1.10. 1 Ports

Mining activities are usually located in remote areas and far from major metropolitan communities who are the end users of the mined products. Shipment of the final ore product beit in the raw form (pending industrialized processing) and concentrates of ores are usually carried out through their transportation channels to the designated port for shipment. The port also acts as the main entry point for mining equipment and materials. The port which is in this context is the sea port may be located on the banks of a navigable river.

The creation of an airport is necessary to support mining activities. This is used in the transportation of miners, contractors, government employees and controllers to the mining site. This increases the time value of production through human resources and stringent availability in time and space. In Cameroon, CAM IRON S.A. located in Mbalam-East Cameroon which is extracting iron ore has enhanced the project for the creation of the Kribi Sea Port which is presently under construction. The creation of the Kribi gas power station is also being undertaken. In addition, the company also intends to construct storage facilities and loading facilities all at the South of Kribi deep sea port.

6.1.10.2. The presence of Available and haulage Roads

Mining activity contributes to create ancillary newly created roads as part of the mine development stage to mining sites and may create access to previously inaccessible forest or wilderness areas. For example, C & K mining Incorporation has graded the earth road that links the village of Mboy I and Mboy II which was for a long time not motorable.[336] The positive effects of this newly created roads to the local inhabitants are varying, including, the facilitation of local subsistence activity of hunting and farming by indigenes of these communities.

Concerning mined ore haulage roads, pipe lines facilities also need to be constructed as haulage roads to enhance the transportation of fuel (diesel or petrol) and water to the mining sites. So far in Cameroon water tanks placed on mining sites by oil Supply Company's achieve this task. Legislation cannot be ignored to impact in the creation of this type of ancillary facility. Nevertheless, the report from the International Mining and Construction Company (MIC) in Cameroon

[336]Observation on the field Mboy I and II, 22/10/2024.

undertaking four quality high Iron ore licenses in the South Region declared that it has started undertaking drilling in Ntem (using 115 Mt. Resources) situated 80km from Kribi. It stated that the metallurgical drilling to better define ore bodies includes the creation of the investigating slurry pipeline.[337]

6.1.10. 3 The contribution of the Railway Sector

Indeed, mining activities require quicker means of getting the minded mineral substances to the industry for processing. Hence the need to minimize traffic on roads which may increase the risk potential when bulk ore is being transported in truck vehicles. As a result of this, there is therefore the necessity to construct a convenient transportation railway.

CAM IRON S.A in its report in 2013 announces the construction of a 2675km railway that will link Mbalam to the Kribi deep sea port. They also made mention of the construction of a railway linking the following iron ore project areas: Ntem, Nkout, Mbarga, Metzimevin, Njweng and Meridional, all located in the Eastern Region of Cameroon. The 2.5 billion infrastructure that covers a distance of 580km, when constructed will go to boost infrastructural development in Cameroon in general and the locality in particular.

6.1.10.4 The positive implications on Mining Town

The creation of a mine slowly sees the creation of a new town because of factors like the lack of towns within relative proximity to the mining site. As a result of this, the surrounding inhabitants in the nearby mining chief town will all flock to this chief town so as to supply labour to the mining company and also render other indirect services. This therefore leads to the growth and development of a new town in that locality. For example, the village of Mbalam that host CAM IRON S.A. and that of Mobilong that host C & K Mining Incorporation have witnessed a rapid growth as a result of mining activities taking place in these localities. The population size, lifestyle and infrastructural development have all improved. Government policies often contribute as the government may use resource development projects in remote areas to contribute to the overall development of a particular region or locality within the state.

Other ancillary advantages that can result from mining activities include; the institution of medical facilities like hospitals, pharmacies

---

[337]Cameroon Exploration Industry Investor's Guide 2014 by the MINMITD on Advanced stage of Mining Projects, Yaoundé- Cameroon, 2014, P. 20.

and health centres. These facilities are usually designed and stuffed to enhance the provision of health services to existing communities as a part of the community development programme. CAM IRON S.A, announces the creation in Mbalam; small business (restaurants, bars, inns, transport companies, micro finance institutions, etc) and social amenities (schools, health centres, play grounds, roads and houses).[338] The effect of mining activities on the local communities in Cameroon ought to be very positive in terms of infrastructural development and welfare of the local indigenes although this might just be a solution to the 'resource curse' which Africa in general and Cameroon in particular are suffering from.[339]The reality today is that, the effect of mining activities in Cameroon is more seen in the negative than in the positive. This is due to the fact that most of the mining companies operating in developing countries in general and in Cameroon in particular do not carry out their activities within the framework of responsible mining.[340]

---

[338]Mbomeda, J.C., and Tekem Tessa, S.C., (2012), ''*Impact of Mining Activities on population in Mbalam, East-Cameroon*'', Available at; http//www.s.free.org/Actes/Synthese_EE_2009/Contenu_Formation/CEIE_02/003-mines/024-TESSA.Pdf.accessed 07/12/2024.

[339]Kelley, J., (2013), ''*China in Africa: Curing the Resource Curse with Infrastructure and Modernization*'', Sustainable Development Law and Policy, Vol. 12 N^{O}. 35, P. 25.

[340]Marta, M., Chambers, D., and Coumans, C., (2005), "*Framework for Responsible Mining: A Guide to Evolving Standards*", Available at; www.frameworkforresponsiblemining.org/pubs/framework-2005/018.pdf. Accessed 19/02/2025.

CHAPTER SEVEN
THE PREVAILING REALITY: DOCUMENTED NEGATIVE CONSEQUENCES OF MINING ACTIVITIES ON THE LOCAL COMMUNITIES IN CAMEROON

The exploitation of mineral resources in any community is usually looked upon as one of the most environmentally and socially disruptive activities undertaken by business. Indeed, many of the environmental disasters or human rights incidents that have contributed to the growing public concerning the actions of companies over the last 40 years have taken place in the extractive industries; the mining sector, therefore, is a key topic in debates about social and environmental responsibility.

7.1. Environmental Degradation: Water, Air, Land, and Biodiversity

This section is based on interviews with respondents, focus group discussion and personal observation of environmental effects of mining in local communities in the Eastern Region of Cameroon. Environmental issue raised by the respondents covered issues of water pollution, air pollution, land pollution and degradation, noise and vibration, climate change, Biodiversity, Soil quality, and impact on wildlife. Personal observations are also included.

7.1.1 The existence of Water Pollution

Water, they say is life. For the local communities, water is a very important resource in their lives particularly in their occupation as farmers. Water bodies in the community serve as a source of drinking water for the people as well as for irrigation on their crops and farms especially in the dry season. It is also used for a wide range of family and household chores and constitutes an important component in the daily activities of the local communities; for example the local inhabitants of Mobilong that host C & K mining Incorporation. This community is blessed with major water bodies such as ''Asuosika'', ''Apensu'' ''Subika'' and ''Atoko'' which were used by the Mobilong people for various purposes. As indicated by the C & K employee interview, mining will inevitably affect the environment including water bodies. Considering the enormous importance of water bodies for the people of Mobilong, they were asked by the researcher how their water bodies have been affected as a result of mining activities by C & K mining Incorporation. Majority of the respondent indicated that their water bodies have not been necessarily polluted but rather they are not using them again because of the warning given to the community by the C & K company and the community leaders to desist from using the water bodies for any kind of activity. It is noted that upon the start of mining operation in Mobilong, C & K warned the people to stop using the water bodies for their activities because of safety and health reasons. Most of the water bodies are still fresh and look quite hygienic except river ''Aspensu'' whose visibility has been polluted by some waste and dust from the community and the untarred roads.

All the local inhabitants of Mobilong were quick to add further that earlier, apart from water bodies that lie in the community that were used for various purposes particularly for drinking, one major source of drinking water for them before mining started in Mobilong was rain water. However, they have stopped using rain water as well because C & K also warned them not to use rainwater because they have been told that some harmful chemicals have been released into the atmosphere from their mines which mixed with rain water and makes them harmful for human and animals. Rainwater is no longer used in Mobilong by the people for fear of dying or getting ill. They complain about the lack of access to potable drinking water and notes that when C & K had not started mining in Mobilong, water was not a problem. Now, people buy water from boreholes and few standing pipes provided by the local authorities and C & K. Alternatively, some also use dug-out wells which are also expensive to afford for many people. The figure below is River ''Subika'' that is heavily polluted as a result of the mining in Mobilong which was observed some few meters on entering the Mobilong community.

Figure 1: Polluted River "Subika" in Mobilong-East Cameroon

Source: Photo: Researcher 5th November, 2024

Intuitively, one can readily observe that using water from the river can have serious consequences on a person's health and safety.

7.1.2. An Aspect of the quality of Air affecting the Mining Sector

Air is a very important natural resource for human, animals and even plant life. Its pollution may have serious consequences on the health. However, access to good and quality air can be challenging and a problem. The local inhabitants of Mbalam were asked if mining operation in Mbalam have resulted in air pollution due to the use of mining machines and other equipment by CAM IRON S.A from the Mining site. Most of the inhabitants indicated that air pollution from the mines is non-existent in the community because the machines used by the mining company do not produce fumes and smoke. However, they intimated that pollution in the atmosphere is basically from huge cars and vehicles that are used by CAM IRON S.A in the transportation of heavy equipment and machines to and from the Mbalam community which produce large amount of dust in the atmosphere because CAM IRON S.A has failed to tar the road linking the communities and CAM IRON S.A plant sites. By observation, the researcher could see huge vehicles owned by CAM IRON S.A parading these untarred roads and producing massive dusty particles into the atmosphere. One has to cover the mouth and nose with a tissue paper or any other material to prevent the direct inhalation of the dust particles. Plants such as Cocoa, palm and cassava farms are visibly seen with dust covering their leaves due to dust produced by the passing vehicles from CAM IRON S.A. Periodically, these untarred and dusty roads are sprinkled with water by CAM IRON S.A. even though the dust keeps coming back within a few days.

However, some of the inhabitants of Mbalam noted that though they seldom see pollution from the mines, they believe that latently, the atmosphere is filled with chemicals and harmful gases which they do not see with their naked eyes. Their response flows from their prevention from the use of rain water by CAM IRON S.A. which did not use to be the case. They believe that blasting of the surface of the earth by the mining company releases some chemicals and dust into the atmosphere though invisible. Rhetorically, one of the inhabitants asked: ''if the atmosphere is not polluted, why have they (CAM IRON) told us to stop drinking rainwater.''[341]

Moreover, another inhabitant of Mbalam noted that in recent times, water stored in barrels and containers changes its colour within a day and that she could visibly see some particles settled on the water surface in the containers. She added that Mbalam used to be vegetative and covered with large forest trees devoid of massive dust particles and as such one could store water for longer periods of time without changes in its colour. However, she believes that the blasting done by the mining company might have resulted in such pollution from dust.

The activities of CIMENCAM in Fiugil have visible environmental effects within the community. The dust cloulds emerging from the CIMENCAM factory are the cause of olfactory and visual disturbance upon arrival in Figuil[342].

7.1.3 The situation of Land Pollution and Degradation

Land is inevitably a valuable asset to many people and for example the people of Lomié in the Eastern Region of Cameroon. This all-important resource is so important to them because it is the very source of their livelihood especially with most of them being farmers. The researcher sought out whether they feel this resource and their livelihood is threatened with mining operation in Lomié?. The majority of the inhabitants indicated that their land is hugely degraded and destroyed by GEOVIC mining operations. Some of the inhabitants also noted that only a small portion of the land has been excavated so far for

[341]Interview, Mr Tekem Johnas, Farmer, Mbalam, 28th October 2025.

[342]Observation ,Figuil, 15/10/2025.

mining and as a result did not see how their land is seriously affected or destroyed. Some of the inhabitants told the researcher that GEOVIC's mining operations do not destroy the land in the way it is destroyed by artisanal illegal mining in the community. A glaring example here is the case of Bétaré-Oya.[343] People who believed in the destruction of the land by GEOVIC's mining operation indicated that huge equipment are used to excavate the land, clearing large areas and digging huge pits that destroy the topography and landscape of the area which they believed would be difficult to reclaim in the future for use. They believed that since illegal miners in Lomié do not use heavy equipment like GEOVIC, their pits can easily be covered and the land levelled easily when the need arises.

On the contrary, GEOVIC's pits are so big and wide with heaps of sand rising to mountain levels and the inhabitants of Lomie believed that such areas would be difficult to cover and levelled for use in the future. Those who believe that only a small portion have been destroyed by GEOVIC's mining operations noted that their lands have not been affected and therefore believed that large lands are still intact as they used to be. Others who thought illegal miners were rather destroying the land believed that since the illegal miners do not obtain permission before mining and also mines indiscriminately without the use of any geographical data, they mine indiscriminately irrespective of whether the areas bears gold or not. They dig pits any where they like only to find no gold deposits and move to other areas and start digging without covering or levelling the land previously destroyed. This has affected the farmers in Lomié greatly and it is almost the same situation with the local farming communities in Ghana.[344]Further questioning reveals that the company is currently undertaking surface mining and account for digging of large pits and trenches although most of the inhabitants indicated that GEOVIC have indicated their plans to start using deep mining. This was confirmed by one GEOVIC employee interviewed who indicated that within the next two or three years from 2015, GEOVIC would start massive deep and underground mining.[345]

---

[343]Tetsopgam, S., Nzolang, C., and Kuepoua, G., (2007), Op. Cit.,

[344]Yamoah Tenkorang, E., (2013), "*The Impact of Gold Mining on Local Farming Communities in Ghana*", Journal of Global Initiative, Vol. 8, N^{O}. 1 and 2, PP, 25-44.

[345]Interview, GEOVIC Employee, Confidential, 23rd October 2025.

7.1.3 The presence of Noise and Vibration

Usually, most people in Cameroon do not consider noise as a form of pollution and have come to accept noise making as part of their everyday living irrespective of where it is coming from. The same can be said of the local communities of Mobilong in the Eastern Region and Lolabé in the Southern Region of Cameroon. However, knowing the dangers associated with noise and the nuisance it can create for the peoples of Mobilong and Lolabé, inhabitants of both communities were asked if mining has increased noise levels particularly from the machines and equipments used in the mining operation in the community. All the inhabitants said that noise levels are relatively down from the mining sites especially from the machines and equipments used by C & K and SINOSTEEL for mining. However, they mentioned two major sources of noise that to them are only periodic but not regular. Noise from blasting the land for mining (usually three times a week in Mobilong) and heavy duty vehicles that transport equipment to and from the plant site were the main source of noise but these are only heard periodically. The inhabitants of Mobilong and its environs like Mparo, Mboy I, Mboy II and Mang, said the heavy vehicles create noise when they pass through the town. But, noise from the blast is the most complained about by the residents in the community and is usually heard during nights when they are sleeping. The inhabitants of Mobilong lament how the blast noise from the mines disturb their sleep and even causes their houses to crack. One inhabitant in describing the noise from the blasting site said:

> *For the blasting, it is not easy especially at night when we are asleep. As we are sleeping, we often booooom!!! And our houses and their foundations are usually felt shaking. If you go round for yourself how most of the houses in Mobilong have cracks because of the blasting. It is very dangerous*[346].

Comparatively, the effect of noise and vibration on local communities in Cameroon is almost the same situation witnessed by the local inhabitants of Kenyasi in Ghana as a result of the activity of Nemont Mining Company.[347]

[346]Interview, Zambo Julitte, Housewife, Mobilong, 5/11/2024.

[347] Opoku-Ware, J., (2010), "*The Social and Environmental Impacts of mining activities on Indigenous Communities: The Case of Newmont Gold (GH) Limited (Kenyasi) in Ghana,*" Masters Thesis, University of Agder, P. 43.

Going round to observe, it was visibly that seven (7) out of every ten (10) houses counted had serious cracks running through the buildings.

Figure 2: Cracks in some Buildings due to site blasting by C & K Mining Company Incorp.

Source: Researcher 5th November, 2024

7.1.4 The negative effects of Wildlife in Managing the Mining Sector

Wildlife is a broad term that refers to all plants and any animals (or other organisms) that are not domesticated. Mining affects the environment and associated biota through the removal of vegetation and top soil, the displacement of fauna, the release of pollutants.

7.1.4.1 Habitat Loss

Wildlife species live in communities that depend on each other. Survival of these species can depend on soil condition, local climate, altitude, and other features of the local habitat. Mining causes direct and indirect damages to wildlife. The effect stems primarily from disturbing, removing, and redistributing the land surface. Some effects are short-term and confined to the mined site while others may have far-reaching, long-term effects.

The most direct effect of wildlife is destruction or displacement of species in areas of excavation and piling of mine waste. This is one of the current environmental issues associated with mining wastes today in the world.[348] Mobile wildlife species like game animals, birds, and predators, leave these areas. More sedentary animals like invertebrates, many reptiles, burrowing rodents, and small mammals, may be more

[348]Djenchuraen, N., (1999), "*Current Environmental issues associated with Mining Wastes in Kyrgystan*", Masters Thesis, Central European University-Budapest, P. 18.

severely affected. If streams, lakes, ponds, or marshes are filled or drained, fish, aquatic invertebrates, and amphibians are severely impacted. Food supplies for predators are reduced by the disappearance of these land and water species.

Many wildlife species are highly dependent on vegetation growing in natural drainages. This vegetation provides essential food, nesting sites and cover for escape from predators. Any activity that destroys vegetation near ponds, reservoirs, marshes, and wetlands reduces the quality and quantity of habitat essential for waterfall, shore birds and many terrestrial species.[349]

The habitat requirements of many species do not permit them to adjust to changes created by land disturbance. These changes reduce living space. The degree to which animals tolerate human competition for space varies. Some species tolerate very little disturbances. For instance, where a particular critical habitat is restricted, such as a lake, pond, or primary breeding area, a specie could be eliminated. Surface mining can degrade aquatic habitats with effects felt many miles from a mining site. For example, sediment contamination of rivers and streams is common with surface mining.

The Mbalam Iron ore mining project, undertaken by Camiron S.A. is surrounded by some protected areas and reserves like the Dja reserve (North West of the site), the Boumba-Bek and Nki National parks (to the South); and the Ivindo National parks in Gabon. This giant mining project will obviously have a negative environmental challenge on these reserves and therefore the international body and Cameroon have to take necessary steps to see how to mitigate the adverse environmental effects on habitat loss in this part of the country.

7.1.4.2. Habitat Destruction

Habitat fragmentation occurs when large areas of land are broken up into smaller and smaller patches, making dispersal by native species from one patch to another difficult or impossible, and cutting off migratory routes. Isolation may lead to local decline of species or genetic effects such as inbreeding. Species that require large patches of forest simply disappear.

[349]Widerland, A., (2014), ''*Environmental Aspects of Mining*'', Masters Thesis, Lulea University of Technology, Sweden.P. 72.

7.1.4.2. Experiencing Biodiversity Loss

Under the Cameroonian law, a separate legal instrument apply to flora and fauna[350] (Plant life and wildlife) conservation values as far as the resulting effects of mining on living organisms to the exclusion of human beings is concerned. Reasons being that, the commencement of a mining project is on land which is the habitat of life out of water is directly linked to a list of hazards which degrade our national environment biodiversity.

7.1.4.2.1 The Concept of Deforestation

Deforestation is basically when trees are cut down from the forest and is understood as the state of the forest being cleared of trees or the removal of trees. The link between mining activities and deforestation is owing to the fact that mining necessitates the cleaning of the mining area at the initial phase. For mining to occur plant life suffers. Indiscriminate felling of trees to clear the wide zones containing the identified mineral resources becomes imminently very indispensable. The magnitude of loss of tropical forest is the subject of great debate. This situation results partly from the shrinking of the tropical forest that represent a great loss for human kind as these forest are the richest and the most divers ecosystems on the planet. Thousands of species are yet to be discovered. Deforestation to enhance mining operation contribute a lot to degrade the forest ecosystems since most mineral deposits are concentrated in the forest rich regions of Cameroon like the South and East Regions.[351] Resulting effects of deforestation include the fact that some key species are even not well known. Endangered and critical endangered species are yet to be fully identified. Since construction cannot be achieved without sacrificing plant life in the process of deforestation, the mining effects of such deforestation extends from destruction of trees and plants to increase possibilities of illegal logging in Cameroon.

7.1.4.2.2. The aspect of Desertification

This is the degradation of land by a number of factors of which mining is obviously included along factors like huge lands cleaning, farming, grazing, deforestation, and salinization of the soil. Desertification also account for a great loss of biodiversity. The effects

---

[350] Ononio, A.B., (2012), *Lois et Procedures en Matiere faunique au Cameroun, L.A.G.A and W.W.F.,* 1st Edition, P. 80.

[351] Funon, K.N., (2014), *"The Impacts of Artisanal Gold Mining on Local livelihoods and the Environment in the Forested Areas of Cameroon"*, Working Paper 150, Bogor, Indonesia: CIFOR, P 30.

on the environment are droughts that lead to migration of persons in large numbers towards the search for fertile land because of dryness and permanent malnutrition. The long term culminated effect of desertification is climate change due to such large scale mining activities.

7.1.4.5 The situation of Climate Change

Every EIA for a project that has the potential to change the global carbon budget should include an assessment of a project's carbon effect. Large scale mining projects have the potential to alter global carbon in at least the following ways:

7.1.4.5.1. Lost Carbon dioxide (CO_2) Uptake by Forest and Vegetation that is cleared

Many large-scale mining projects are proposed in heavily forested areas of tropical regions that are critical for absorbing atmospheric carbon dioxide (CO_2) and maintaining a healthy balance between CO_2 emissions and CO_2 uptake. Some mining projects propose long-term or even permanent destruction of tropical forests. EIAs for mining projects must include a careful accounting of how any proposed disturbance of tropical forest will alter the carbon budget. The EIA should also include an analysis of the potential for the host country to loss funding from international consortiums that have and will be established to conserve tropical forests.[352]

7.1.4.5.1 Carbon dioxide Discharged by Machines

Machines used in mineral exploitation usually emit heavy carbon dioxide that affect the climate negatively. The EIA for such project should include a quantitative estimate of CO_2 emissions from machines and vehicles that will be needed during the life of the mining project. These estimates can be based on the rate of fuel consumption (typically diesel fuel) multiplied by a conversation factor that relates units. (Typically litters or gallons) of fuel that is consumed and units (typically metric tons) of CO_2 that is emitted.

7.1.4.5. 2 Carbon dioxide Released by the Processing of Ore into Metal

This situation also leads to climate change especially by the process of metallurgical versus hydro-metallurgical techniques. An example is found in an assessment by CSIRO mineral of Australia which used the life cycle assessment methodology to estimate the life

[352]Nazhi, C., (1995), *Environmental Challenges and International Responses,* MIT Press, London, P. 431.

cycle emissions of greenhouse gases from copper and nickel production, including mining. This assessment found that life cycle greenhouse gas emissions from copper and nickel production range from 3.3kilograms of CO_2 per kg of metal for copper produced by smelting to 16.1kg of CO_2 per kg of metal for nickel produced by pressure acid leaching followed by solvent extraction and electro winning. The bottom line is that metal mining generate more than 1 kg of greenhouse gas for every 1 kg of metal that is produced, and this does not take into account lost carbon uptake of cleared forest.

7.1.5. Soil Quality

Mining can contaminate soil over a large area. Agricultural activities near a mining project may be particularly affected.[353] According to the study commissioned by the European Union: ''Mining operations routinely modify the surrounding landscape by exposing previously undisturbed earthen materials. Erosion of exposed soils, extracted minerals ores, tailings, and fine materials in waste rock piles can result in substantial sediment leading to surface waters and drainage ways. In addition, spills and leaks of hazardous materials and the deposition of contaminated windblown dust can lead to soil contamination.

7.1.5.1. Soil Adulteration

Human health and environmental risk from soils generally fall into two categories: (1) contaminated soil resulting from windblown dust and (2) soils contaminated from chemical spills and residues. Fugitive dust can pose significant environment problems at some mines. The inherent toxicity of the dust depends upon the proximity of environmental receptors and types of ores being mined. High level of arsenic, leads, and radio nuclides in windblown dust usually pose the greatest risk. Soils contaminated from chemicals spills as fill materials, ornamental landscaping, or soil supplements and residues at mine sites may pose a direct contact risk when these materials are misused as fill materials, ornamental landscaping, or soil supplements.[354]

7.2 Social Disruption: Livelihoods, Conflict, and Cultural Erosion

The social effects of large-scale mining projects are controversial and complex. Mineral development can create wealth, but this can also

[353]Adjei, E., (2007), ''*Impact of Mining on Livelihoods of Rural Households: A Case Study of Farmers in the Wassa Mining Region, Ghana*'', Masters Thesis, Norwegian University of Science and Technology, P. 85.

[354]Warhas, A., (1999), "*Mining and the Environmental Development: Case Studies from the Americas*", International Development Research Centre, Canada, P. 325.

cause considerable disruption. Mining projects create or may create jobs, roads, schoolsand increase the demands of goods and services in remote and impoverished areas, but the benefits and costs may be unevenly shared.

To be able to fully establish the extent of social effects of mining on Cameroonians in general and the host local communities in particular, the researcher found it extremely important to use certain basic social indicators which can easily be identified and analysed by the researcher. Among the major social impacts experience by the local communities in Cameroon which all the inhabitants noted affects them in one way or the other are high prices of goods, services and food commodities, increase in certain types of crimes, prostitution, population growth, high levels of poverty, employment problems, infrastructure development, business or economic activities in general, dispossession and deprivation of land rights and loss of control over resources, resettlement, conflict, migration and health.

7.2.1 Goods and Services

One important aspect of social life that is affected in communities where mining takes place is the price of goods and services. On prices of goods, services and food commodities, majority of the inhabitants of Kongo, and Lomie that host the GEOVIC Cameroon PLC lamented how the start of a mining operation in the community have resulted in escalated prices of goods, services as well as food commodities which hitherto were cheap. It is realized that the mere perception of the people about cobalt, nickel and manganese mining firm to them indicates that workers of such companies are very wealthy people and as a result are willing to pay any amount for a commodity they need. As a result, providers of basic services, petty traders and prices of general goods are so high with the view that workers of GEOVIC Cameroon PLC would be ready to pay for them when they need them. Community residents who usually complain about the high prices are usually told to leave if they cannot afford them even at such higher prices. By observation and actual confirmation, we decided to buy a sachet of water which according to the local inhabitant some years cost 50 FRS CFA but now being sold for 100 FRS CFA. Apart from the fact that most of the residents saw us as a researcher, in their minds, they also wondered if we were not a disguised GEOVIC worker and as a result sold the water to us at that high cost which we knew do not cost that much even in the cities like Douala and Yaoundé. A local inhabitant of Kongo for instance indicated to us that:

> *A few years ago, when I gave 1000FRS CFA to my wife, she could buy plantains, cassava and fish to prepare a meal for the entire household. But now I have to give her about 2000FRS CFA and then go to the farm to get other vegetables to add to that. If not, the whole family will starve and you see, we are farmers and our farms have been collected by GEOVIC for mining. No work for us too. Where do we get the money to cater for our family? We are suffering.* [355]

Similar responses were given by most of the responses and the passion with which they expressed themselves in relation to high prices of goods and services in Kongo land Lomie is particularly interesting to observe.

Figuil is a major source for cement production in Cameroon and is marketed mainly in other parts of the country and in neighbouring countries like Chad. Despite the production of cement in Fuigil, it is paradoxical that cement is more expensive there than other major towns in the north of Cameroon, making it inaccessible to the majority of the local population. A bag of cement in Figuil costs between 6500 and 8000, while in the neighbouring town of Garoua, cement costs between 4500 and 5000.

7.2.2 High Crime Wave

Social vices are noted to be a necessary by-product in communities where mining takes place. These vices including various types of crime and criminal activities as well as prostitution is usually rampant in communities where there are economic activities, influx of stranger such as mining areas. Questions about crime and criminal activities in the community since mining operation began were asked and the responses from the respondents are at best ''mixed''. Taking as a case study the localities of Yokadouma and Bétaré-Oya, a crime that is noted to be common is stealing from farms and assault. However, very heinous crimes such as murder and burglary are very uncommon. In fact, only few inhabitants indicated having heard about someone caught stealing from someone's farm or any other property. They however, attributed the low level of crime rate especially murder to the

[355]Interview, Mr, Gbamine Jacques, Farmer, 15/10/2025.

existence of certain traditional folklores and taboos in the community that provide for serious consequences for people who engage in such criminal acts. For instance, the belief in the existence of a river god who watches their deeds and reward or punish people accordingly.

7.2.3 The Situation of Prostitution

Prostitution is usually describes as ‘‘an old age’’ profession. It employs people in most countries although its widespread could be very devastating and could have a long term social and health impact for any society if not properly controlled especially when certain categories of people are involved. Views about the subject of prostitution have been very diverse and in some societies, its discussion is much closed. In Cameroon, the discussion of the subject matter of prostitution evokes morality and as such it is not usually discussed in public circles. On prostitution which we believe was quite sensitive and much closure exist in terms of its discussion, in both interviews, the focus group discussion and personal observation especially at night provided very revealing insights although to some extent we expected a certain trend in that direction. Interestingly, almost all the local inhabitants in Mbalam interviewed and the general response in the interview and agreement during the focus group discussion indicated an upward and significant increase in prostitution and other forms of sexual relationships that have developed in the community with the start of CAM IRON mining in the community. Usually, the responses go thus:

> *Hmm! That one, huh! It is so common that even young girls and children are involved in the practice. Now all our girls are been deceived into it because of money. It is the money they want because we are poor and they have to cater for their needs as well. At least, they do that for a living. Even this Christmas, you can see them at night.*[356]

Observing at night, I could easily see young girls standing around some major guest houses and hotels in Mbalam with some of them also moving in and out of the hotels with men, some of them being expatriates, supposedly, top officials of CAM IRON resident in the community. Usually girls of ages ranging from 16 years to 35 years are mostly spotted. In fact in the focus group discussion, it was particularly revealing when one member of the group retorted:

---

[356]Interview, Confidential, Mbalam, 12/12/2024.

Now these CAM IRON people have "collected" all our girls and wives and they are sleeping with them indiscriminately because they have the money and we are poor. For instance, when we give 1000 FRS CFA to our wives, the CAM IRON men will give her 10.000 FRS CFA. Because of them, our wives nowadays do not respect us because they think we are poor and we can't give them what they want. Most of our wives are divorcing us and marrying the CAM IRON workers and the young girls are just getting pregnant. As for me, if any of them should come near my wife, I will shoot them.[357]

This comment affirmed responses from majority of the inhabitants that the presence of CAM IRON and their mining activities have increased divorce rate in the community since the employees of CAM IRON according to the inhabitants have the money to provide for all the need of the women they have an affair with which they themselves lack.

7.2.4. Population Growth

Population growth is usually expected in communities where mining takes place because of the increased presence of mine workers in such communities. The effect of mining in Figuil, Bidzar and North Biou, all in the Northern part of Cameroon hosting ROCAGLIA and CIMENCAM mining companies on population growth is very visible. In their responses, all the local inhabitants stated that over the past four to five years, the population of these localities has increased significantly. In an attempt to seek clarity and to account for the reasons for that trend, they were asked what really accounted for such population increase in the communities over the past few years. Basically, two major reasons were assigned to the trend namely increase in birth rate and migration into the community by strangers who are either workers of ROCAGLIA and CIMENCAM or come to the communities with the hope of getting jobs in these mining firms. However, most of the local inhabitants indicated that the increase was basically due to the migration into the communities by strangers and foreigners from different parts of Cameroon who are there for jobs in the mines.

---

[357]Interview, Confidential, Focus Group Discussion, Mbalam 12/12/2024.

7.2.5 The presence of Poverty

The general believe is that the presence of mining companies in any particular area would inject massive capital investments into the area or community which would in effect trigger capital catch flows, put more money in the system and hence reduce poverty since economic activities would be generated. This belief we can say to a large extent account for the high prices of goods, services and food commodities in Mobilong because it is not uncommon to hear people say something like ''oh, diamond, is here and as such people here are rich''.

In order to confirm this assertion and belief that is dominant in the community and even among people living outside the Mobilong town, inhabitants were asked if the start of diamond mining have resulted in a reduction in poverty levels that is dominant in the community. From the responses all the inhabitants indicated that poverty levels have rather increased in the community since mining started in Mobilong. However, few of the local inhabitants were quick to add that families who have any of their relatives working at C & K mining company have had an improvement in their levels of poverty. Some of the local inhabitants also indicated that those whose lands were taken for mining were compensated with quite huge sums of money and as such they believed such people are also living quite better lives now.

On the contrary, local inhabitants who have had their lands taken over by C & K for mining when asked about the improvement in their poverty situation noted that the money was not enough and as such could not cater for their needs which have brought untold hardships on them, even much worse than before. A few indicated that they invested the money in building of houses but added that at some point, the money was not enough to complete such projects. Others also indicated using their money to buy lands for future use. Some of the local inhabitants also indicated that they extended their houses by building extra rooms for rents which they now depend on for their livelihood. The general feeling from the focus group discussion and the interviews is that poverty levels have rather worsened since mining began in the community since people whose lands were taken over by the mining firm do not have any other place to farm for their subsistence and the compensation given to them is woefully inadequate to make any serious life time investment which they can derive their daily livelihood. In an interview with one female respondent, she angrily said:

The C & K mining people have made our lives very miserable. They have taken over all our lands and now we do not have any place to farm and sell our products to feed our families. Now, we cannot buy meat or fish for our meals and we have to go to the bush to catch crabs as meat for our dinner. Why? Look at me and the children there, how do we feed them? At first, when we sell our farm products, we get money to feed them and send them to school; but these people (C & K mining company) have collected our farms and on top they failed to employ our children.[358]

This comment affirmed responses from majority of the respondents that the presence of C & K mining company and their mining activities have instead worsened poverty situation in the community since most of the inhabitants have been deprived of their means of livelihood. Comparatively, the situation in Mobilong is similar to that felt by many communities in Ghana and Tanzania as a result of the effects of mining activities on their lands.[359]

7.2.6 The promises of Employment to the local communities

The promises of jobs have been one of the major incentives for most communities to open up mining activities. In order to confirm the responses on high levels of poverty, local inhabitants of Mobilong were asked about employment situation in the community because most of the local inhabitants had earlier indicated that families who have any of their relatives working at the C & K mining company have had an improvement in their livelihood. The aim was to draw a link between employment levels and the prevalence of poverty in the community as indicated by the local inhabitants. Initially, local inhabitants were asked if there was any promise from authorities or management of C & K mining company for the provisions of jobs to the members of the community before mining began in the community. In fact, C & K report states that ''their labour recruitment discourages excessive migration from outsiders to local communities due to their policies of

---

[358]Interview, Madam Balolo Amare Jacques, Farmer, Mobilong, 5/11/2024.

[359]See the following; Jemilatu Yaro, I., (2010), ''*The Impact of Mining on livelihoods of Local Communities: A Case Study of Newmont Ahafo South Mining Project of Brong Ahafo Region of Ghana*'', Masters Thesis, International Instituttе of Social studies, the Netherlands, P. 45, Kitula, A.G.N., (2006), ''*The environmental and socio-economic Impacts of Mining on Local livelihoods in Tanzania: A Case Study of Géita District*'', Journal of Cleaner Production, Elsevier, P. 414.

hiring local people''.[360] As a response to this question, all the local inhabitants indicated affirmatively ''Yes'' and indicated that the promise of jobs for the people of Mobilong at the mines was a major reason for accepting the proposal for the company to start mining in the community. They believed that employment in the mining firm would alleviate their financial problems and poverty and therefore accepted that promise readily.

In a sequel to this question, local inhabitants were asked if they or their children have been employed in the mining firm since mining operation began. Most of the local inhabitants reacted angrily to this question and stated that they have not been provided with the promised employment. Neither their children nor any relative had been promised with any form of employment linked with mining activities in the community. Only two (2) local inhabitants stated that they have one of their relatives working with the company. Further probing these local inhabitants revealed that they were relatives of the Mobilong chief and as a result the chief supposedly used his influence as the community leader to get them employed in the company. In a discussion with the chief of Mobilong, he told the researcher that C & K is currently employing many youths from the village, but there is still mass unemployment in the village.[361]

Further, the local inhabitants were asked to give explanations as to why they have not been employed by the mining firm. They indicated that the mining company failed to employ them because they complained that the local people do not have the relevant and requisite skills to work in the mining companies. Few of the local inhabitants also attributed the situation to bribery and corruption (particularly impersonation) on the part of the community leaders and C & K officials (mainly Cameroonian Managers) to employ people who can pay. All of them however stated that since the company tells them that they do not have the skills and competence to work in the mines coupled with their inability to pay the bribes that are requested by some C & K officials for employment, most of their children have become miserable and frustrated because they do not have anything to do and also cannot farm because the land has been taken over by the mining company. One

[360] C & K Mining Company Incorporation Sustainability Report (2011) ''*Now and Beyond 2011*'', A C& K Mining Inc. Publication, Cameroon.

[361] Steven Fox, (2011), ''*Opacity: A Socioeconomic Study of Diamond Mining in South–Eastern Cameroon*'', IST Collection Paper, 728, P, 55.

interviewee stated this when assigning reasons as to why they are not employed:

> *C & K people are saying that we have not gone to school and we are illiterate. They say they need people who have gone to school and have knowledge about how to do mining. For us here, we are only farmers and we are not educated. So if you want your son or daughter to work at C & K, then you have to give a bribe.*[362]

Local inhabitants of Mobilong were asked about the type or kind of people who are working at C & K. Most of them indicated that workers of C & K are basically not local people from Mobilong but rather migrants from other mining areas in Cameroon particularly Lomie, Kongo and Bétaré-Oya where mining company like GEOVIC have operated for quite long periods of time and the people have somewhat high educational levels and standards. Only a few people from the community have managed to give bribes and have got employment as unskilled and semi-skilled labourers in other related services of the mining operation like catering and driving of vehicles. Observation from the community confirms the fact that only few local men and women are employed at C & K and hence, they can be seen readily loitering about in the community or playing football or other forms of traditional games without work. Interviews with the employees from C & K Company also confirmed that most of the local people have been denied employment because they are illiterates and lack the skills to work in the mines where huge machines and equipments are used. He even advised me to tell them to acquire education if they are to get employment in the mining firm if not directly at C & K or with other subsidiary services associated with the mining operations in Mobilong.[363]

On the contrary, a review of C & K's documents indicates that the company has been committed to their promise to the community by hiring 100% of unskilled labourers from the local communities and have given priority to local community members in jobs where skills and experiences are required.[364] This same report notes that by July 2011, the mining firm is committed that 35% of their operational workforce will be local people from the surrounding villages like

[362]Interview, Confidential, Mobilong, 5/11/2024.
[363]Interview, C & K Mining Company employee, Confidential, 5/11/2024.
[364]C & K Mining Company Incorporation Sustainability Report (2011), Op. Cit.,

Mobilong, Moboy I and Moboy II. This is in sharp contrast to the local inhabitant's responses and what was observed as well as the response on employment from the C & K employee interviewed. According to C & K its employment rate has been increasing since 2010 with an initial start of 706 employees, rising to 2,693 and 4,803 for the year 2011 and 2012 respectively with a national employment rate in the mines being 50% whereas local employment rate is 30%.[365] It can therefore be realised that comparatively, more people from other parts of the country are employed than local residents of Mobilong and confirms the respondent's responses that more outsiders are employed by the mining firm than local Mobilong residents.

The failure of C & K to employ local people has resulted in grief, frustration and hatred from the people towards the mining company and its employees resulting in some minor conflicts and tension. In the focus group discussion, members indicated that there is a simmering tension in the community between the youths especially and the mining company and that any least provocation can trigger a clash. One of the members in the discussion stated that they had been a time when the youths tried to kill one of the employee drivers of the firm when passing by with the company's car. They smashed all the screens of the car and had attempted to kill the employee's driver but for the early intervention of one opinion leader. It is particularly revealing when one other local inhabitant responded in an interview:

> *Let me tell you, when you come to Mobilong here, all of us have guns in our rooms waiting for a day when tension sparks. That day, only God knows what will happen to these people (C & K workers).*[366]

This comment we believe shows the extent of grief and frustration that has filled the hearts and minds of most of the people in the community.

7.2.7 Infrastructural Expansion

Infrastructure basically refers to those physical structures that enhance the life and living conditions of people in any place. These especially include electricity, roads, schools, and social amenities etc that make life comfortable. Local communities in Cameroon where mining is taking place lack certain facilities and infrastructure comparable to bigger cities in Cameroon like Yaoundé or even Bertoua,

---

[365] Ibid .

[366] Interview, Confidential, Mobilong, 5/11/2024.

which is the regional capital of a region that hosts most of the mining companies in Cameroon. However, popular thinking in local communities in Cameroon like Mobilong as in many other mining areas in the world is that the presence of big mining firms like C & K mining company would inevitably lead to a massive infrastructural development in the community due to the massive injection of capital and infrastructural investment in such communities.

Local inhabitants were therefore asked to indicate whether mining in the community have impacted significantly on infrastructural development in the community. Responding initially to this question, most of the local inhabitants noted that one major reason for accepting the proposal for mining to take place in the community was the promise made to them by the company, the government and community leaders about provision of certain basic infrastructure and social amenities like good drinking water for households, provision of electricity to houses, building of hospitals, schools, tarring of untarred roads and other physical structures that can open up the area ready for variety of economic activities and hence, create employment and reduce poverty. When asked whether such infrastructure have been provided, most of the local inhabitants interviewed said that such infrastructures have not been provided or the existing ones improved in the community since mining started. They rather indicated that the few that already exist have rather been worsened or destroyed because of the pressure that the company has brought into the community due to the large number of migrants and strangers moving into the community who compete with the local people for few existing ones.

This is confirmed by a report prepared by C & K mining company which states that the presence of mining in the community has ''increased pressure on social services, health, education and sanitation due to new residents''.[367] Specifically, they mentioned a promise to build a hospital for the community but so far, C & K has not built one. Instead, the company has only rehabilitated part of the community clinic that was built by Cameroonian government some years back.

These same respondents said that facilities like drinking water and community roads are very deplorable and there are no plans by the company to improve and maintain them or to provide new ones for the community.

[367]C & K mining Company Incorporation Sustainability Report, (2011), Op.Cit.,.

Contrary to popular responses by the respondents which indicate that no major infrastructure investments had been made in the community since mining started, a review of C & K documents however, contradicts these responses and notes that as at 2011 and 2012, C & K has committed US$ 358, 841 in monetary community investments with the largest allocation of US$ 222, 222 made for civil projects followed by US $ 132, 000 on education. Another report also notes that in 2003 alone, the mining company spent US$ 110,000 on community investments primarily on health, education and social infrastructure with community leaders involved in directing investments.[368]

Following the report of C & K, the researcher sought to observe the above-named facilities provided by the company but was unable to see them in the community. All attempts made to contact the company authorities were in vein despite the numerous appointments they gave us. The conclusion we can draw from this drama is that most mining companies are there to protect their interests and the natural resources found in Africa in general and Cameroon in particular end up as a grief to the people.[369]

7.2.8 Economic and Business Development

It is noted that mining can be a major propellant of economic activities in most mining communities by creating wealth, providing jobs and stimulating business ventures for community members. A good example here is the situation in the Americas[370] and in Ghana.[371] The researcher took the case study of Mbalam community and tried to see the impact of CAM IRON S.A on economic and business development. The local inhabitants were asked if mining in this community has created a conducive economic environment for stimulating business, creating wealth and providing personal jobs for the people in the community. Some of the local inhabitants indicated that mining has generated petty business in the community. Others were of the opinion that mining has created some local jobs and business but

---

[368]Ibid .

[369] Mpacko Priso, A., (2010), "*Où Sont Passée les Ressources qui manquent pour le Développement de l'Afrique?* ", La Revue Sub Saharienne d'Economie et de Finance, P. 119. See also, Reed, E., and Marta, M., (2007), ''*Assessment of the Mining Sector and Infrastructure Development in the Congo Basin Region,''* W.W.F, Washington DC, P. 18.

[370]Gary. M., (2001), *Large Mines and the Community: Socioeconomic and Environmental Effects in Latin America, Canada and Spain, the World Bank, Washington DC*, P. 145.

[371]Antwi, F., (2010), ''*An Assessment of the Impact of Newmont Gold Ghana Limited (NGGL) on the Socio-Economic Development after six years of Operation in the Birim North District.''*, Masters Thesis, Kwame Nkrumah University of Science and Technology-Ghana, P. 65

not as many as expected. Another fraction was on the stand that business in the community were already existing before mining started. Most of the inhabitants are people whose lands and farms were taken over by CAM IRON and were given compensation. Such people they added for fear of not getting their daily bread decided to invest in petty business ventures that could provide them with a source of livelihood since it is their main livelihood which was their farms that had been taken over by the mining company. By observation, the researcher noticed that most of the businesses in Mbalam were mainly table top businesses like selling toffees, and roasting of ripe plantains. It is also common to see people doing business in telecommunication particularly selling phone credits, cards and credit transfers.

7.2.9 Withdrawal and Denial of Land Rights

Findings show that there is the continued denial of the local communities to own, control and enjoy their lands and natural resources. An example of such local community is the Baka located at Mobilong in the East of Cameroon. The impact of the exploitation of diamond by C & K mining company has result to dispossession and deprivation of their land rights and loss of control of resources. The government does not provide adequate protection to these vulnerable indigenous people nor recognise their rights, which are linked to their status as indigenous peoples under international law.[372] The land ownership legislation in force does not take into account the traditions, customs and land tenure systems of indigenous peoples or their way of life.[373] The Baka-the original natives of the region, since the introduction of reserves of timber by mining companies in the region, have felt their access to their traditional forest shrinking. The Baka's original ability to freely roam the forest in search of food has evaporated. They have muddled perception of the mining occurring around them.[374]

The creation of reserves and parks and the allocation of timber and mining concession simply is a huge takeover of hunting and

[372] Nah Tetinwe, A., (2016), "*Translating policies on the rights of indigenous communities into concret practice to mitigate conflicts over natural resource exploitation in cental Africa: Case study of the Baka people in Eastern Cameroon*", Journal of studies of sociology of science, Vol.7, N° 6, P.5.

[373] Centre Pour l'Environnement et le Développement, (2013), ''*A Proposal by Traditional Rulers on Land Tenure Reforms in the Rural areas of Cameroon*'', Messa Press, Yaoundé. See also Nyuyinui, M., ''*Droit foncier et droit des Communautés: les enjeux de la reforme au Cameroun*'', A Paper Presented at the International Conference on ''Gouvernance des Ressources Naturelles et Droit des Communautés au Cameroun de 1994 à 2014: Bilan et Perspectives'', Organized by Centre Pour L'Environnement et le Développement, Yaoundé, Hôtel Mt Fébé, du 13 au 16 Avril 2015.

[374] Steven Fox, (2011), Op.Cit., P. 22.

agricultural land previously cultivated for domestic purposes, affecting the livelihoods of the Baka community. As per agreements and contractual issues leading to the commencement of natural resources exploitation by companies, all the lands in the area are under concession and companies possess the legal right to demarcate it for any natural resources exploitation related activity. Based on this concession, companies hold the right to acquire any previously occupied land and to resettle or compensate the affected group under already documented rules and guidelines satisfying to all parties and interest group but which are never well implemented.

What has generated agitations and conflicts is the fact that Companies have taken over large portions of land, installed equipments and fenced the explorative areas to prevent any encroachment on the area. By implication, most of the lands belong to this company (C & K mining company). The effects has been loss of productive agricultural and hunting, fishing and foraging land for indigenous peoples, thus limiting the expansion of the community and impoverishment resulting from the loss of their livelihood. For instance, diamond mining at Mobilong in South-Eastern Cameroon has created a negative lifestyle change for local peoples as the company has been making great use of the fauna as nutrition for their workers, taking away from the Baka's food sources.[375]

Today, the Baka have been restricted by zoning and are no longer allowed to wonder freely into their former hunting grounds which are now under the logging and mining companies. Under the United Nations Declaration on the Rights of Indigenous Peoples, the current situation the Bakas are facing seems to be contradictory. Under Article 26, indigenous Peoples have the right to land, territory and resources which they have traditionally possessed and resided in. Article 29 declares that indigenous Peoples have the right to preservation and protection of their environment as it is used for production of resources.

7.2.10 Relocation/ Dislodgment

A total of about 300 households were impacted/ displaced by the mining activity in Mobilong by the C & K mining company.[376] The majority of the people are farmers who depended on the environment for their livelihood and source of income. The implications of such displacement on these Baka inhabitants have been acute food shortage

[375]Ibid, P. 40.

[376]C & K Mining Company Incorporation Sustainability Report, (2011), Op. Cit.,

and heightened levels of poverty. Resettlement/relocation also contributed to the breakdown in family relations and disruption of social cohesion. The resettlement areas do not have the same conditions and facilities as previously inhabited areas. This necessitates the need to provide all relevant social services and facilities to support their wellbeing in the newly inhabited places.

As a result of the numerous problems which the Baka of Mobilong diamond project are facing, the researcher wanted to know the opinion of other stakeholders on these problems by posing the question of potential problems with affects of mining on the Baka, a high-level administrator in the mining sector responded:

> *There is no problem. People want to create problems. People want to shout and do not give any help to those pygmies, they just shout. There is no problem. They want development, they want like everyone else. Bring development, don't talk and don't talk too much. There is no problem.*[377]

This comment simply to an extent show the lack of willingness on the part of mining officials to deal with the effects of mining activities on the vulnerable people like the Baka in the Mobilong diamond mining site. Beside this, is the issue of wife snatching. Some Baka community members reported of their wives being snatched by C & K workers. Some company workers had capitalized on the inability of some community members to secure jobs after losing their livelihoods to the mine to snatch their wives away from them by providing them with money and packed lunch. As one Baka member said:

> *As for this company people, they are not good, they have taken our lands and now they are even snatching our wives from us. When they get your wife, you are finished. What they do is to provide the ladies with money and take away.*[378]

7.2.11. Conflict

Natural resources have been shown to be linked to the conflicts that have plagued a number of Central African countries over the last decades, both motivating and fuelling armed conflicts.[379] Natural

[377]Interview, Confidential, Yaoundé, 10/11/2024.

[378]Interview, Confidential, Mobilong, 5/11/2024.

[379]Hallesson, D.N., (2009), "*An Analysis of Natural Resources Related Conflicts in Central Africa and the Gulf of Guinea*", Cameroon Journal on Democracy and Human Rights, Vol. 3, N^{O}. 1, P. 47.

resource revenues allocated to catchment communities are mismanaged, compromising peace as armed groups buys over the legitimate claims of indigenous peoples who are discriminated against in natural resource management. Even when conflict give way to a fragile peace, control over natural resources and their revenues often stays in the hands of small elite and not used for broader development.[380] In consequence, both national and international measures to avoid the detrimental impact of resources endowment have increasingly been discussed and implemented[381] however with little achievements.

Despite being endowed with some of the most demanded natural resources in the world, Africa has failed to transform its enormous natural wealth into tangible benefits. Instead, the abundance of the natural resources has become what some analysts described as a ''curse'' or a ''peace liability'',[382] fuelling violent conflicts over access to, and control of, natural resource wealth.[383] Recent experiences from resource-endowed countries such as the Democratic republic of Congo and Central Africa Republic have demonstrated the critical linkage between the exploitation of natural resources and violent conflict.[384] Natural resources promote conflict through three mechanisms: first, resources can motivate conflict as violence results from disputes over the benefits of the costs[385]of resource extraction. Second, natural resources provide opportunities for violence by financing warfare. Third, resources can cause conflict through indirect mechanisms: resources may weaken political institutions and impair the effectiveness of public bureaucracy, as they increase the incentives for corrupt behaviour.

In the United nations secretary General's seminar report to the General Assembly and the Security Council in 1998 on the causes of conflict and the promotion of durable peace and sustainable

---

[380]United Nations Expert Group, (2006), ''*Natural Resources and Conflict in Africa: Transforming a Peace Liability into Peace Asset,* '' United Nations Expert Group Meeting, Conference Report, Cairo, Egypt, P. 7.

[381]Mähler, A., Shabafrouz, M., andStrüver, G., (2011), ''*Conflict prevention through Natural Resources Management?": A Comparative Study,*'' Working paper N° 158, German Institute of Global and Area Studies, Hamburg-Germany. Available at www.giga-hanburg.de/workingpapers Accessed 20 July 2025.

[382]United Nations Expert Group, (2006), Op.Cit., P. 62.

[383]Ganesan, A., and vines, A., "*Engine of War: Resources, Greed, and the Predatory State",* Available at http://www.hrw.org/legacy/wrzk4/download/14pdf. Accessed on 15/7/2025.

[384]Network of Global Agenda Councils, Natural Riches?Perspectives on responsible Natural Resource Management in Conflict-affected Countries, World Economic Forum, Geneva, Switzxerland, 2013, PP, 6 and 7.See also, Owona Mfegue, K.F., (2005), Op. Cit., P. 50 .

[385]Example, ecological damages, and socio-economic stress

development in Africa, among the key factors identified as fuelling conflict was the illegal exploitation of natural resources and non-payment of compensation to the catchment communication to mitigate the adverse effects of exploitation.[386] In 2005, in the Secretary General's Progress report to the 60th session of the General Assembly on the implementation of the recommendations contained in the above report, the secretary General reiterated that illegal exploitation of natural resources in conflict-prone and conflict-ridden countries continued to be one of the contributory causes of conflict and if its recurrence and cited the example of Angola, the Democratic republic of the Congo, Sierra Leone and Liberia, where natural resources had provided major funding for the perpetuation of war[387].

Although natural resource exploitation has been presented as impetus to economic growth, the consequence on catchment communities has been alarming. Often, the blame has been laid on governments and companies perceived as indifferent to sustaining communities and addressing the enormous negative impact of their operations. This ''devil may care'' attitude of mining industry is well presented in the media, civil society and international organizations.[388] Cameroon, like some other Central Africa Countries has been beset by a number of conflicting claims regarding rights over the management of natural resources, leading at times, to loss of ancestral lands, inter-ethnic conflicts damages and loss of property, lives and the aggravation of the poverty situation in rural areas.[389]

Although there has not been real conflicts in Cameroon as a result of the exploitation of natural resources, some degree of tension has often arisen in some local communities between the youths and the mining company. In this light the youths of Lolabé located some 30 kilometres from the town of Kribi in the South of Cameroon on 28 of August 2008 mounted a road blockage against the activities of SINOSTEEL CAM, a mining company that is exploiting Iron Ore on the Mountain of Mamelles.[390] These angry youths expressed the non-recruitment in the mining activity and non-respect of the promised made by the company to the villagers as regards the provision of basic

---

[386] United nations Expert Group (2006), Op. Cit., P. 62.
[387] Ibid.
[388] Mensah, S.O., and Okyere, S.A., (2014), Op. Cit., P. 69.
[389] Amungwa, F.A., (2011), '*The Evolution of Conflicts related to Natural Resource Management in Cameroon,* '', J Hum Ecol, 35(1), Kamla-Raj, P. 54.
[390] Joseph Abena, ''*Les villageois Barrent la Route aux Engins de la SINOSTEEL CAM*'', Le Jour, Vendredi 28 Août 2008.

social amenities like water, electricity, and health unit. Even if the local community of Lolabé and the Baka may not be at conflict or war in the technical sense of those words; it is nonetheless anarchic and riddled with claims that stems from the fact that natural resources have not or are not benefiting them.

7.2.12. The Situation of Migration

One of the most significant impacts of mining activity is the migration of people into a mine area, particularly in remote parts of Cameroon where mines represents the single most important economic activity. For example, the population of Kongo increased in 2003 due to the presence of GEOVIC in the locality. Most of these migrants were in search of greener pastures at the mines but surprisingly most of their dreams were never met since the jobs they came in search for are not available. Comparatively, at the Grasberg mine in Indonesia the local population increased from less than 1000 in 1973 to population of the squatter settlements around Porgera in PNG, which opened in 1990, has grown from 4000 to over 18,00. This influx of newcomers can have a profound impact on the original inhabitants, and disputes may arise over land and the way benefits have been shared.[391].

Sudden increases in population can also lead to pressure on land, water, and other resources as well as bringing problems of sanitation and waste disposal. Migration effects may extend far beyond the immediate vicinity of the mine. Improved infrastructures can also bring an influx of settlers. For instance, it is estimated that the 80-meters-wide, 890-kilometers-long Ocean to the Carajas mine in Brazil created an area of influence of 300.000 square kilometres.

7.2.13. Health Implications

The medical community is starting to see the issue of mining as a serious threat to the general health of the population. Be it in Mbalam, Mobilong and Bétaré-Oya, the health effects of mining remain alarming. In Mobilong, the people were asked about the effect of mining upon their health. A lot of people were able to say the sickness and the diseases they suffer from are as a result of mining activities. A lot of people came out to say that the majority of them suffer from malaria since they are unable to cover the pit after mining which serves as a breeding place for mosquitoes which cause malaria. Apart from malaria, people also complained of having cholera, diarrhea, cold, flu,

[391]These were among the factors that led to violent uprisings at Grasberg in the 1970s and the 1990s.

headache and skin rashes which might also be as a result of the use of certain chemicals during mining which affects their water bodies. Comparatively these are similar health hazards affecting the local inhabitants of Akwatia town in Ghana as a result of the activity of mining industry.[392]

Contamination of the environment is not a major health problem in Mobilong since diamond mining does not involve much chemical use. There are some health related matters as a result of the mining activities. The mining activities carried out by both C & K and artisaner operators create large pits which are filled with water during rainy season. Stagnant water, which serves as a breeding site for anopheles mosquitoes the vector which causes malaria in Africa are all over in Mobilong. This has really increased the rate of malaria in Mobilong and some see it to be normal. Malaria affects more people in Cameroon but the mining industry has also helped in the increasing number of cases in that community.[393]

Again, the community believes that due to the influx of immigrants there has been an increased rate of teenage pregnancy, sexually transmitted diseases, assault and other respiratory tract infections since most of the youths die from contracting one of the above mentioned diseases.[394]This was revealed by Mr Ekuda who works in the Public Health Unit of St. Dominic's Hospital, Mobilong. HIV/AIDS are also killing a lot of people in the Eastern region of Cameroon, where Mobilong is found.

The researcher in the zeal to find out the health effect of artisanal mining activity in Bétaré-Oya discovered that, most of the miners on this site appear to be physically well fit although, they said back aches, muscle aches are very common including hernia and respiratory affections. Malaria is also very persistent especially in the rainy season due to the proximity of numerous abandoned pits that are later filled with water.[395]

---

[392]Kwateng, G., (2012), ''*Environmental Impact of Mining and the Well-being of the People in Akwatia: A Case Study in Akwatia Town, Ghana,*'' Masters Thesis, Swedish University of Agricultural Sciences, P. 45.

[393]Randhem, J., (2008), ''*Environmental Impacts and Health Aspects in the Mining Industry*'', Masters Thesis, Chalmers University of Technology, Sweden, P. 35.

[394]Njilah, I.K., ''*Mining and Public Health: Case of HIV-AIDS Prevalence in Mining Communities*'', A Paper Presented at the 2nd Cameroon International Mining Conference and Exhibition on ''*Developing Central Africa's Sustainable Mining Sector*'', Organised by Ametrade and MINMITD, Yaoundé, Conference Hall, 27-29 May 2015.

[395]Focus Group Discussion Bétaré-Oya, 17/08/2024.

CHAPTER EIGHT
COMMUNITY RESILIENCE AND COPING STRATEGIES IN THE FACE OF ADVERSITY OF MINING ACTIVITIES IN CAMEROON

This chapter is specifically the result of personal interviews with local communities on company and survival mechanisms developed by the community residents themselves in response to the environmental and social impacts that are experienced in their communities. It also finds out the nature of the survival or coping mechanisms and how these mechanisms were developed or obtained in order to adjust to the impacts.

8.1 Navigating the Social Landscape: Community Strategies for Mitigating Mining Impacts

Naturally, it is common for people to device measures to deal with effects of a particular phenomenon on their lives. This is what is usually called coping and survival mechanisms. This can also be said about effects of mining and it resultant effect on people especially when such effects threaten their very survival and livelihood. For the people of Mobilong for example, managing and developing alternative coping and survival mechanisms is a natural outcome of the effects that are experienced in the community as a result of mining activities. As noted above, the social effects exerted by mining activities in Cameroon is mainly centred on issues of crime, prostitution, population growth, escalating prices of goods and food commodities, employment, poverty, minor conflicts with company workers and staff, infrastructure development as well as business (economic activities).

In finding out from the local community what mechanisms they have adopted to adjust or mitigate these social effects, most of the respondents readily responded that they do not have any technical capacity to mitigate their social effects since they believe that its effects are beyond their control. At best, they merely have to adjust. For instance, they stated that issues of crime control and prevention, prostitution, conflicts and infrastructure development to a larger extent is the main responsibility of the government and the responsible institutions of state and can only complain and draw the attention of those state institutions responsible for controlling and managing them.

However, for employment in particular, most of the local inhabitants indicated that since they need to survive, they quickly have to develop an alternative means of survival. Most of the local inhabitants indicated that a major coping mechanism to their employment problem is to engage in illegal artisanal mining. Under this method gold has been exploited without recourse to environmental concerns. The youth in the area are manly involved as a means of employment in their desperate quest to survive. When asked, most of the respondent said:

> *Please, the artisanal ''is our life wire now. Now is what we depend on mostly to survive because when we wake up, we and our children go there to dig and mine gold so that by evening time, we will get something to eat. Had it not been this illegal mining, most of our children would have been armed robbers by now. They should leave us alone to do our ''artisanal'' because they did not employ us.*[396]

Observation at the illegal artisanal mining site revealed large number of young men and women as well as old ones involved in gold mining on site without any environmental consideration. As noted by most of the respondents, many of the young workers on the illegal mining site noted they have engaged in that work as a means of survival since they have not been employed by C & K Mining Company Incorporation and their farms have also been taken over for mining purposes.

Apart from engaging in illegal mining as an alternative to their employment problems, few of the local inhabitants also noted that as an alternative to employment, they have entered into agreement with other community members whose farms have not been taken over by the mining company to form and share the products of the farm with the owners of the land. Again some of the local inhabitants stated that now they are engaged in petty business of some sort since their farms were taken over by C & K for mining.

8.2 Local Monitoring and Mitigation of Mining's Environmental Impacts

Since most local communities in Cameroon interact with their environment to survive, the researcher stay in some of the mining communities in Cameroon like Mobilong, Mbalam and Lomie

[396]Interview, Confidential, Mobilong, 5/11/2024.

prompted him to find out how they are coping and adjusting to the environmental effects that mining in the community is having on them. For example, effects on land, air and noise pollution, most of the inhabitants in these above mentioned communities indicated that like most of the social effects, they only have to adjust or accept such effects since he communities do not have the means to deal with the effects but to accept them. However, for effects on water, it is clear that some measures have been taken by the people in response. Since most of the water bodies have been rendered unusable since mining began, most of the local inhabitants indicated that they have resorted to the digging of deep wells in their homes to provide them with water bodies previously used. Few of the inhabitants noted that they make use of water pipes provided by the mining companies like C & K Mining Company in Mobilong at a fee. They complained that the digging of wells in their homes and the buying water from pipes is very expensive and further adds to their poverty woes. Those of the Mobilong lament how they could initially easily access water from rivers like ''Subika'' and ''Atoko'' without having to pay any money.

On mining effects on air, most local inhabitants noted that mechanisms developed to adjust and mitigate its impacts are done by mining companies like C & K in Mobilong which involves the periodic spraying and sprinkling of the roads with water from water tankers. However, the spraying is done at long intervals and one could easily see dust particles in the atmosphere at Mobilong especially during the day.

8.3 Corporate response: the limits of corporate social responsibility

This section is based on interviews with the communities' inhabitants as well as mining companies' employees and text analysis on the awareness of mining companies to the social and environmental impacts of mining activities on local communities. Specifically, measures devised and developed by the company are elicited from the companies' employee and some text analyses of such measures and strategies also reviewed.

8.4 Mining Companies' Awareness of Their Environmental and Social Impacts

One most important first step in dealing with any problem is the acceptance and knowledge of the existence of the problem. To be able to device strategies and measures to deal with the effects of mining on the local communities, the management of the mining companies first need to be aware of the existence of any such effects and then be able to develop strategies to migrate or help people to adjust them. As a result, local inhabitants hosting some of the mining companies were asked if in their major social and environmental effects of mining companies operation in their communities have come to the attention of the management of the mining firm. From the responses given, almost all the respondents said that the companies is fully aware of the effects that their activities are having on the communities because of two major reasons. For example in Mobilong, the officials of the company have been having some meetings with the community and their representatives periodically and secondly, there is the existence of information centres for C & K that the community residents' lodge complains and grievances. On the other hand, few indicated that not all the effects are known by the company because they believe the most important and real problems on the ground in the community are not communicated to the C & K management by the chiefs and their community leaders. One interviewee when asked about C & K awareness of most of the environmental and social problems the community faces since mining started said:

> *When you go to the information centres and tell them your problems, they do nothing about them. Our representatives are also bribed and so they don't tell them the real problems facing us.*[397]

Asked the same question, the C & K employee interviewed noted that most of these effects have already and earlier been anticipated by the company even before the start of the operation and they continue to develop strategies to mitigate and help people adjust to them.

When asked further if apart from the community leaders, the Mobilong inhabitants cannot make complain to C & K themselves, most of the respondents indicated that some people had on their own tried to meet C & K officials themselves but had difficulties meeting them. However, they added that most people are afraid to complain to C & K officials directly. When asked why they were afraid, most of them noted that there is likely to be a contradiction in what their chief tells C & K officials and what the community residents will also tell the officials. The disgrace that will result they indicated cost them either lives or other forms of punishments from the community leaders. One respondent in the interview said that:

[397]Interview, Confidential Mobilong, 5/11/2024.

Who am I to tell C & K or the chief what to do? We cannot complain much. Those who complain are punished by the chief and in extreme cases are killed. For me I don't want to die early.[398]

8.5 CSR as a Framework for Sustainable Mining Practices

This section is based on how the mining companies manage the social and environmental effects of its activities through responsible business practices like corporate social responsibility. Thus, we shall vividly consider the notion and definition of Corporate Social Responsibility (CSR) on the one hand, and on the other hand, examine the extent to which mining companies do practice CSR.

8.5.1 The Doctrine of Social Responsibility in Business

Emphatically, CSR is a precursor of social contract which understand men as being able to act freely in a civil society united by a general will or ''Volonté Géneral''.[399] Therefore, social contract signifies the relationship between the society and the business. According to the contract, society recognizes organizations as agents, particularly in the eyes of the law, and authorizes them to use land, natural resources and offer employment. From the business point of view, they improve the quality of life of a society. One can take the argument of the social contract further by adding to it that business socially, morally and politically ''bounded'' to improve the quality of life of society: they are expected to enhance the life of consumers and workers to promote justice by avoiding deception or fraud, respect their workers and avoid harming any other social groups.[400] It is, however, the manner in which the social contract has been conducted, particularly on behalf of corporations during the past one hundred years, that makes the issue of CSR so prominent and important nowadays. It may be that the reason behind the ''misconducts'' of the social contract is the different understanding and explanations developed around the notion of CSR. The social contract is just one ''plausible'' explanation of what is CSR. Many competing arguments that justify the nature and scope of CSR have been developed over the years, resulting in offering different discourses of the notion.[401]

---

[398]Interview, Confidential, Mobilong, 5/11/2024.

[399]Rousseau, J., *The New Encyclopaedia Britannica,* Chicago, Vol. 26, P. 942.

[400]Bichta, C., (2000), '' *The key Determination of Environmental Performance- Case Studies from the Chemical/Fertiliser and Metal Sectors,''* PhD Thesis, School of Management, University of Bath –United Kingdom, P. 75.

[401]Bichta, C., (2002), ''*Corporate Social Responsible Practices in the Context of Greek Industry'',* Corporate Social Responsibility and Environmental Management Journal, Vol. 5, P. 24.

A commonly accepted illustration of CSR is Carroll's[402] four component model of economic, legal, ethical, and discretionary responsibilities. The four components could be depicted as a pyramid.[403] The pyramid starts with the ''economic responsibilities'' as the foundation and the first and foremost responsibility of business. As the basic unit in society, a business is responsible to provide goods or services and make profit to create wealth. At the same time, rules and regulations are set for the business to operate within certain limits. Meeting these rules constitutes the ''legal responsibilities of the business. Besides the ethical norms embodies in the first two categories, there are additional ethical actions which are not included in law but expected by the society. The importance of ''ethical responsibilities'' has been well noticed although it is always an issue to judge what is and is not ethical. It is reasonable to say that the ''ethical responsibilities'' are the expectations above legal requirements that the society has of the business. ''Discretionary/philanthropic responsibilities'' are even vaguer than ethical responsibilities. Society leaves these to the judgement and choice of the business. To fulfil these responsibilities, the social role of the business is voluntary. The decision to assume them is not required by law and also above and beyond the sense of ethics. It is only led by the business's desire to be involved in this role and contribute to the society.[404] Carroll[405] suggests that although the four components are not mutually exclusive. To view the components separately could give managers an idea of different types of responsibilities. This could help managers to see the conflicts between components, such as a conflict between components, such as a conflict between the economic and the other three responsibilities indicated by Carroll[406] as concerns for profits versus concern for society.

8.5.2 Conceptualizing Corporate Social Responsibility: Beyond Philanthropy

Bowen's book,[407] ''Social Responsibilities of the Businessman'', is considered the first definitive book on the CSR concept. In it, CSR was defined as an obligation to pursue those policies to make those decisions, or to follow those lines of action that are desirable in terms

---

[402]Carroll, A., (1979), ''*A Three-Dimensional Conceptual Model of Corporate Performance*'', Academy of Management Review, 4(4), P. 505.
[403]Ibid.
[404]Carol, A., (1979), Op. Cit., P. 497.
[405]Ibid, P. 120.
[406]Ibid.
[407]Bowen, H., (1953), *Social Responsibilities of the Businessman,* New York, Harper and Row, P. 17.

of the objectives and value of our society. Many other researchers have contributed to the development of the concept by following it.[408] It is also defined as the continuing commitment by the business to behave ethically and contribute to economic development while improving the quality of life of the workforce and their families as well as of the local community and society at large.[409] Basically, CSR is often defined as its components and applications. It is suggested that responsible corporations will perform activities and application beyond profit and legal reasons.[410] Business when identifying CSR issues, normally consider the influence of their operations and activities on society.[411] Examples of those topics include problems of pollution, poverty, racial discrimination, transportation and industrial health and safety.[412]

An important point asserted by many scholars as a part of the CSR definition is to balance the interest of different groups.[413] That is to say, to whom is a business responsible? According to Marrewik,[414] this interest group approach can take three forms to address the question. The ''shareholder approach'' is referred to as the classical view of the CSR. The sole responsibility of a business is to make profit and create wealth. The shareholders of the business should be the focal point. The business should be concerned with CSR to the extent and only to the extent that it creates value for the owner. In this approach, only the economic dimension is considered.[415] The ''shareholder approach'' indicates that a business is not only responsible to its owners but also has obligations to various stakeholders, such as employees, customers, business partners, government and non-governmental organizations.[416]

---

[408]Carroll, A., (1979), ''*A Three-Dimensional Conceptual Mode of Corporate Performance*'', Academy of Management Review, 4 (4), P. 505; Marrewilk, M., (2003), ''*Concepts and definitions of CSR and Corporate Sustainability: Between Agency and Communication;* Journal of Business Ethics, Vol. 44, P. 105; Vidal, N.G., and Kozak, R., (2008), ''*Corporate Responsibility Practices in the Forest Sector*'', Journal of Corporate Citizenship, 31, P. 75.

[409]Holme, L., and Watt, R., (2008), ''*Making Good Business Sense*, ''World Business Council for Sustainable Development, New York, P. 30.

[410]McGuire, J., (1963), ''*Business and Society*'', New York, McGraw-Hill, Davis, K., (1960), ''Can business afford to ignore Social Responsibility?,'' California Management Review, 2(3), P. 76.

[411]Davis, K., (1967), ''*Understanding the Social Responsibility Puzzle*'', Business Horizons, 10(4), PP. 45-51

[412]Carrol, A., (1979), Op.Cit., Vidal, N.G. and Kozak, R., (2008), Op.Cit.,

[413]Quazi,A., O'Brien, D., (2000), ''*An Empirical Test of a Cross-National Model of Corporate Social Responsibility*'', Journal of Business Ethics, 25(1), P. 51.

[414]Marrewijk., Op.Cit., P. 105.

[415]Friedman, M., (1962), Capitalism and Freedom, Chicago University Press; Garriga, E., & Mele, D., (2004),'' *Corporate Social Responsibility Theories: Mapping the Territory*'', Journal of Business Ethics, 53 (½), P. 71

[416]Juslin, H & Hansen, E., (2003)., Strategic Marketing in the Global Forest Industries, Authors Academic Publishing, Corvallis, Oregon, P. 610; Rinne, T., Hansen, E., and Juslin, H., (2006)., ''*Corporate Responsibility: Balancing Economic, Environmental and Social Issues in the Forest Industry,*'' Forest Product Journal, 56(2), P. 12.

The ''Social approach '' is a broader view of CSR. It suggests that a business is a part of the society and responsible to the society as a whole. It should serve to meet the needs of the society constructively. Thus Carroll's[417] pyramid and Marrewijk's[418] interest group, incorporate economic and non-economic concerns of CSR. They could be encompassed by the three concentric circles[419] approach developed by the Committee for Economic Development (CED) in 1971.

Some writers claim that the term social responsibility suggests the effort that the business should make to be socially responsible.[420] They argue that Social responsiveness is a better term to adopt since it implies going beyond obligations. Sethi[421] describes this concept based on a three-state schema: (1) social obligation, (2) social responsibility, and (3) social responsiveness. The schema illustrates the adaptation of corporate behaviour to social demands. Social obligation is defined as the adaptation of corporate behaviour to market forces and legislation. The only criterion for corporate behaviour here is legal constraints. However, it may be that the legal criterion is not sufficient. Dowling and Pfeffer[422] suggest three reasons why the legal criteria are not sufficient. Firstly, due to the dynamic of social norms, the legal change is often delayed because of its formal nature. Secondly, social values might conflict with each other while laws are assumed to be consistent. Thirdly, during a transitional period, certain activities might be hardly tolerated by the social system while the law confers the social acceptance on the legal code. Thus, legal criteria are necessary but not sufficient to address this concept.[423] In order for a business to be socially responsible, it must perform at a level of congruent with the dominant social norms and expectations. Compared to social obligation, social responsibilities are just more proactive. Corporations adapt behaviour before it becomes legally required. Social responsibilities in general are short-term adaptations.[424] The third stage

[417]Carroll, A., (1979), Op.Cit., P.34.

[418]Marrewijk, M., (2003), Op.Cit.,P.56.

[419]The inner circle only involves the basic economic function; the intermediate circle includes the awareness of changing social values when implementing their economic function; and the outer circle encompasses the responsibilities that corporations should assume in order to be more involved in improving society.

[420]Sethi, S., (1975), ''*Dimension of Corporate Social Performance: An Analytical Framework*'', California Management Review, 2(4), P. 75

[421]Sethi, S., (1975), Op.Cit., P.45.

[422]Dowling, J., & Pfeffer, J., (1976), ''*Organizational Legitimacy: Social Values and Organizational Behaviour*'', The Pacific Sociological Review, 18(1), P. 136.

[423]Sethi, S., (1975), Op.Cit., P. 34.

[424]Ibid.

described by Sethi is Social responsiveness.[425] Social responsiveness involves long-term adaptation. The idea of social responsiveness is not about how the corporation should adopt to current social norms, but about the long-term role business should play in the social system. Corporations are supposed to predict the changes that might take place in the social system and be ready for the challenge. The Social Responsiveness-related activities are anticipatory and preventive, while the social responsibilities-related behaviours are prescriptive.[426]

The European Commission Green Paper on CSR equally defines it as ''a concept whereby companies describe voluntarily to contribute to a better society and a cleaner environment''.[427] CSR can also be called Corporate Consciences, Social performances, and sustainable responsible business. Responsible business is a form of corporate self-regulation integrated into a business model.[428] Its policy functions as built-in, self-regulating mechanism whereby a business monitors and ensures its active complaints with the spirit of the law, ethical standards and international norms while its goal is to embrace responsibility for the company's actions and encourage a positive impact through its activities on the environment, consumers, employees, communities, stakeholders and all other members of the public fare who may also be considered as stakeholders. It basically, means that a company needs to be socially responsible and environmentally sustainable.[429]

Although the various approaches to defining CSR can tend a better understanding of this concept, there is no universal agreement on the topic. Votaw[430] suggest that the meaning of CSR is not the same for everyone. The socially responsible activities and topic areas might also change over time. For example, the idea of CSR is also referred to as Social Responsibility, sustainable development, corporate citizenship, corporate responsibility and business ethics.[431] Also Sethi asserts that it is conceptually and methodologically dangerous to investigate CSR

---

[425] *Ibid.*

[426] *Ibid.*

[427] Promoting a European framework for CSR (2001), Green Paper, Com (01), 366 final.P. 5.

[428] Wood, D., (1991), ''*Corporate Social Performance Revisited,*'' The Academy of Management Review, 16 (4), P. 25.

[429] http://www.wikipedia,%20th%20free%20encyclopeadia.webarchieve/CorporateSocialResponsibility; by Social Responsible, means the company's activities should benefit the society and the environmentally sustainable, means the activities of the company should not harm the environment

[430] Votaw, D., (1972), ''*Genius become Rare: A comment on the doctrine of Social Responsibility*'', California Management Review, 15 (2), P. 31.

[431] Marrewijk, M., (2003)., ''*Concept and Definitions of CSR and Corporate Sustainability: Between Agency and Communion*'', Journal of Business Ethics, 44, P. 105.

without considering the context within which business operate.[432] It depends on the context and specific situation. Contextual characteristics such as social, cultural, political and economic characteristics of the operating environment of the businesses are critical considerations when addressing CSR related issues.[433]

8.5.3 CSR in practice: A critical assessment of Mining Companies in Cameroon

This section looks at the positive effects as well as opposing views about mining companies activities in Cameroon in terms of their corporate social responsibility. Some of the mining companies like C & K provide employment to the local inhabitants of Mboy I and II though there is controversy on the type of employment provided. Vocational training covering masonry, mobile phone repairing, carpentry etc was on- going as at the time of this study. This affirms that C & k Mining Company has shown some level of commitment in corporate social responsibility. In Lolabé, some 30km from the chief town of Kribi found in the Southern Region of Cameroon, SINOSTEEL CAM involves in the exploration and exploitation of iron ore initiated a training programme in carpentry, painting, masonry and wielding during theproject construction stage. Under the project's apprenticeship programme, nineteen (19) graduates have been trained and are pending employment in the company. Other programmes were scholarship packages for needy students. These items included 35 school bags, books, balls, pens and some didactic school materials.[434] As one of the local inhabitants attested:

> *In fact SINOSTEEL CAM is one step ahead of other companies in terms of ensuring sustainable development because they have initiated a lot of programmes such as scholarship packages for needy pupils. SINOSTEEL CAM has a better chance because they are doing well in terms of their Corporate Social Responsibility. If they are able to enforce it, the community will benefit.*[435]

---

[432]Sethi, S., (1975), Op.Cit.,P. 45.

[433]Vidal, N., &Kozak, R., (2008), '*'Corporate Responsibility Practices in the Forestry Sector.*", Journal of Corporate Citizenship, N^{O}.31, P. 75.

[434]Interview, Jean Hubert Bessala, Op.Cit.,

[435]Ibid.

The above comment indicates that mining activities could have positive impacts on local communities depending on how they implement their CSR.

The researcher again struggled to find out from the inhabitants of Mbalam if apart from their own coping and survival mechanism generated by themselves for their survival, other bodies particularly the government or its related agencies, non-governmental organization or the mining company itself has provided them with a means to adjust or mitigate the social effects so identified. Most of the respondents indicated that it is only CAM IRON S.A that has taken some steps to deal with the poverty situation in the community through CAM IRON's vulnerable programme by providing some families whose farms have been taken over by the company with household consumables such as cooking oil, canned drinks, rice and corned beef to supplement their diet and the livelihood empowerment. However, they added that the distribution of the consumable under vulnerable programmes is very selective with CAM IRON officials only classifying some people as vulnerable and non- vulnerable without any clear criteria for the households. Only those in the wisdom of the CAM IRON officials who are seen as vulnerable are given such products to the neglect of many other households. For instance, one respondent stated:

> *When they came here, they said some of us are not vulnerable. They usually asked how many children you had. If you had eight or less children and you had a mobile phone, they said you are not vulnerable because you can buy phone and put credits to make calls. If you had more than twelve children, they said you are vulnerable and they give you rice and cooking oil. But how do they know if i am vulnerable or not even if I have one child? I learnt they sell the remaining consumables and they also gave some to their girlfriends.*[436]

Interview with the CAM IRON employee as well as a review of CAM IRON's documents confirmed the vulnerable programme and states that the programme is born out of the conviction of CAM IRON that some households are directly impacted by their activities which have caused some changes in their lives and hence putting them in

[436]Interview, Confidential, Mbalam, 12/12/2024.

vulnerable positions. The official noted that the vulnerable programme food basket involves Rice (400kg), beans (85gams), canned fish (34.1grams), cooking oil (1 litre) and whole milk powder (8grams). However not all these items are given to the households according to the respondents.

Despite all the above mentioned gestures by some of the mining companies in Cameroon, the researcher was left wondering alone as all the catchment communities' cannot boost of a drop of pipe-born water provided by a mining company. In addition, they lack basic social amenities like health districts, electricity, schools and a host of infrastructures that can make life worth living. Therefore, if some of the mining companies in Cameroon are doing corporate social responsibility, then more have to be done to make it significant.

Generally, social expenditures are portrayed as philanthropy by most companies. Local communities have the mistaken belief that all projects implemented by companies are voluntary gifts. The rhetoric by companies does not always match the practice in the field where they operate. On Lafarge Group (CIMENCAM), website for instance, it is stated that the group participates in the construction of low cost housing. CIMENCAM's contribution is limited to the sale of cement for housing projects as it does for any other customers and therefore such information on CIMENCAM providing social housing can be misleading if we consider the housing situation in the locality of Figuil. It is paradoxical that the description of a commercial transaction in this instance leaves the impression that the sale of cement is a social venture. However, the construction and equipment by CIMENCAM of classrooms and administrative block at the Government Technical High School Bidzar is visible.[437] The company has also built a borehole to provide water to the local inhabitants near Bidzar.

Even though the exploitation of mineral resources have a positive effects on the national economy of Cameroon, these positive effects are not significant to insist on. Rather than being in a joyful state, the local communities are paying the price for the presence of mineral resources on their lands. The prices are in terms of the effects felt by the local communities. These effects of mining on the local communities are dual. The social and environmental effects are very glaring. However, the social effects resulting from mining on the local communities in

[437] Observation, Bidzar, 16/10/2025.

Cameroon is very widespread and severe in comparison to the environmental effects although both situations interact and it is very difficult to delink the environmental effects from the social effects because of their linkage.

Furthermore, it should be stated categorically that although some of the mining companies like C & K and SINOSTEEL CAM have made some giant strides and moved through Corporate Social Responsibility to managing the effects of the activities on the local communities, most of their impact management strategies can best rather be described instead as ad-hoc in nature and highly unsustainable. This is because most of the local inhabitants whom these impact management strategies and measures are developed to serve are not benefiting from them. Hence, these strategies are not achieving the right purposes and have resulted in the development of some form of apathy among the local inhabitants in participating in any project that serve to manage the effects of mining on them. This is particularly the result of the fact that most of these effect management strategies do not address the specific needs of the people in the communities and are largely based on assumptions and early experiences of the mining company elsewhere in their operations.

CHAPTER NINE
TOWARDS TRANSPARENT AND EQUITABLE GOVERNANCE: FRAMEWORKS FOR MANAGING MINERAL WEALTH IN CAMEROON

The right of Cameroonians to sovereignty over their mineral resources necessarily imports an entitlement to demand that government should manage these mineral revenues for the maximum benefit of the people. It equally demands that the exploitation of hard minerals should be carried out with due consideration for the environment. This chapter argues that the existence of rights means that corresponding duties are also attached. The chapter therefore examines the demonstrably inadequate efforts that are being made by the government and mining companies to discharge their various duties. In this connection, the chapter discusses the Extractive Industries Transparency Initiative (EITI) and the Global Reporting Initiative (GRI), which are Multi-Sectorial and Multi-stakeholder initiatives aimed at fulfilling, protecting and promoting the human right to development and the human right to a healthy environment, and transparency in the management of mineral revenue.

Sub-National Extractive industries Revenues allocation to the local communities in Cameroon are important to make them benefit from the wealth of the nation. But, the payment of mining royalties to local communities seems to be an illusion due to some obstacles.

9.1 From Rights to Duties: The Government's Fiduciary Obligation

It has been correctly observed that ''if the phrase 'rights of peoples' has any independent meaning, it must confer rights on peoples against their own governments.''[438] In line with the Hohfeldian conception of legal relationships and obligations, the peoples' right translates to government's correlative duties.[439] Indeed, ''it is a deeply

[438]James Crawford, *Some Conclusions, in The rights of Peoples* (James Crawford ed. 1988) at 56, See also Gillian Triggs, *The Rights of 'Peoples'' and Individual Rights: Conflict or Harmony?*, In The Rights of Peoples, (''If peoples' rights are to have any meaning beyond state's right, they must include the right of a ''People'' against its own Government.'').

[439]Wesley NewComb Hohfeld, (1923), *Fundamental Legal Conceptions as Applied in Judicial Reasoning and other Legal Essay*, P. 38. Examples of the extensive corpus of legal Commentary and Critique of Hohfield's work in this area include Walter Wheeler Cook, (1919), *Hohfeld's Contributions to the Science of Law;* Yale Law Journal, P. 721.

rooted presumption of international law that rights and duties are correlative.[440]Therefore, the right of people is transformed into a duty of the states.[441] Primarily, this duty would restrain irresponsible use and management of resources by public officials and oblige them, as agents of the state, to utilize positively, the resources for the peoples' benefit.[442]

Even if one were to assume a situation where the right to sovereignty over natural resources resides in the state and are not attached to peoples, it will not necessarily follow that the state is without responsibility in how it chooses to manage the resources. States' rights over natural resources are accompanied by a corresponding responsibility that cannot be easily shirked. In a report on the Spanish Zone of Morocco claims, President Huber of the permanent Court of International Justice stated, ''Responsibility is the necessary corollary of a right. All rights of an international character involve international responsibility.''[443] By the same strand of reasoning, all rights of a national character involve national responsibility. Similarly, in the **Barcelona Traction case**, the International Court of Justice emphasized that ''responsibility is the necessary corollary of a right.''[444]

A simple way of describing responsibility of a state here is to view it as obliging the government to administer public assets in the interest of the people and for national development. In the 1952 debates on a draft resolution regarding the right over natural resources, the representatives from Iran premised the argument in support of the concept on the interest of the people.[445] According to Professor W. Michael Reisman, the central idea relating to the declaration on permanent sovereignty over natural resources is that ''the national

---

[440]Nico Schrijver, (1988), Op.Cit., P. 29.

[441]Paul Peters et al., (1988) *Permanent Sovereignty, Foreign Investment and State Practice, in Permanent Sovereignty over Natural Resources in International Law*, P. 96.

[442]Ibid. P. 259.(Suggesting, however, that there is not always a clear concurrence between rights and duties in International Law. ''Legal rights generally denote benefits conferred on its holder and the ability to enforce the correlative duties of another subject although sometimes (especially in International Law) there is a lack of correspondence between rights of one subject and duties of another.'') .

[443]G.A.Res. 626 (VII), U.N.Doc.A/2361 (Dec. 21, 1952); Ian Brownlie, (2003), Principles of Public International Law, 6th edition, P. 437.

[444]Barcelona Traction, Light & Power Co., Ltd. (Belg. Spain), 1970 I.C.J. 3, P. 36 (Feb. 5).

[445]He stated that ''certain industrialized countries would have to realized that in the modern world a policy of exploiting the resources of another country against the interest of that country's inhabitants could not be justified.''

community in which the resources are found is to be a significant beneficiary of their exploitation''.[446]

In 2003, the British government announced its position on this matter in its principles and Agreed Actions on the Extractive Industries Transparency Initiative,[447] affirming that the ''management of natural resource wealth for the benefit of a country's citizens is in the domain of sovereign governments to be exercised in the interest of their national development''.[448] The statement continued to posit that not only should governments proactively use resources for the benefit of people, they were also prevented from exercising permanent sovereignty in a way that would cause substantial harm to their peoples.[449]

In Africa, the shift from past emphasis on states right aspects of PSNR, started in the case of **Social and Economic Rights Action Centre (SERAC) v. Nigeria.**[450] In that case, the African Commission on Human and People's Rights Interpreted Article 21 of the African Charter to encompass a duty on governments. This interpretation can be viewed as setting an important precedent on the African continent and a great eye-opener for Cameroonians in general and local communities in particular.

The issue under discussion could also be analyzed from the perspective of the government occupying the position of a trustee or an agent in relation to the country's natural resources. As a trustee or an agent, the government has a responsibility to discharge its obligations in good faith. She is in a fiduciary relationship with the citizens, such that she cannot be permitted to abuse the relationship. Implicit in this trust or agency relationship, is the expectation that the political leadership will not divert the national wealth they hold on trust for their personal use[451] and that they will not allow their duties as agents to conflict with their personal interests.[452] The numerous duties of trustees

---

[446]W. Michael Reisman, (1989), ''*Harnessing International Law to Restrain and Recapture Indigenous Spoliations,''* American Journal of International Law, N^O^. 56, P. 57.

[447]For a discussion on this initiative, see Cynthia A. Williams, (2004), *''Civil Society Initiatives and ''Soft Law'' in the Oil and Gas Industry''*, N.Y.U. J. Int'l L. 8 Pol, P. 457. Cameroon adhered to this initiative in 2005

[448]*Ibid. (citing EITI, statement of Principles and Agreed Actions, 2003, at http://www.dfid.gov.uk/pubs/files/eitidraftreportstatement.pdf. Accessed July 15 2025*

[449]Subrata Roy Chowdhury & Paul J. I.M. de Waart, *Significance of the Right to Development: An Introductory view, in the Right to Development in International Law,* P. 15.

[450]Soc.& Econ. Rights Action ctr & ctr. for Econ & Soc. Rights V. Nigeria, African Commission in Human and Peoples' Rights, Commission N^O^.15/96 (2001) at http://www1.Umn.edu/humanrts/africa/comcaseS/155-96.html.(Accessed July 15 2025).

[451]Kofele-trale Patrimonicide, P. 98.

[452]G.H.L. Friedman, (1983), *The Law of Agency* (Agents duties arising from fiduciary nature of the relationship).

and agents would apply to the extent possible.[453] It is imperative to institute appropriate mechanisms in International Law by which nationals can enforce their rights under this trust and agency relationships.

In carrying out her duty, the government has to take positive steps so as to come up with a paradigm specific and legally consistent with the legal rights of Cameroonians. The government has to involve the local communities in the transparent management of the revenue generated from its exploitation as well as to setting up arrangements that will enable the generated revenue to reach the masses, so as to uplift them from the economic doldrums. The transparent management of the mining revenue is her recognition of the duty it owes to Cameroonians in general and local communities in particular, to enable them enjoy the right to development and the right to live in a healthy environment. Yet, much still has to be done to achieve the desired goal.

9.2 The Imperative of Transparency in Curbing the "Resource Curse"

There has been a growing recognition over the last two decades of the importance of transparency and strong governance for economic growth and social development, particularly in natural resources producing economies. The high demand of these natural resources like gold and diamond coupled with an increase in price at the international market has strengthened calls from the civil society and a broader range of stakeholders for greater transparency and accountability. The International Monetary Fund has recently published a Guide on Resource Revenue Transparency,[454] while the U.K.-led Extractive Industries Transparency Initiative (EITI) has garnered increasing International support in both natural resource producing and consumer countries. The EITI aims at fostering voluntary cooperation between governments, private mining companies, and civil society to enhance transparency in the oil and mining sectors. While substantial efforts have already been undertaken to strengthen transparency, continued and sustained action is necessary to address the remaining gaps in this area. Some argued that there is an association between resource riches and poor economic performance (the ''paradox of plenty'' or ''resource curse''), and a significant body of literature has sought to explain the

[453] For an explanation of the powers and duties of a trustee in the administration of a trust, see L. A. Sheridan & George W. Keeton, (1983), *The Law of Trusts*, 11th Edition, P. 250.

[454] The guide was first issued in June 2005 and revised in April 2007.

relationships between resources and abundance and economic performance.[455] But the resource curse is not inevitable: a range of countries with prudent and transparent management practices (including Botswana, Canada, Chile, and Norway) have benefited from resource wealth.[456] The key question for a large number of countries is how they can ensure that their abundance in resources remains a blessing. The answer lies, at least in part, in the transparent management of mining revenue.

Empirical work, particularly in the last decade, has demonstrated the importance of transparency and good governance to effective policy making, economic growth and poverty reduction.[457] The prevalence of weak transparency and corruption in public management is not limited to natural resources producing countries. The mining sector is prone to mismanagement and abuse because of the magnitude of the revenues at stake and its enclaved-sector nature with few people involved.[458]

Strengthened effort to enhance transparency in the mining sector can therefore be instrumental in changing the overall perceptions about governance in the country. Currently, assuming the accuracy of figures reflecting a relatively modest level of government revenues from mining, Cameroon's ability to ensure quality spending is deemed sufficient to make immediate use of mining revenue. Quality spending, that is productivity-enhancing expenditures, is essential to ensure that future generations benefit in a manner consistent with their rights from the mining wealth (which would take the form of a man-made wealth).

---

[455]Auty (1997), for instance, examines the relationship between broadly defined resources, rich groups of countries over the period between 1960-90. Sachs and Warner (2000), show a robust inverse relationship between growth and resource riches for a sample of 97 countries over the period 1970-1989. However, the above mentioned view has not remained unchallenged. Hansman and Rigobon (2003), while supporting the generally inverse relationship point out that natural resource rich countries performed well economically in the 1980s contrary to what would be expected under the "Dutch disease" hypothesis. Lederman and Maloney (2003) , raised doubts about the robustness of the Sachs and Warner findings, and subsequently in Natural Resources: Neither curse nor Destiny (2007) argue, on the basis of case studies, that resource wealth combined with appropriate policies and institutions can contribute significantly to long-term growth.

[456]The importance of institutions as an explanatory variable is stressed by Sala-i-Martin and Subramanian (2003), who provide evidence to show (both in a cross-section study and in the case of Nigeria) that the impact of resource wealth is strongly linked to its impairment of institutional quality, and that little of the effect arise from natural resource endowments per se.

[457] For example, Kaufmann, Kraay, and Zoidolobaton (1999), and subsequent surveys carried out by the World Bank (www.worldbank.org/wbi/governance).

[458]A World Bank staff while preparing the Report on the observance of standards and codes in 2000, commented that while Cameroon has a legal framework that meet a number of transparency criteria, "the complexity and cumbersomeness of the system (and enforcement thereof) are such that Cameroon is at present unable to fulfil the various principles set out in the code of Good Practices on Fiscal Transparency".

9.3 Cameroon's EITI: Identifying Institutional and Operational Shortcomings

It remains factual that Cameroon is among the great producers of hard mineral resources in Africa. Being a mining destination for investors in Africa, Cameroon is a member of the Extractive Industries Transparency Initiative, EITI, since March 2005. Despite this, the oil and now the mining industry in the country remains near opaque in the violation of the principles of the initiative. A few factors, however, are identified as accounting for the lack of transparency in Cameroon's mineral industry.

Transparency is perceived to be lacking as a result of the limited dissemination of information which undermines public scrutiny and accountability. Publication of data on the mining sector has been very limited in Cameroon thus preventing effective public scrutiny and an active debate on the use of mineral resources. In order to hold policy makers accountable and to strengthen governance, the public (particularly researchers, parliament and civil society organizations) needs information on how mineral resources are generated and spent (or saved). Involving directly experts and/or nongovernmental organizations can also contribute to promote the public debate as these actors can help explain the complex issues involved in the sector. Furthermore, encouraging active parliamentary engagement, particularly at the time of the discussion of the budget law can support effective oversight.

9.4 Strategic Hurdle

Within the past two decades, considering the shortcomings of the transparency initiative, and recognizing the need for greater transparency, the government has taken steps to strengthen transparency in the budgetary process, as well as encouraging public scrutiny and debate. The most significant of these efforts has been the adherence to the EITI in March 2005.

9.5 The Extractive Industries Transparency Initiative (EITI): A Global Framework

The EITI is a multi- stake-hold dialogue, involving governments, oil, mining companies and NGOs, motivated by the publish what you pay coalition of 120 NGOs, led by Global witness, an NGO in the U.K., and several other founding members.[459] The aim of this initiative was

[459]Global witness statement to the Extractive Industries Transparency Initiative (June 2003), at http://www.globalwitness.org/reports/show.php/en.0043,html. Accessed on July 15th 2025

to redress the huge distributional disparities in resource-rich-yet-poor countries, where government corruption and lack of concern for the country's people could so often lead to enormous wealth for a very few people in the host countries, combined with a populace that is, on the whole, desperately poor.[460] On its part, the driving force behind the publish what you pay campaign was to instigate changes in international stock market and accounting rules so that oil, gas, and mining companies would be required to disclose, on a country-by-country basis, their net payment to governments in each country from which they extract natural resources.[461] The basis of this was that revenue transparency will help to promote government accountability and reduce corruption in many resource-rich-yet-poor countries. From the onset of this initiative, Cameroon erroneously was not considered as falling among these countries. Erroneous because Cameroon is a resource-rich-yet-poor country so one would find no justification for not including it among such a category of countries. This might be attributed to the lack of information on the issue.

The EITI initiative actually began in June 2002 with conversations between Global witness and major British oil companies, such as BP and shell, asking them to voluntarily disclose their net payments to host governments. The companies responded by agreeing in principle with the concept of disclosure and readily recognized that their economic interest would be promoted by stable political conditions in countries in which they do business. This stability could be promoted by greater disclosure and a resulting increase in public accountability.[462] Yet, there were a number of practical concerns that prevented BP and SHELL from agreeing to take the lead on this issue. First, many of their contracts had confidentiality provisions that prohibited the companies from disclosing this information without the host governments consent. Second, each had a concern about competitive disadvantages if only a few companies participated. That is if SHELL and BP insisted on disclosure, to the host government's

[460]Ibid .

[461]Publish what You Pay, Publish What You pay, at http://www.publishwhatyoupay.org. Accessed July 15th 2025.

[462]Howard Cater, CEO, ISIS Asset Management, Address at the Extractive Industries Transparency Initiative (EITI) London Conference (June 17, 2003) (Transcript available at http://www.dfid.gov.uk/news/news/files/eiti_draft_report_isis.htmtop). ISIS is a $100billion asset management company that uses corporate governance and corporate social responsibility measures and engagement across its entire portfolio. It was one of the first institutional investors to support the Publish what You Pay Campaign. Ultimately, ISIS spoke in support of the EITI on behalf of institutional investors from the U.K , United States, Continental Europe, and Canada who together with ISIS, manage about $3 trillion of client funds.

perceived disadvantage, there would still be a number of other large companies prepared to negotiate for the same concession to extract resources without requiring disclosure. Thus, this was an area that Global witness quickly recognised would need government intervention, such that there would be a level playing field among competitions.

The campaign got a serious boost when billionaire investor and social activist George Soros became interested in the issue and wrote to Prime Minister Tony Blair asking him to promote government regulation to require extractive industry transparency. Using a soft Law approach, Prime Minister Blair and British Government then took the lead in 2002 in pulling together oil companies, mining companies, international organizations such as the IMF and the World Bank, investors, and NGOs to address revenue transparency through what became the EITI. The EITI was launched by Prime Minister Blair at the World Summit on sustainable development in Johannesburg, South Africa, in September 2002, where he encouraged all oil mining (Public, Private, and state owned), international organizations and NGOs to work together to develop a framework for reporting extractive revenues and payments.[463] At Evian, in early June 2003, the effort got another boost from the G-8 countries' growing concern about fighting corruption, which is coming to be understood as ''one of the key obstacles to social and economic development,'' and their parallel concern about economic mismanagement.[464] The G-8 agreed on an action plan that included intensified, yet still voluntary, attention to transparency and accountability issues in countries where extractive industries revenues are important.

On June 17th 2003, the British Government held a conference on the EITI where its principles and Agreed Actions were publicly announced.[465] Among the principles are:

- A share ''belief that the prudent used of natural resource wealth should be an important engine for sustainable growth that contributes to sustainable development and poverty reduction, but if not managed properly, can create negative economic and social impacts:

[463]Http://www.dfid.gov.UK/News/News/files/eiti_guide_b.pdf. Accessed July 15, 2025.

[464]Extractive Industries Transparency Initiative, Statement of Principles and Agreed Actions & II (June 17, 2013), at http://www.dfich.gov.UK/pubs/files/eitidraftreportstatement.pdf.Accessed July 15, 2025.

[465]Ibid .

- An affirmation that the ''management of natural resource wealth for the benefit of a country's citizens is in the domain of sovereignty government to be exercised in the interest of their national development;
- A recognition that ''Public understanding of government revenues and expenditure over time could help public debate and inform the choice of appropriate and realistic options for sustainable, development;''
- An emphasis on ''the importance of transparency by governments and companies in the extractive industries and the need to enhance public financial management and accountability;
- A belief that ''payments disclosure in a given country should involve all extractive industries companies operating in that country'',
- An affirmation that in ''seeking solution, we believe that all stakeholders have important and relevant contributions to make- including governments and their agencies, extractive industry companies, service companies, multilateral organizations, financial organizations, investors and non-governmental organizations.''

Among the agreed actions were the following:

- That participants would work to develop and test ''methods payment disclosure, revenue disclosure and publication in the extractive industries in countries heavily dependent on natural resources;''
- That participants would work at the country level ''to implement reporting guidelines consistent with EITI principles, agreed between each host government and companies working in its country, along with support from the civil society, international institutions and other relevant players.''

A striking feature of the initiative perhaps, is the broad ranges of countries, companies, NGOs and investors that signed the statement of principles and Agreed Actions and are participating in the EITI.[466] In

[466]Cynthia A. Williams; the companies include Anglo-American PLC, Arera, BG Group, BHP Billiton, BP, Chevron Texaco, Conoco Phillips, Debeers, Exxomobile, network mining, NNPC, Repsol YPE, Rio Tinto, shell, SOCAR, Sonangol, Statoil, and Total. The Governments, Convened by the United Kingdom, include those of Azerbaijan, Belgium, Democratic Republic of Congo, Equatorial Guinea, France, Germany, Ghana, Indonesia, Italy, Japan and the United States. International Organizations include the IMF, the OECD, the U.N. Development Program and the World Bank. A broad range of NGO Initiated and supported the EITI, including the following signatories: CAFOD, CARE International, Global witness, Human Rights Watch, open society institute, Publish what you pay coalition and Transparency Kazakhstan.

addition, institutional investors with $3 trillion of funds under management signed onto the principles, representing a broad spectrum of U.K., U.S., continental European, and Canadian Investors, led by U.K. investors.[467]

The rapid growth of this idea promoted by NGOs and today broadly supported and sponsored by governments can be explained on three counts. Firstly, companies, developing countries, and investors recognized as leaders in corporate social responsibility such as BP and shell, have adopted code of conduct that do not permit paying bribes and therefore want a level playing field, including broadly applicable bans on bribery. This will permit them to compete effectively. Thus, disclosure rules that discharge the payment of bribes by requiring their disclosure (at least in theory) are in the economic self-interest of responsible companies.[468] Secondly, many host governments now recognise that being perceived as corrupt, as insufficiently serious about the rule of law, or as mismanagers of their economies, lower foreign direct investment and can, therefore reduce important sources of support, economic development and revenue.[469] So, measures that support good government are increasingly welcome, again, at least in theory. Lastly, Institutional investors in the United Kingdom, where the campaign began, recognised that extractive industries entails long-term infrastructural investment and as a result, is subject to significant financial risk where corruption, conflict and desperate poverty intersect. Thus, the political and social stability of countries in which companies invest is understood by these investors to be of paramount concern.

This initiative was developed without high-level involvement from the U.S state department, and without serious support from the U.S government. To keep the U.S companies, and the U.S government involved, the British government was pressured into backing away from supporting mandatory disclosure initiative, and the support of important U.S players such as Chevron Texaco was explicitly premised on the initiative remaining voluntary. Moreover, for this reason, campaigners from Global witness and Catholic Relief Service do not expect the EITI

---

[467]EITI, part V.

[468]A recent World Bank survey indicated that 40% of 3600 companies' surveyed paid bribes. David Hess and Thomas W. Dunfee, (2000), ''*Fighting corruption: A Principle Appraoch: The C^2 Principles (combating corruption),''* Cornell International law Journal, P. 596, citing Thomas Omestand, (1997), ''*Bye-Bye to bribes: The Industrial World Take Aim at official corruption''*, U.S News & World report, December 22, PP. 39-42. Yet Public opinion is turning against this practice, even as International development organizations and NGOs are recognizing the huge corrosive effects on sustainable development and poverty reduction of corruption.

[469]Ibid.

to work. According to one Global witness spokesperson, "the purely voluntary approach will not work in the countries where it is most needed because many political and business elites have major vested interests in a voiding transparency".[470] Cameroon, like most developing countries, seems to be paying lip service to the initiative so as to buy favours from multilateral financial institutions like the World Bank and the International Monetary Fund. According to a member of the Cameroonian Publish What You Pay Coalition, "there is a perception that the government is using EITI to gain heavily indebted poor country (HIPC) status, but is not really committed to implementation.[471]

9.6 The Cameroonian EITI Experience: A Critical Review

Convinced by the advantages of the EITI, namely the fight against corruption, the promotion of good governance, the promotion of transparency and accountability, and the improvement of the investment climate, Cameroon announced its intention to join the initiative in March 2005 in the EITI conference in London. The announcement was followed by June 2005 by a decree[472] creating the monitoring and Implementation Committee for EITI principles. The committee which reports to the Minister of Finance as chair is the steering and decision-making body for EITI issues. The Monitoring Committee technical Secretariat was created in September 2005,[473] to coordinate, plan and monitor initiatives to implement the EITI. Its mandate also included the production and publication of reconciliation statements. To date, several reports have been published.[474]

The monitoring and implementation committee is comprised of the following members:

A Chairperson in the person of the Minister of Finance; members representing the public and Para-public sectors:

- A representative of the Presidency of the Republic;
- A representative of the Prime Ministry;
- The Minister in charge of hydrocarbons or his representative;
- The Minister of Justice or his representative

[470]Charlotte Denny, Scramble for Africa: Corruption and Chaos: True Cost of New oil Rush, Guardian (Manchester), June 17, 2003, at 1 (quoting Simon Taylor of Global witness).

[471]Eye on EITI, Civic Society Perspectives and Recommendations on the EITI, Publ sh What You Pay, 2006, P. 8.

[472]Prime Ministerial Decree N° 2005/2176/PM of June 16, 2005.

[473]Ministerial Decision N°. 002328/MINEFI/ CAB of September 15, 2005.

[474]2013 EITI Validation Report for Cameroon.

- The General manager of the National Hydrocarbons Corporation (SNH);
- The President of the National Anti-Corruption Commission

Members representing the Private Sector:

- The General Manager of TOTAL E & P Cameroon;
- The General Manager of PECTEN Cameroon;
- The General Manager of PERENCO Cameroon;
- The General Manager of GEOVIC Cameroon;
- The President of the chambers of Commerce, Industry and Mines

Members representing the Civil Society:

- Two members of Parliament, one from the ruling party and one from the opposition;
- The President of Transparency International Cameroon;
- Three Representatives of non Governmental Organizations;
- Three representatives of Decentralized local collectivities;
- The President of the Union of Journalist in Cameroon;
- Two representatives of the Religious Communities

The committee meets at least once every semester on the convocation of the president, who may on his own accord, or at the instance of other members invite any other persons to take part in the deliberations by virtue of their various competence, related to the subject being discussed. Invitations for meetings, which are supposed to be addressed to members at least seven days before the meeting indicating the time, date, venue and agenda of the meeting, must be accompanied by working documents. A quorum of the committee is formed when at least half of the members are present. Its resolutions are adopted by a three-quarter vote of the members present.

The mission[475] of the Monitoring Committee consists in:

- Ensuring the follow-up of the implementation of the Principles and measures developed within the framework of the EITI;
- Elaborating a governmental action plan for the implantation of the EITI principles and to ensure their application;
- Identifying any obstacles constraining the smooth application of the EITI principles and proposing to the government, appropriate solutions for eliminating these obstacles;
- Ensuring the auditing of extractive industries by international auditors and also making sure that extractive industries show

[475]Http://www.eticameroon.org. Accessed on June 29, 2025.

proof of payments made to the government and that the government show proof of sums effectively registered as coming from extractive industries;

- Ensuring the publication of the government website and in the media of comprehensive and exhaustive information on the payments received by the state from the extractive industries, as well as EITI International reports showing the conformity of such payments;
- Searching on behalf of the government for technical and financial assistance necessary for the putting in place of the EITI principles, as well as participating in EITI international meetings.

Comparatively, the mission of the Cameroon monitoring committee is similar to that of the Nigerian Extractive Industries Transparency Initiative Act of 2007.[476]

When a country intends to adhere to the EITI principles, it has to go through three different stages; it must first of all acquire the status of an engaging country, when it officially declares it intention to adhere. Cameroon acquired this status in March 2005. Secondly, the status of a candidate country is acquired when the country concerned has fulfilled the four conditions or requirements put in place, namely, that there has been an official declaration to that effect, and that there has been the designation of a national monitoring and implementation committee; that the country has committed itself to work with civil society organizations, and that the country has elaborated a plan of action. Cameroon acquired this status in March 2008. Lastly, a country acquires the compliant country status when the EITI board issues a favourable report after examining the level of implementation of the initiative's principles. A country has a maximum of two years to become a complaint country after acquiring the status of a candidate country. Cameroon was supposed to go through the validation exercise in view of acquiring the compliant country status in March 2010. However, at her request, this date was changed to September 2010. It was until 17 October 2013 that Cameroon was admitted as a compliant country. In May 2013, the EITI Board adopted a new EITI standard in order to move from a process that only encourages publishing company payments and government receipts from the extractive industries, to a process that encourages improved governance of the extractive industry

[476]Ewere, A.O., (2012), *An Evaluation of the NEITI Act 2007.''*, Benue State University Law Journal, N°. 1, Vol. 4, Bellan Press, Makurdi, P. 160.

sector.[477] This new standard involves monitoring the entire extractive industry value chain from exploitation to distribution of revenues generated. The new standard accords special attention to the end of the value chain: value which covers the management of expenditure generated from the exploitation of extractive resources.[478]

9.6.1 The Observing and Executing Committee

The overall objective of the EITI is to ensure a transparent management of natural resource mining revenue so as to ensure socio-economic development and enable the citizens to enjoy the human right to development. The success of this initiative in Cameroon will depend on how committed the monitoring and implementation committee is to the principle of the initiative. The principle demands amongst others that each country should appoint a leader with the time, bureaucratic skills, and political influence to drive EITI implementation. The appointment in Cameroon of the Minister of Finance to lead the Initiative seems problematic. This is in the sense that the Minister of Finance already has a very busy schedule to be given such a demanding assignment. This definitely has an effect on the execution of the programme of action of the initiative. One of the principles also demands that each state should recognize the fact that genuine civil society participation is a requirement of EITI. Hence, states should support their active engagement at each critical step of the EITI process. The Cameroon government has not been very committed to this principle. EITI meetings at times are organized hastily and as such, documents are not circulated as required, making it impossible for members to participate effectively in deliberations. A member of the Publish What You Pay Coalition from Cameroon pointed out that: ''the civil society did not get a chance to make contribution on the working plan. The government came with the documents to the meeting and went through them at the meeting... the civil society representatives did not have the chance to prepare because the documents were not made available before the meeting. As a result, there was no basis for an informed decision on the part of the civil society.''[479] With respect to the membership of the Monitoring Committee, one of the EITI principles demands that every state should ensure that the civil society representatives be genuine members of that sector and not chosen from

---

[477]Extractive Industries Transparency Initiative Source Book, U.K., 2015.

[478]Ibid.

[479]Discussion, Confidential, Member of Publish What You Pay, Yaoundé; 1/02/2025.

representatives of the interest of political parties, companies, or the like. While appointing members of the civil society in Cameroon, two members of parliament are considered as representing the civil society, knowing fully well that they are politicians. The legislature is supposed to occupy a prominent position in the monitoring of the transparency process in the mining industry. In constituting the membership of the committee, the executive (representatives of the Presidency and the Prime Minister) and he judiciary (Minister of Justice) are placed as members of the public or Para-public sectors, and the legislature is planned as a member of the civil society. A call from the EITI for the institutionalization of EITI into statutory law to help ensure continuity and sustainability, demands an independent role from the legislature than one accorded by the government.[480]

The government's adherence to the EITI is an attempt to discharge a duty incumbent on her to manage mining revenue in a way that will permit the local communities to enjoy the human right to development.[481] This EITI is being supported by the Publish What You Pay (PWYP) coalition of civil society organizations. On the other hand, the right to the healthy environment imposes a duty on mining companies to conduct their extractive activities having regard for socio-economic and environmental issues. The Global reporting Initiative makes the monitoring of the discharge of this duty easier. Before examining this initiative, it is necessary to take a look at the role the PWYP Coalition in the transparency framework.

9.7. The Role of Civil Society: The Publish What You Pay (PWYP) Campaign

In December 1999, Global witness published a report called A Crude Awakening; an exposé of the apparent complicity of the oil and banking industries in the plundering of the state assets during Angola's 40 year civil war. It became clear that the refusal to release financial information by major multinational oil and mining companies aided and abated the mismanagement and embezzlement of the oil and mining revenues by the elite in the country. The report concluded with a public call on the oil and mining companies operating in Angola to ''Publish What You Pay''.

[480]Shulika Binla, S., ''*The Extractive Industries Transparency Initiative (EITI) Implementation Process in Cameroon''*, Parliamentary Awareness Workshop on EITI, 14 June, 2012.

[481]Implementing the Extractive Industries Transparency Initiative: Applying Early Lessons from the Field, A Report of the World Bank and EITI, 2008.

It was clear, however that the lack of transparency in the extractive industries was also a significant concern in other resource-rich but poor countries. In June 2002, therefore, Global witness along with other founding members[482] launched the world wide PWYP campaign, calling for all natural-resource companies to disclose their payments to governments for every country of operation. From a few, mostly UK-based groups, at its launch, PWYP members today span 60 countries, with PWYP national affiliated coalitions in 31 of these. The rise in civil society participation can be attributed primarily to the great thirst for change in resource-rich developing countries among civil society groups, given the devastating impact of the resource curse. The campaign is largely consistent with ongoing local priorities regarding good governance, corporate accountability and poverty reduction and thus has served as a useful vehicle for local groups to continue to push for greater access to information and accountability.

PWYP's call for companies to ''Publish What You Pay'' and for governments to ''Publish What You Earn'' is a necessary first step towards a more accountable system for the management of natural resources revenues. However, it is impossible to ensure proper management of natural resources wealth by looking exclusively at revenues. PWYP members therefore also call for transparent and accountable management and expenditure of public funds as an essential way to addressing the poverty, corruption and autocracy that too often plague resource rich countries. This is, the campaign's ''Publish What You Spend'' objective.

A further call of PWYP is for the public disclosure of extractive industry contracts and for licensing procedures to be carried out transparently in line with best International practices. This is central to any effort to trace revenues and expenditure in the extractive industries as contracts determine the benefits, obligations and indeed, the transparency of the agreements between countries and industry. This is the campaign's ''Publish What You don't pay/ should Pay'' objective. Since the launch of the Publish What You Pay campaign in 2002, the coalition has grown in both scope and geographical presence and has established itself as the industry transparency issues. From its inception,

[482]They include CAFOD, Open Society Institute, Oxfam GB, save the children U.K. and Transparency International UK. This small founding coalition of NGOs was soon joined by others such as Catholic Relief Services, Human Right watch, Partnership Africa Canada, Pax Christi Wetherlands and Secours Catholique/CARITAS France, along with an increasing number of groups from developing countries.

PWYP's objectives have been for companies to "Publish what you pay" and for governments to "Publish what you earn" as a necessary first step towards a more accountable system for the management of natural resources revenues.

9.7.1 Transparency of Contracts and Licensing Procedures

Publish what you pay (PWYP) members promote the public disclosure of extractive industry contracts and call for licensing procedures to be carried out transparently and in line with best international practice. The contracts between governments and mining companies are central to any effort to trace revenues and expenditures in the extractive industries. Extractive Industries Contracts determine the benefit, obligations and indeed the transparency of the agreements between countries and the industry. The anticipated mining boom will result in high profit for many companies. But if there is no transparency of contracts and licensing procedures, the government budget will remain meagre, while the high poverty level will persist and development indicators will remain dismal. If citizens are to know whether payments and receipts from extractive companies reflect a fair deal for the country, the contracts on which they are based must be made transparent as well. Unfortunately, the use of the confidentiality clause protects mining contracts from this much-needed disclosure. Companies usually claim that payment information is proprietary and would either cause commercial harm if made public or would lead citizens who lack an understanding of industry dynamics and investment risks to demand overly generous terms. Likewise, policy makers who commit their countries to bad deals based on poor information, advice or outright corruption fear a political backlash if they make these contracts public.

9.7.2 Transparency of Government Expenditure

Publish what you pay (PWYP) members work towards open, participatory and transparent budget processes at national, regional and local levels, in order to ensure effective allocation and management of mining revenues. It is impossible to ensure the proper management of natural resources wealth by looking exclusively at revenues. Transparent and accountable management and expenditure of public fund is essential to addressing the poverty and corruption that plague the country. Citizens must have the data and tools to assess the revenue flowing into the government's coffers. But the revenue information produced from exercises like the Extractive Industries Transparency

Initiative (EITI) is useful only insofar as citizens and policy makers can use it to analyze the management, prioritization and spending of these funds for economic growth and human development. The adoption of revenue transparency standards has resulted in more data being produced and disclosed, and more demand for attention to government spending and development outcomes. Thus, PWYP members promote not only transparency in resource revenue payments and government receipts, but also the accountable and transparent management and expenditure of those revenues.

9.7.3. Transparency of Company Payments and Government Revenues

Publish What You pay (PWYP) members work to achieve transparency of mining company payments to governments where they extract, and of government revenues to local authorities, as a necessary first step towards a more accountable system for the management of mining revenue.

Two thirds of the world's poorest people live in countries rich in natural resources. In most countries, sub-oil minerals belong to the state. But in many countries, there is an inverse relationship between this public resource and public welfare. The links between resource wealth, poverty, conflict and corruption- the so called ''resource curse''- are well documented. Effective and responsible governance of natural resources can generate revenue that foster economic growth and reduce poverty. Public information and public accountability are the best guarantees that a country's resource wealth will translate into lasting benefit for its citizens.

Mining companies make payments directly to governments in the form of royalties, bonus payments and taxes, providing the state with an autonomous flow of funds that is independent of its citizens. These windfalls reduce the need for additional taxation and thereby eliminate a key motivator for citizens' scrutiny of public finances. Extractive incomes give governments' ample resource to buy political support through patronage, and legislatures often have little or no budget oversight. Thus the connection between citizens and the public purse is weakest in resource-rich countries where the need for well-informed, vocal and active public oversight of government funds is greatest. Citizens have little or no access to information about these payments, because resource contracts customarily are shrouded in mutual confidentiality clauses forbidding either party from disclosing information without prior permission from the other. In the absence of public awareness or participation in government processes for revenue collection and distribution, corruption and mismanagement of public finances are free to thrive.

Today, the global community can see a coalescing movement to promote transparency and accountability in the mining industries. Worldwide Public awareness of this industry's impact on governance, human development, the economy and the environment has never been higher, and leaders and communities now understand that progress is possible if the extractive sector can be opened to public scrutiny.

PWYP- Cameroon adopted a new communication strategy in April 2010. As part of this, the NGO (PWYP-Cameroon) published a bi-annual magazine. The first issue (May 2010), entitle ''Industries Extractive en Toute Transparence'', aimed at generating discussion and debate on the extractive industries among a wider public audience. The primary focus of the PWYP-Cameroon coalition is to play an effective role as a watch dog of EITI implementation in Cameroon.

9.8 Corporate Accountability: The Global Reporting Initiative (GRI)

The Global reporting Initiative (GRI) is a multi-sector, multi-stakeholder partnership that is working to create and refine a consistent, comparable format for companies to report voluntarily on the economic, environmental, and social impact of their actions, that is, to produce a sustainability report.[483] It was established in 1997 by an NGO in the United States, the coalition for Environmentally Responsive Economies (CERS), an organization which uses share holder activism to get commitments by companies to produce environmental reports and implement environmental management systems.[484] The GRI reporting format has been developed for the most part by companies around the world, NGOs, accounting firms, institutional investors, and labour, with the involvement of some government agencies (such as the U.S Department of labour, International Labour Affairs Bureau, and the French Ministry of the Environment) and the U.N. Environment Programme (UNEP).[485]This affiliation with the U.N. Environmental Programme brings an International standing and close partnership with

[483]Global Reporting Initiative, GRI at a Glance, at http://www.globalreporting.org/about/brief.asp.Accessed May 25, 2025.
[484]Ibid., at http://www.globalreporting.org/about/faq.asp. Accessed November 15, 2024.
[485]Ibid .

the U.N, that is, a priority for a global institution such as GRI. UNEP ensures the involvement of fellow UN agencies as appropriate, depending on the relevant sustainability issue addressed. The continued partnership with UNEP includes collaboration on technical, outreach and regional development activities associated with GRI's sustainability Reporting Guidelines.[486] Moreover, it has been endorsed by the U.N. world summit on sustainable Development, and the reporting format has been endorsed by securities regulators in countries as diverse as Australia, France, and South Africa. As late as 2002, the GRI was established as an independent organization, with headquarters in Amsterdam, the Netherlands.[487]

As of march 4th, 2004, 416 companies in the automotive, utility, consumer products, pharmaceuticals, financial, telecommunications, transport, energy, and chemical sectors, in addition to public entities and non-profits, have published reports that adopt part or all of the guidelines.[488] Since the effort is voluntary, companies can adopt the GRI reporting guidelines as they wish. Thus, there is a range of adaptation of the GRI Guideline, as well as some companies that follow them in all particulars. If a report is prepared ''in accordance with'' the GRI, meaning that every indicator to disclose the specified economic, environmental, or social information has been set out, or its absence explained, then the company can include the following statement in its report, signed by the CEO or Board: ''This report has been prepared in accordance with the 2002 GRI Guidelines. It represents a balance and reasonable presentation of our organization's economic, environmental and social performance.''[489] Most reporters are ''following'' the GRI, or ''using it'', or ''basing their reports on it,'' but are not reporting ''in accordance with'' its guidelines.

The reporting format on environmental matters is the most highly developed of the GRI indicators and seeks to provide a picture of a company's ''impact on living and non-living natural systems, including ecosystems, land, air and water.''[490] Environmental reporting using the GRI format requires a company to produce and disclose specific information on its global usage of energy, water, and material per

[486] Http.//www.globalreporting.org. Accessed July 20, 2025.

[487]Press release, Global Reporting Initiative Update, October 2002 at http://www/globalreporting.org/news.

[488]Http://www.globalreporting.org. Accessed July 20, 2025.

[489]Global Reporting Initiative, Sustainability Reporting Guidelines 2007, Reporting Expectations and Design (2007), at http://www.globalreporting.org/guidlines.Accessed July 20, 2025.

[490]Ibid.

million dollars of sales, its emissions to air and water, its waste management profile, the environmental profile of its products and services, its suppliers' environmental performance, and its effects on land use and biodiversity.[491]

Companies, particularly large global companies, participate in GRI and produce citizenship reports outside the GRI framework because many NGOs and civil society organizations generally in Europe, the United Kingdom, the United States and Africa are demanding transparency by global companies about their economic, environmental, and social impacts. They are calling for more corporate attention to social responsibility issues such as sustainability and growing inequality. One of the solutions to this can be through payment of sub-national revenue to the host or catchment communities and effective and transparent management of these revenues.

9.9. Ensuring Local Benefit: The Challenge of Sub-National Revenue Sharing

Sub -National Extractive Industries Revenues (EIR) are payments allocated by central governments to local and/or regional governments or private actors such as landowners. These payments originate from the overall state share of revenues from extractive industries projects. There are three widely used mechanisms for allocating EIR revenues of sub-national actors:

1) Derivation- a percentage of revenues generated by EI projects are given directly to sub-national entities while the rest are managed at the national level through the normal budget process;
2) Formula- the national budget process include a formula uniquely to redistribute EIR to sub-national entities;
3) Budget process- In this case, there is no special mechanism and thus EIR are re-distributed via the normal budget process.[492]

There are five generally accepted rationales for sharing revenues with regional or local governments:

i) Compensation for the depletion of the natural resources of the land belonging to its inhabitants, especially if these have been occupying the land before the establishment of the contemporary state;

[491]Ibid.

[492]Morgandi, Matteo, (2008), "*Extractive Industries Revenue Distribution at the Sub-National Level: The Experience in Seven Resource-Rich countries.*", RWI, P. 15.

ii) Replacing the existing revenues with sources for economic development for the future generation;
iii) Redressing environmental damage caused by the extraction;
iv) Pre-empting autonomous taxation efforts by local authorities if not duly compensated, and in worse cases;
v) Preserving harmonious political relations between the central government and the periphery.[493]

In countries such as Nigeria and Indonesia, sub-national EIR distribution is clearly a political economy solution to appease constituencies' that have strained relations with the central government. However, more and more governments are realizing that communities hosting large EI projects experience negative impacts ranging from price inflation to environmental destruction and therefore have the right to some form of compensation. No matter the reason, sub-national EIR must tangibly contribute to poverty alleviation and local development.

9.9.1 Significant Ideologies for Sub-National Extractive Industry (EI) Revenue Distribution

The International Monetary Fund (IMF) developed a code and implementation guide for best practice management of natural resource revenue. In this light, the IMF guide as regard sub-national EIR states:

> *Clear Rules and Principles should guide whatever sub national revenue sharing arrangement is chosen...similar principles of transparency to those recommended for other parts of the government budget should apply to the processes of planning, allocating, spending, and reporting of resource revenues. The social feature of the resource revenue, however, requires that governments give particular emphasis to policy clarity with regard to explicit treatment of risks arising from the resource base, transparency of accounting, and control of receipts and spending.*[494]

Some of the best practice principles recommended by the IMF and others to make sub-national EI payments a success include:

1. Clear Rules

The mechanism for determining sub-national revenue sharing should be widely discussed and publicly approved. The laws and regulations governing sub-national allocations should be thorough and

[493]Ibid .
[494]International Monetary Fund Guide on Resource Revenue Transparency, 2007.

publicly disseminated in a format comprehensible to the average citizen.

2. Traceability and Transparency

Governments should implement a ''traceability'' system whereby EIR can be traced throughout the entire value chain from the collection of taxes to sub-national allocations and all the way to expenditures at the local level. This requires a strong tax-collection effort and sound internal mechanisms of finance ministries to track funds. Documents detailing EI revenue allocations and expenditures should be easily accessible by the general public at all levels of government.

3. Lessening Instability

The extraction industries sectors are quite volatile and therefore government receipts from extractive projects can vary greatly from year to year. Central governments often struggle to deal with the volatility of EI revenues and sub-national governments are even more vulnerable. National government should protect local governments from volatility by creating ''smooth'' revenue streams at the sub-national level while monitoring sub-national governments' expenditures and debts.[495]

4. Fair Sub - National Distribution

Many countries adopt sub-national payment schemes to compensate communities impacted by EI projects. However, beyond impacted communities, governments should consider allocating EI revenues to regions or localities with the greatest need. Special attention should be paid to distribution schemes to ensure that a minority of resources ''producing'' regions do not receive an overly large share of payments. Impoverished ''non-producing'' areas should also benefit from sub-national EI payments.[496] Government should pay special attention to the vertical and horizontal distribution of EIR. Vertical distribution refers to sharing between different levels of government (national, regional, local), while horizontal distribution refers to distribution across one level of government (sharing between local councils in producing and non-producing regions for example).

5. Strong Local Development Planning, External Monitoring and Citizen Monitoring

Sub-national entities should produce short and medium term local development plans as a condition for receiving EI payments. Expenditures should be in line with development plans and

[495]Ibid .

[496]Payments to poor areas that do not produce natural resources is often referred to as ''equalization''.

concentrated on investments, not consumption. Thorough external auditing of expenditure should be conducted to detect administrative weaknesses and corruption. Citizens must have the power to refer cases of mismanagement/corruption to the judicial system since they are the intended beneficiaries of sub-national payments.

9.9.2. Mining Royalties in the Localities of Figuil and Yokadouma

Today, Cameroon government has opted to open up its mining sector to industrial mining projects which will provide additional revenues for local councils and communities via the local mining royalties. This can only be practicable if the government pays royalties to the host communities.

9.9.2.1Mining Royalties in Figuil

Created by Decree N^{O}.82-455 of 20th September 1982 establishing councils and amended by Decree N^{O}. 82/557 of 5th November 1982, the town of Figuil is located in the Mayo Louti division of the North Region of Cameroon. The name Figuil is derived from the first inhabitant of the area called FIGUIRMA. Figuil is located 32km from Guider which is the divisional headquarters of the Mayo Louti Division and is the terminal of the Northern part of national road N^{O}.1 which connects the North and the far North regions of Cameroon. Figuil is made up of (04) cantons (Bidzar and Indjode, Lam, Biou, and Figuil) comprising of fifteen (15) participatory planning units (PPU). The population of Figuil is estimated at 700.000 with women representing 53% of the entire population and a young population with an average age of 35.[497]

The situation in the town of Figuil and the establishment of new communities has been influenced by two extraction companies-ROCAGLIA and CIMENCAM. Many migrants from neighbouring countries notably Chad and Nigeria live in the town. These people settled in search of fertile lands for farming and also fishing. Figuil is made up of diverse ethnicities notably: Guidars, Bororo, Mambayes, Moundang Sara Toupouri, Guiziga, Massa, Mousgoum, Mada and Zoulgo. Far from being an impediment, multiplicity of ethnic groups has not particularly posed a problem despite the fact that Figuil is at the crossroad where different cultures coexist.

The agricultural sector is the first response to the vital needs of the locals, but due to unpredictable agricultural seasons and low support

[497] Plan de Développement Communal de Figuil, 2009.

of farmers by the government, the population is poor and has no stable and sure income source. Animal husbandry is practised as a secondary activity and a principal source of income. Animals are raised in response to the demand in the local market. Due to the tensions between the farmers and the herders over access to land, there is a decreasing supply of animals from the region in the national market.

The main sources of energy are wood, water, dung, kerosene, coal and electricity, which are not available in the entire council area but only in the centre of Figuil. The rate of literacy in the Northern Region is respectively 27.21% and 54.53% for women and men according to a UNESCO report for education for all published in 2000. The town has two technical schools (Government Technical High Schools Bidzar and Figuil), three general education schools of which only two are functional and thirty-eight primary schools and one private school.[498]

In the health domain, Figuil had eleven health facilities in 2007. These include six integrated health centres, district hospitals, two Catholic health centres and two health posts but with no pharmacy in the area. The hospital in Figuil had about four doctors and twelve nurses. All communities in Figuil recognize that HIV/AIDS is spreading rapidly, especially among women and girls. Their low educational levels partially account for this. The Figuil council experiences difficulties with access to drinking water. The nature of its climate with five (5) months of rain per year, the scarcity of drinking water sources and poor maintenances of existing ones indicates the difficulty of access to water for the population. Despite the fact that National Road N°. 1cuts across the city of Figuil, access to various villages is a critical problem due to the poor road conditions and this poses real concerns. The isolated nature of the area makes it difficult or impossible for local residents to transfer their produce to markets. The area is richly blessed with quarry resources including an estimated 600.000 tons of limestone reserve and just over 2.5 million tons of marble found only in the Bidzar deposit.[499] These resources are mainly exploited by CIMENCAM and ROCAGLIA.

9.9.2.1.1 Analysis of Mining Royalties in Figuil

EITI conciliation report remains the only valid document where information on sub-national revenue payments and transfers can be obtained. Successive EITI conciliation reports, notably from 2009,

---

[498] Ibid.

[499] Ibid .

2010 and 2011, presented figures of the ad valorem/extraction tax paid by CIMENCAM and ROCAGLIA. From these figures, the share of revenues for councils and local communities in Figuil can be calculated. The table below presents the expected share of sub national royalties for the council and local communities in Figuil.

Table1: Expected Distribution of Mining Royalties to the Figuil Council and Local Communities from ROCAGLIA and CIMENCAM Royalties Payments

Year	Company	Ad Valorem Tax/ Tax extraction	25% of Ad Valorem taxes/ tax at extraction	15% to the Figuil council	10% local communities
2009	ROCAGLIA	0	0	0	0
	CIMENCAM	85.930.656	21.482.664	12.889.598,4	859.3965,6
2010	ROCAGLIA	0	0	0	0
	CIMENCAM	90.290.689	22.572.672,25	13.543.603,35	9.029.068,9
2011	ROCAGLIA	2.779.208	694.802	416.881,2	10.033.782,9
	CIMENCAM	100.337.829	250.84457,25	15.050.674,35	10.033.782,9
TOTAL		**279 338 382**	**69.834.595,5**	**41.900.757,3**	**27.933.838,2**

Source: Data from Cameroon EITI Reports 2009, 2010 and 2011

From the above table the Figuil council was expected to receive 41.900757.3FCFA between 2009 and 2011 while the local communities were expected to receive 27, 933 838.2 FCFA as their own share of the extraction paid by the two extraction companies operating in Figuil. But it cannot be ascertained that these amount reached the local councils or the local communities.[500]

Following the CelPro[501] correspondence to the Ministers of Finance, Mines and the Environment on the 13th of March 2012 raising the issue of non-transfer of royalties, no response from the competent authorities was received. 41.900.757.3FCFA expected as sub national revenue transfers represents 51.09% of the Figuil council budget for the financing of different projects. Budgetary provisions for the women promotion centre, creation of community forest, and improvement of the lake to facilitate counter season crop production and drinking water for cows was budgeted at 20.000.000, 15.000.000 and 5.000.000FCFA

[500]Bissou, M., Bamenjo, J., and Koagne, A., (2014), Sub-national Payments and transfers from quarry exploitation in the locality of Figuil, RELUFA, Yaounde, P. 45.

[501] Cellule de veille et de protection des victimes des activités miniers de l'arrondissement de Figuil. This is a local base NGO.

respectively. Sub-national transfers alone, if effectively transferred, could have financed all three of these projects.

9.9.2.2 Mining Royalties in Yokadouma

Yokadouma is a colonial town in the East Region situated some 300km from Bertoua and 650km from Yaoundé, the political capital of Cameroon.[502] It is the headquarter of the Boumba and Ngoko Division. Yokadouma sub division covers a surface area of 10.100kms with a population estimated at 64,000.[503] People engage principally in subsistence agriculture, fishing, animal husbandry and hunting. The Yokadouma council is one of the largest councils in the East Region with a total of forty-one municipal councillors, a mayor and four assistant mayors.[504] The council and local communities have benefited from one of the largest municipal budgets over the past 15 years following the introduction of Annual Forest Royalty (AFR) payments to communities around industrial logging forest concessions. Despite the huge revenue flows into the council and local communities, Yokadouma has not shown any visible signs of meaningful development.[505] The infrastructure in the council area remains rudimentary with no tarred roads. The Yokadouma council has also been in the spotlight for the embezzlement of council funds by the former mayor and local treasure.[506]

9.9.2.2.1 Analysis of Mining Royalties in Yokadouma

Based upon our research, there is an alarming lack of sensitization and planning around the mining royalties in Yokadouma. Many locals are unaware of the existence of mining royalty and had no knowledge that the C & K diamond mine had already gone operational.

However, local delegates from the Ministry of mines designated the seven villages closest to the mine as the beneficiaries of the 10% of royalties allocated to local communities.[507] Based on our discussion during field study, each village expressed the desire to have their own revenue management committee with a separate bank account (as opposed to creating one committee to manage royalties in all seven).

---

[502] Gervais Zoa, http://www.fao.org/docrep/article/wfc/x///0163. Accessed 14/01/2025.

[503] Cameroon Population Census of 2005. Rapport de Présentation des Résultats Définitifs. Http://www.statistics-cameroon.org/downloads/Rapport.de presentation 3 RGPH. Pdf. Accessed 14/01/2025.

[504] http://www.feicom.net. Accessed 14/01/2025.

[505] Observation during field study.

[506] 2009 state department country report on Human Rights http://www.state.gov.igidrel/ris/hrrpt/2009af. Accessed 14/01/2025 the former mayor and municipal treasure were recently sentenced to 30 years of prison terms each for embezzlement.

[507] The Villages that will receive Mining Royalties are: Mang, Masscembo, Long, Mparo, Mobalo, Mboy I, and Mboy II.

The Baka indigenous Community was particularly insistent that they have their own community since they do not benefit from AFR payments. Each group also expressed the desire to work with authorities and civil society to create local development plans as a basis for mining royalty expenditures. They agreed that the mayor participate in the committee, but should not be president to avoid over concentrating decision making power in the hands of one individual.

Yokadouma currently receives sub-national payment from diverse sources, but non has been done when it concerns mining. All stakeholders involved in the mining sectors need to urgently commit to dialogue at the local level. Yokadouma has an obvious need for pilot dialogue platforms described in the Cameroon mining code.[508]

Thus, if Yokadouma can successfully implement a system to manage mining royalties, this system could be applied to other natural resource sectors. Furthermore, as Cameroon pursues its decentralization process, localities like Yokadouma will begin to receive sub national payments in other sectors such as health and education. The zone's developments will hinge on its ability to transparently and efficiently translate these revenues into human development for its residents.

---

[508]Bamenjo, J., (2012), *Sub-National Resource Revenue Management in Cameroon: Forest and Mining Royalties in Yokadouma, East Cameroon,* RELUFA, Yaoundé, P. 58.

CHAPTER TEN
SYSTEMIC HURDLES: OBSTACLES TO EFFECTIVE ROYALTY DISTRIBUTION AND MONITORING

The mining sector in Cameroon holds significant potential for economic growth, job creation, and government revenue. However, the promise of this wealth is often stifled by a series of deep-rooted, systemic hurdles that prevent the transparent, efficient, and equitable distribution and monitoring of mining royalties. These obstacles form a complex web that involves governance, technology, infrastructure, and socio-political factors. While many actors wish to be integrated in the monitoring of social expenditures and sub-national payments and transfers, there is some serious lack of coordination.

10.1 Sub-National Transfers: An Unfinished Agenda

Under Cameroon's 2023 Mining Code (Law No. 2023-006 of 25 July 2023), the distribution of mining royalties is clearly outlined. The key article governing this is Article 147.

10.1.1. The Overall Royalty Rate

First, it's important to note that the royalty is calculated as a percentage of the "minehead value" (valeur à la tête du puits) of the mineral produced. The standard rate varies by mineral but is typically:

- 2.5% for precious stones (e.g., diamonds, sapphires)
- 5% for metallic substances (e.g., gold, iron ore, bauxite) and precious metals
- Other rates are specified for construction materials, industrial minerals, etc.

10.1.2. The Distribution Key (How the 100% is Split)

The total royalty revenue collected from a mining project is distributed as follows:

Table 2 : Distribution of mining Royalties

Recipient	Percentage Share	Primary Use of Funds
State Budget (Trésor Public)	**50%**	Enters the central government's consolidated revenue for national expenditure.
Council Royalties (Redevance minière communale)	**25%**	Allocated to the **municipal council(s)** where the mining activity is physically located.
Council Royalties (Redevance minière communale)	**15%**	Allocated to the **municipal council(s)** of the **Division** (Department) where the mining activity is located.
Special Fund for Local Development	**10%**	Paid into the **Special Inter-Communal Support and Development Fund** (FSACI).

Source : 2023 Mining Code

10.1.3 Detailed Explanation of Each Share

The royalties is being share between the state, local council and the special fund for local development.

A. The State's Share (50%)

This half of the royalty income goes directly into the central treasury of the Government of Cameroon. It is used to fund national priorities, infrastructure, and public services that benefit the entire country, not just the mining region.

B. The Local Council Shares (40% Total)

This is the most significant change and a major point of emphasis in modern mining codes, including Cameroon's. It is designed to ensure that communities directly affected by mining activities benefit from the revenue.

- 25% to the Host Council(s): This portion goes to the specific municipality (commune) where the mine's extraction, processing, or transport infrastructure is situated. This direct injection of funds is meant for local development projects like building schools, health centers, roads, and providing clean water.
- 15% to the Divisional Council(s): This is allocated to the broader department (département) where the mining activity takes place. This recognizes that a large-scale mine has impacts and benefits that extend beyond the immediate host municipality.

C. The Special Fund for Local Development (10%)

This 10% is paid into the Special Inter-Communal Support and Development Fund (FSACI - Fonds Spécial d'Appui et de Développement Inter-Communal). This fund acts as a redistributive mechanism. It is managed at the national level and is intended to support development projects in other mining communities across Cameroon that may not currently have an active mine but have potential or historical mining activity. It aims to ensure a more equitable distribution of mining benefits nationwide.

10.1.4 Fundamental Considerations and Prerequisites

Transparency and Accountability: A major challenge, not unique to Cameroon, is ensuring that the funds allocated to local councils (the 40%) are used effectively, transparently, and for their intended developmental purposes. The new code emphasizes the need for proper management and reporting of these funds.

1. **Local Development Plans:** The code encourages, and in some cases requires, that the use of council royalties be aligned with the local council's development plan, promoting coordinated and strategic investment.
2. **Other Financial Obligations:** Royalties are just one part of a miner's fiscal obligations. They also pay:
   - **Corporate Income Tax** (CIT) at 30% on profits.
   - **Land Tax.**
   - **A surface royalty (redevance superficiaire)** for the land area used.
   - **Various other fees and contributions.**
3. **Stability Clause:** Mining Convention holders (typically large-scale projects) benefit from a fiscal stability clause, which protects them from unfavorable changes to the fiscal regime (including royalty rates) for a period of 10-15 years.

In essence, the **2023 Cameroon Mining Code** splits the mining royalty income into a **50/40/10** structure:

- **50% for the Central State**
- **40% for Local Governments** (25% to the direct host municipality, 15% to the host department)
- **10% for a National Fund** for inter-communal development in mining regions.

This structure reflects a global trend towards ensuring that a significant portion of mining revenue is directed back to the local communities that bear the social and environmental impacts of mining operations, while still providing substantial revenue for the national treasury.

Despite the efforts made in modifying the law, there are still unanswered questions since there is no clarity on how the share allocated to local communities will be handled once the transfer of the revenues has been made to the account of the municipal treasurer. In view of the foregoing, the lack of an operational regulatory framework raises difficulties of effectively monitoring sub-national transfers and use in Cameroon. It is imperative to harmonize the approach and modalities for payment and management of sub national revenue transfer in Cameroon.

10.2 The Fissure between Practice and Administrative Organization

Municipal councils have the mission to promote economic, social, health, educational, cultural and sports development within their collectivities and therefore require the necessary resources to achieve these objectives. Rendering effective sub-national revenue transfer and reframing the social expenditure framework of companies could add some impetus and provide additional resources for councils concerned. The information gap between services of ministries located in the various regions and divisions and the central level services does not help matters. A contract signed with the companies is the preserve of the Central authorities. It is paradoxical that lower levels of the same administration do not have access to the same information existing at the central level, in order to use and check the activities of companies. The consequence of this approach is the inconsistencies witnessed in the field when supervising the activities of the companies. The idea of committee or a platform for actors and stakeholders at the local level to monitor sub-national payments, transfers and social expenditures of companies could be a move in the right direction.

10.3 The Absence of Traditional personalities in the Course

As auxiliaries of the administration and custodians of culture, traditional leaders can play an important role in the EITI process. They understand the socio-cultural contradictions of a particular anthropological community and act as administrative reference points in a village or a group of villages. But their role is not put at the forefront in the management of mineral resources, the monitoring of sub-national payments and transfers, or decisions on social expenditure of the companies. This is the same problem that is facing the villages of

Eyumojock and Tinto communities in the South West Region of Cameroon as regard the management of AFR.[509]

For example in Figuil, communities are organized in Lamibes, each headed by a Lamido who is both the traditional chief and religious leader. In Figuil, the Lamido of Biou where the ROCAGLIA quarry is located could represent an important voice. The EITI is still not well known by local communities as a tool to hold companies accountable. The Cameroon coalition of Publish What You Pay and the Union of Cameroon Journalists (UJC) conducted a study entitled "knowledge, perceptions and expectation of communities affected by extractive projects on the EITI" conducted in late 2012 concluded that less than 9% of the populations are aware of the EITI. Involvement of traditional authorities and local communities can boost the EITI process at the local level.

10.4 The Inconsequential involvement of Local Organizations

The Cameroon coalition of Publish What You Pay (CCPWYP) is one of the major civil society movements monitoring the Extractive Industry Transparency Initiative. Currently, the CCPWYP is in the process of extending its membership to also include local organizations like development without borders in Ngaoundere, Celpro-Figuil, and CEFAIG-Yokadouma. The involvement of local actors where the extractive projects are executed is a desire by PWYP Cameroon to bridge the gap and engage the real local actors so as to have legitimacy in their campaign. This is the logic that should be reflected in the composition of the EITI committee-to involve local organizations which are currently not involved in monitoring the implementation of EITI in Cameroon CelPro-Figuil is very active in campaigning for the rights of local communities affected by exploitations but it is out of the EITI process. The admission of CelPro-Figuil in 2014 as member of the Cameroon coalition of PWYP will reify their voice in better protecting the rights of the local population affected by ROCAGLIA and CIMENCAM projects.

The management of natural resources for the benefit of its local inhabitants has been of dismay in African in general[510] and Cameroon in particular. An examination of the Extractive Industries Transparency

[509]Kang Ekome, E., (2005), "*Grappling with the use of Annual Forestry Royalties in Cameroon: The need to look beyond rules*", Annales de la F.S.J.P, University of Dschang, Tome 17, P. 456.

[510]Ochola, O., (2010), *Managing Natural Resources for Development in Africa: A Resource, Book*, University of Nairobi Press, Kenya, P. 408.

Initiative (EIT) and the Global reporting Initiative (GRI), which are multi-sectorial and multi-stakeholder initiatives aimed at promoting transparent management of natural resources for the benefit of its citizens, show that Cameroon pays only lip service to them. The consequences of this failure are that the catchment communities in Cameroon continue to live in abject poverty and in unhealthy environments despite the abundance of mineral resources exploited from their lands. The local communities deserve as of right the payment of compensation through royalties but suppressingly this is hardly the case.

Ascertaining the rights holder over mineral resources in Cameroon is very important. Belonging to the local communities suggest that a duty assigned to some person or entity and action will obviously lie both under international as well as domestic law in case of any breach. The local communities have the right to development and a healthy environment. The reality is that, these local communities are still enclaved and the environment in which they live degrades everyday as a result of the activities of mining companies. If these rights are being constantly violated without any voice of the communities being heard, the reason might be that the local communities do not know of the existence of these rights. The exploitation of mineral resources in Cameroon has not yet brought any development on the lives of the local inhabitants. Instead they are constantly paying the price through the ''resource curse'' syndrome. Even though some of the mining companies are managing the effects of their activities on the local communities, most of their impacts management strategies (corporate social responsibility) are not enough and are highly unsustainable. The best way in which this can be handled can be through the signing of the Community Development partnership agreement or contract between the mining company and host community. Also the transparent management of revenue from mineral resources can help change the story of the local communities. Unfortunately, Cameroon's adhesion to multi-sectorial and multi-stakeholder initiatives has not yet made the management of these revenues transparent. If these revenues paid to the state coffers are being managed well, the local communities will benefit from them. The payment of mining royalties to catchment communities could have helped make them feel some positive impacts of the mining exploitation from their lands.

CHAPTER ELEVEN
CONCLUSION: SUMMARY OF FINDINGS, POLICY IMPLICATIONS, AND RECOMMENDATIONS

From the foregoing, we discovered that mining companies in Cameroon do operate within a well-defined legal framework. There exist both domestic and international regulations and institutions which provide benchmarks for best practices by corporate entities engaged in the mining industry. International legal instruments through ''hard'' and ''Soft'' Law, have provided extensive benchmarks for the operation of mining companies wherever they operate. Added to these international legal instruments are some international institutions put in place in order to better implement the law. Nationally, Cameroon has succeeded to provide a legal and institutional framework to regulate mining activities in the country. In this light, the mining code and its decree of Application are indeed the main laws that address mining related issues in Cameroon. This business friendly code in addition to other investment legislation has helped to attract investors in the mining industry.

In the light of the legal and administrative requirements to obtain a mining permit in Cameroon, we clearly discovered that an operator has to fulfil both requirements before he can ever be granted this mining permit whether industrial or artisanal. In this vein, we find that the mining application process is long, expensive and difficult to navigate due to a wide range of institutions and documents to furnish to this effect. The long nature of the mining application process is very visible especially at the level of the administrative requirements at least with regards to the award of the industrial permit. This is because the industrial permit is issued by the president of the Republic after the recommendation of the Minister in Charge of Mines. So, an applicant of an industrial permit would have to wait for the President of the Republic to issue a decree before he can carry on exploitation. The code does not state in any of its dispositions the time frame upon which the president must sign a decree granting an industrial permit. This gives the impression that an applicant may wait for so many years before ever commencing his exploitation operations if the said permit is ever granted to him. Furthermore, both legal and administrative requirements to obtain a mining permit entail that the applicant spends some amount of money either in terms of the fixed fee to pay at the state treasury in prelude to obtaining a mining permit, and equally bears the financial charges when experts of the Ministry in charge of Mines conduct visits to the project site to attest whether the applicant has conducted studies in accordance with the provisions of the law in force.

The granting of a mining permit by the state to a mining company or operator, gives the bearer some rights and obligations in the course of its activities. These rights and obligations which are usually spelled out in the mining code and mining convention or agreement which is intended to bring some order in this sector, end up not achieving this objective. This is in a situation where one of the parties to the mining agreement fails to honour its own obligations. In this connection, the state of Cameroon, which ought to grant a mining concession to a mining company, does not do this. This failure of the state to honour its obligation puts mining companies in Cameroon in a difficult situation with landowners since they have to negotiate afresh for a portion of land in question. On the other hand, the protection of the mining environment must be given attention by the mining companies. For this to succeed, the state must ensure that mining companies comply with their environmental protection obligations. ESIA which have to be carried out before a mining activity commences, usually takes place only when the company has began exploitation. This demonstrates the weak respect of the laws by the mining companies and also weak monitoring capacity of the state towards the mining companies' obligations. Therefore, mineral exploitation can be done in a sustainable manner only if the state takes proper measures to monitor and control the activities of mining operators within its national territory. In this connection, the state of Cameroon has put forth mechanisms by which they can control the activities of mining operators. The state has done this at the national and international levels. Nationally, the state enjoys the principle of permanent sovereignty over its natural resources, a principle which the state use to control abusive exploitation of its natural resources by mining operators. The state has also enacted laws and institutions to better follow up the activities of mining operators. The worry is whether these control organs created by the state do perform their missions given the fact that they are mounted with inadequate human resources and infrastructure. At the international level, Cameroon is a member of EITI and Kimberly Process

Certification Scheme which both have the reputation of controlling the activities of extractive industries wherein they operate. The work of NGOs and civil society Organizations as watch-dogs on the activities of mining operators cannot be underestimated. All these control mechanisms, have lead to the discovery of some infringements committed by mining operators. These offences range from direct to indirect offences and deserve some sanctions. However, it is regrettably that the mining code has not yet provided any sanction for the environmental offences out-lined in the code.

The research gap that this research set out to fill relates to the reason why in spite of the presence of laws providing benchmarks for the best practices, Cameroonians in general and local or catchment communities in particular have not witnessed any enhancement of their rights to development and to a healthy environment. In an attempt at providing a solution to this problem, this research based on the principle of permanent sovereignty over natural resources, first of all established that hard mineral exploited from Cameroon belongs to Cameroonians with the government being only a trustee who is supposed to manage the revenue for benefit of the citizenry. The local communities' rights to development and to a healthy environment are ascertained as an inalienable one and in consequence, need to be promoted and fulfilled. One of the objectives of this work was to investigate whether legislation exists, imposing obligations on mining multinationals to respect the rights of local communities. To achieve this objective, we examined some national as well as international instruments in that respect. After this examination, the research concludes that there exist provisions in these instruments which impose obligations on mining companies to respect the right to development and to catchment communities in particular.

This research also sets out to determine the extent to which the activities of mining industries violate the right to development and to a healthy environment of local communities. In an attempt at answering the question whether these activities actually violate such rights, we explained the content of the rights; bringing out the violations, thus concluding that the rights are actually violated by the activities of the mining industry. Also, in determining whether these rights are justiciable, we did examine the whole concept of the justiciability of the rights. Although the research did not find any case brought by

Cameroonians against mining multinational for violating such rights, it nevertheless concludes that the rights are justiciable.

The research findings have confirmed one of the hypotheses on which the work was based namely; that hard mineral exploration and exploitation in Cameroon has an impact on the lives of Cameroonians in general and host communities in particular. Although ''all paths to development have social, environmental and economic implications which must be evaluated and understood by decision makers, and communicated to those potentially affected'', it is important that such decisions about particular development process must be made in such a way that people's lives do not become worsened off. The effects of mining activities which can be social and environmental as demonstrated in this work is a major source of devastation for peoples' lives especially in communities where mining takes place. Increased frustration among the people especially the youths is the outcome of mining activities. Basically, this resulted from the disappointment of mining companies to provide the people with employment and jobs and overall development of the community for the reason that they are unskilled and uneducated to work in a mining company's set up. This has indeed increased the unemployment situation in the communities since those whose farms were taken had the hope that they would get jobs in return and continue to have a source of livelihood. There is a sense of deception lingering in the minds of many mining communities due to this disappointment. The researcher realized from the findings that this frustration and sense of deception has created some form of tension and hatred for mining companies employees and as a result catchment or host communities would attempt to attack mining companies and its employees or officials at the least provocation. There is simmering tension in the communities because most of the residents of the host communities are aggrieved. The researcher therefore finds a misfit in what communities are promised before mining takes place and whether such promises are fulfilled in reality.[511]

This thesis has argued that if Cameroonians are involved in the management of the mining industry, they will also derive benefits there from. Looking at EITI and GRI, which are multi-sectoral and multi-stakeholder initiatives aimed at promoting transparent management of natural resources for the benefit of its citizens.It shows that Cameroon

[511]Observations in Mobilong, Lolabé and Mbalam.

pays only lip service to them. As a result of this, the host communities continue to live in abject poverty and unhealthy environment. If at least mining royalties are being paid to them, this could have changed some of the deplorable situation they are facing as a result of the exploration and exploitation of minerals on their lands.

- **Possible Reforms for the Mining Sector Activities in Cameroon**

Simplification of Procedures in Acquiring Mining Permit

One of the fundamental problems encountered by mining companies comes at the level of the legal and administrative procedures[512] in acquiring mining permits which is a vital formality to embark on the exploration and exploitation of hard mineral resources. In fact, the procedures for acquiring mining permits in Cameroon are costly and time consuming.[513] To this end, we are proposing that the difficulties encountered in acquiring mining permits caused by complex administrative and legal procedures be reviewed. In fact, the procedures should be in such a way as to enable potential mining companies to be in possession of required mining permits within the shortest possible time and that should also be at a very comprehensive moderate costs so as to encourage more investors to invest in the exploitation of hard mineral resources. This will considerably help to limit the use of unofficial channels that cause serious setbacks on the state in terms of revenue collection. In fact, the procedures should be in such a way as to enable a potential investor to be in possessions of the mining permits within fifteen days from the date of the submission of his request.

The Improvement of Inter-Ministerial Synchronization and Communication

The mining industry is one of the sectors upon which the state can greatly rely to attain proper growth if all the stakes and challenges surrounding the sector are taken into fervent consideration. This does not in any way warrant that all the institutions in the state be involved. In fact, technical ministerial departments and institutions should thus be given the prerogatives to intervene in the mining sector whenever need arises. The many governmental departments and institutions[514] involved in the mineral sector in Cameroon often disagree on how the mineral resources should be managed leading to conflicts and gridlocks.

[512]As seen in Chapter 2.
[513]Ibid .
[514]As seen in Chapter 1.

To eradicate this, it becomes imperative for the existing laws to limit the number of government departments involved in the issuing of mining permits to be at least three. This may significantly help reduce the duplication of procedures and the expenditures that mining companies are subject to and thus encourage their involvement in the exploitation of hard mineral resources in Cameroon. Added to this, is the fact that there should be collaboration between departments and institutions of the same ministry. For example, in the Ministry of Mines, the Directorate of mining and CAPAM should instead work together rather than being seen as two opposing camps. Also, the Ministry of Mines, Forestry and Environment should constantly communicate and work together so as to avoid the problem of overlapping natural resources permits which threaten protected areas.

Talking on the Issue of Timorous and Frozen Mining Legislation

The Cameroonian mining code is timid and frozen. This can be seen in Article 50 of the 2010 Law amending certain provisions of the 2001 Law. This article provides that every exploitation of small mineral must be constituted of at least 40% of national interest. The modalities for the participation of nationals shall be defined by the regulation in force. However, it must be stated that until now there exist no regulation in force defining the modalities for the participation of nationals to this effect. This unequivocally demonstrates that the existing mining legislation is timid and frozen and thus slows down national operators who intend to engaging in this sector.

We are therefore proposing that more comprehensive and objective instruments be adopted to meet the realities with which the law regulating mining companies involvement in the exploitation of hard mineral resources. To this end, whenever a law is to be revised, it should be more concrete if the law in question is revised alongside its decree of application to avoid any ambiguity that may arise in the short, medium or long run. When they are simultaneously revised, it may curb the problems facing mining companies which are nursing the idea of engaging in the sector, but who may be limited due to incomplete pieces of legislation in the area.

Augmenting Transparency

We are equally recommending that there should be transparency of mining contracts through the systematic publication of the said contracts in order to enable the local population to monitor and evaluate the execution of such contractual money paid in by mining companies.

This will in turn promote good governance and reduce corruption. Cameroon by becoming a compliant country in October 2013 under EITI initiative, simply demonstrates her willingness to make the extractive industry more transparent. The mining code should make the publication of mining contracts an obligation. This will enable access of information to the public especially researchers. For the company, the publication of its contract will enable them to create an enabling environment with the host communities since they will not be surprised by the presence of strangers on their ancestral lands.

Enhancing Local Development of Catchment Communities

The absence of an organized framework hinders effective channelling of the expected benefits of exploitations to the council and local communities. The Cameroonian mining code in a vague manner[515] talks on the development of host communities without giving details on how it is going to look like or which aspect of development. The vagueness of this article plays to the advantage of mining companies who do not comply to it. To this end, it is important that extractive companies establish Development Partnership Agreement with local communities. The partnership or Community Development Agreements between companies and local communities can contribute to local development if effectively implemented. Under the present context of the revision of the mining legislation in Cameroon, there is need to make community development agreements between companies and local communities an obligation. In this connection, the future mining code should state the necessity for these documents to be included in appendices of contracts/agreements. Community Development Agreement (CDA) also need to be framed and should operate within an organized framework. In countries like Nigeria[516] and

[515]Article 16 of the 2010 Law amending the 2001 Mining Code.

[516]Article 116 of Nigerian Minerals and Mining Act, 2007 is to the effect that:

''(1) Subject to this section, the holder of a mining concession, small mine or quarry shall, prior to any development activities in the concession area, concluded with the host community where operations are performed an agreement called Communal Development Agreement or any other agreement for the transfer of social and economic benefits to the community.

(2) The Community Development Agreement shall contain binding clauses n social and economic contributions the project will bring for the sustainability of the community

(3) The Community Development Agreement must meet all or some of the following issues related to the needs of the host community:

(a) Scholarship, learning, technical training and employment opportunities for indigenous communities;

(b)The financial forms or other forms of contributory support for infrastructure development and maintenance such as education, health and other community services, roads, water and electricity;

(c) The creation of development and support for small and medium enterprises;

(d) Agricultural products, marketing; and

(e) Methods and procedures for environmental management and local governance and socio-econcmic.''

Guinea[517] CDA are subject to legal provisions and so we do recommend the Cameroonian legislator to integrate this in the upcoming revision of the mining code.

Enhancing Practical Approach vis- à vis Communication and Consultation with the Public and Reintegration of the Mining Sites

Unless information about basic ESIA procedures is made available in English and French and translated as well into local languages, the Cameroon populace will undoubtedly be placed at a disadvantage in ESIA decisions. On this score, the fundamental effectiveness of public inquires can be compromised. Towards this end, it is recommended that the ability of the Cameroonian public to effectively and efficiently participate in public consultation meetings will be enhanced if literature and all the relevant documentation describing envisaged projects are made available in English and French and translated as well into the local languages concerned. The ESIA Law does not stipulate at which stage of the ESIA process the consultation should take place. It is thus imperative that the public at large be considered at the early stage of the ESIA process. This can be achieved through a clear stipulation of the stages at which the public is to be consulted.

In the exploration phase, ESIA impacts can be aspiring already. The 2001 mining code and its amendment in 2010 have not provided any solutions for a mining company to conduct ESIA at this stage. This is in contradiction with the 1996 law on Environmental management in Cameroon which stipulates that all activities capable of producing an impact on the environment shall be subject to ESIA realisation. We do hereby humbly recommend that the Cameroonian legislator should make the realisation of ESIA during the exploration phase.

The Cameroonian mining code also has not adequately handled environmental impacts that can arise as a result of mining activities. The code just as other ministerial departments concern with mining activities is silent on the rehabilitation of many sites which today

---

[517] Loi N° L/2011/006/CNT du 9 septembre 2011 Instituant le Code Minier de la République de Guinée. This Code is to the effect that companies seeking an industrial or semi-industrial license to present in the constitutive documents, a Community Development Plan annexed to the convention on Local Development, which covers, among other things, aspects on training, medical, social, education, road infrastructure... water supply, electricity. The signing of this convention on Local Development intervenes upon obtaining the mining license (Article 30). Also under Article 130 of the same code,'' the holder of a mining title must contract a Local Development Agreement with the Local Community residing on or close to the mining title. (...)''. The purpose of the Local Community Convention is to create the conditions for an effective and transparent management of the Local Development contribution paid by the holder of mining title to build capacity of the Local Community Planning and implementation of Community Development Programme.

present themselves as the major environmental impact of mining activities in Cameroon. We recommend that rehabilitation of mining sites should be given priory in the upcoming revision of the mining code and a commission or institution should be created to follow-up to ensure that these mining companies actually rehabilitate the sites after exploitation. Cameroon like Ghana should impose a creation of a rehabilitation fund by mining companies before a mining exploitation permit can be issued. The purpose of this fund shall be to rehabilitate the site created by the said mining company in case it fails to carry out the rehabilitation.

Create a Commission of Experts on the Rights of Local Communities /Indigenous Peoples over Natural Resource Exploitation in Cameroon

The commission of experts hereinafter referred to as the commission shall undertake a comprehensive review of conflicts relating to natural resource governance in Cameroon. Members of the commission should consists of representatives of indigenous peoples, African Commission on Human Rights, the African Court of Human Rights, persons of high moral standing, impartial and competent with recognised professional reputes.

The mission of the commission should be to undertake a field trip to these communities to pursue the dialogue on the theme, identify the claims of the peoples, and to find lasting solutions for the effective implementation of the rights of these populations. This, the commission will do by visiting and organizing meetings during which the commission gets abreast with the problems of the peoples. At the end of the exercise, the commission will draw up a report to be submitted to the African Commission on Human Rights which should be empowered to coordinate the work of the former. Upon receiving the Report, the African Commission on Human Rights will again empower the Commission to concert with the indigenous peoples on the projects they would like to receive in return for the exploitation of natural resources on their ancestral lands. The projects shall be agreed upon in order of importance. The commissions shall present the projects to the African commission on Human Rights which shall forwards same together with the first report to the respective governments who upon receiving and concerting with the African commission on Human Rights disburse royalties allocated to indigenous peoples to the commission. The latter will oversee and supervise the execution of these projects.

Improving the Responsibility of the various Mining Companies

It is recommended that mining companies operating in Cameroon become more accountable to the people by making known to the community in which they operate various development initiatives and programmes that are rolled out by the company. As it stands currently, most local inhabitants are not aware of programmes and initiatives that are undertaken by mining companies to which the local inhabitants can benefit. It is not in anybody's interest to keep such programmes in the dark from community access. Mining companies should take a conscious effort to market their development programmes, initiatives and investments in host communities. The use of the media like brochures and leaflets is not adequate since the illiteracy rate is very high. However, the use of radio programmes, information vans to announce such programmes in host communities, community durbars are very useful means that can be employed by mining companies to market their programmes and to educate and inform local communities about them. In this way, mining companies could be accepted by local communities since most of them would appreciate the efforts the company is making to improve lives and increase community awareness. This in the end would improve mining company's corporate image and reduce any negative perception dominant in the community about the company. If this is done effectively, mining companies would be better placed as companies that do not renege on its corporate social responsibilities in communities of its operation and better be placed to contribute to sustainable development of its mining communities.

Enhancing the Respect of Developmental Potentials made by Mining Companies

In terms of promised developments and other social benefits made to local communities that invariably serve as a social license for mining companies to operate in host communities, it is demonstrated by our findings that to a larger extent, this has not been met by many mining companies. It is therefore recommended that mining companies take steps in fulfilling its promises of infrastructural development and investment particularly in water, electricity, hospital and social amenities at little or no cost to the local inhabitants. In addition, the few existing ones can be expanded to provide and cater for the needs of the teaming number of communities' inhabitants which often increases tremendously as a result of the mining activities in a particular community, thereby putting more pressure on the existing facilities and infrastructure resulting in its destruction and demise. Adding more facilities and expanding the existing ones would in the long run ease the pressure on the few ones and prolong its lifespan in the long ran.

In line with unfulfilled promises to local inhabitants, it is recommended that great attention be paid to the massive unemployment situation caused largely as a result of the displacement of local inhabitants from their farms which basically served as the major source of employment and livelihood for them since they are predominantly farmers.

SELECTED BIBLIOGRAPHY

A) TEXT BOOKS

1. Abilabi, N.C. (2012), *The Rights of Indigenous Peoples over Natural Resources: The Case of the Ndian Division of Cameroon*, Lambert Academic Publishing, Germany.
2. Aboki, Y. (2004), *Introduction to Legal Research Methodology: A Guide for Writing Long Essays, Thesis, Dissertations and Articles*, 2nd Edition, Tamaza Publishing Limited, Kaduna.
3. Ackerman, R.W. (1975), *The Social Challenge to Business,* Cambridge, M.A: Harvard University Press.
4. African Development Bank (2009), *Oil and Gas in Africa*, Oxford University Press.
5. An Ansomes, and Stefaan, M. (2011), *Natural Resources and Local Livelihoods in the Great Lakes Regions of Africa: A Political Economy Perspective,* Palgrave Macmillian, New York.
6. Anglice, (1971), *Imperialism, Sovereignty and Making of International Law,* Heinemann Inc, London.
7. Anoukaha, F. et al. (2002), *OHADA, Sociétés Commerciales et GIE,* Bruylant, Bruxelles.
8. Anyangwe, C. (1987), *The Cameroon Judicial System*, CEPER, Yaoundé.
9. Aryee, E.B. (2003), *Trends in the Small-Scale Mining of Precious Minerals in Ghana: A Perspective on its Environmental Impacts,* Elsevier Press.
10. Atiyah, P.S. (1998), *Eassies on contract,* 10th Edition, Sweet and Maxwell, London.
11. Bakandeja, G. (2009), *Droit Minier et des Hydrocarbures en Afrique Centrale,* Editions Larcier, Bruxelles.
12. Bakken, M. (2008), *The Mining Law of 1872: Past Politics and Prospects*, New Mexico Press.
13. Bales, R.L. (1984), *Dictionary of Geological Terms,* Doubleday Publishing C°., New York.
14. Bamenjo, J. (2012), *Sub-National Resource Revenue Management in Cameroon: Forest and Mining Royalties in Yokadouma, East Cameroon,* RELUFA, Yaoundé.
15. Bandoki, S. (2008), *Le Droit Minier et Pétrolier en Afrique*, Edilivre, Paris
16. Barbier, E. (2005), *Natural Resources and Economic Development*, Cambridge University Press, United Kingdom.
17. Bateman, A. (1990), *Economic Mineral Deposits,* 2nd Edition, John Wiley Books, New York.
18. Beaud, S. (2008), *Guide de l'enquête de Terrain: La Découverte,* Grands Repères, Paris.
19. Bissou, M. Bamenjo, J. and Koagne, A. (2014), *Sub-National Payments and Transfer from Quarry Exploitation in the Locality of Figuil,* RELUFA and Natural Resource Governance Institute, Yaoundé.
20. Bissou, M. et al. (2014), *EITI and Mining Governance in Cameroon: Between Rhetoric and Reality,* RELUFA and NRGI, Yaoundé.
21. Biya, P. (1981), *Pour le Libéralisme Communautaire*, édition P.M.
22. Boivin, J.P. et Lavaire, C., (2008), *Carrières et Granulats*, Editions du Moniteur, Paris.
23. Bonnie, C. (2004), *Enjeux des Nouvelles Réglementation Minières en Afrique*, Nordiska Afrinkainstitutet, Uppsala.
24. Briely, J.L. (1958), *The Busts of Obligation in International law*, Oxford Clarenda Press.
25. Burke, M.E. (1999), *Corporate Community Relations: The Principle of the Neighbour of Choice,* Quorum Books, London.
26. Campbell, B. (2010), *Ressources Minière en Afrique: Quelle Réglementation pour le Développement?* Presses de l'Université du Québec, Québec.

27. Carbonnier, J. (2001), *Flexible Droit*, L.G.D.J., 10éme édition, Paris.
28. Centre Pour L'Environnment et le Développement, (2013), *Proposal by Traditional Rulers on Land Tenure Reforms in the Rural Areas of Cameroon,* Messa Press, Yaoundé.
29. Colins, C., and Winfield, M. (2000), *Environmental and Mining Law Policy in Canada,* Hart Publishing, London.
30. Collier J., and Lowe. (1999), *The Settlement of Disputes in International Law: Institutions and Procedures,* Oxford University Press.
31. Collin, P.H. (2000), *Dictionary of Law*, 3rd Edition, Peter Collin Publishing, London.
32. Craik, N. (2008), *The International Law of Environmental Impact Assessment,* Cambridge University Press, United Kingdom.
33. Csurgai, G. (2006), *Les Enjeux Géopolitiques des ressources Naturelles,* Edition l'âge d'homme, Lausanne.
34. Devaux, C.J. (1987), *Droit Minier des hydrocarbures: Principes et Application,* Edition Technip, Paris.
35. Dze-Ngwa, W. (209), *History of Cameroon*, SOPECAM, Yaoundé.
36. Essaga, S. (2013), *Droit des Hydrocarbures en Afrique: Recueil Commenté de Textes,* L'Harmattan, Yaoundé.
37. European Bank for Reconstruction and Development, (1993), *Investor's Environmental Guidelines,* Graham and Trotman Limited, United Kingdom.
38. European Bank for Reconstruction and Development, (1994), *Environmental Impact Assessment Legislation,* Graham and Trotman Limited, United Kingdom.
39. Fanso, V.G. (1989), *Cameroon History for Secondary Schools and Colleges: The Colonial and Post-Colonial Periods,* Vol.11, Macmillian Cameroon, Limbe.
40. Feh L, P. (2010), *Environment and Natural Resources*, Ferguson Publishing, New York.
41. Folorunsho, T. (2005), *The Criminal Liability of Bodies Corporate in Nigerian Law,* Chenglo Limited, Enugu.
42. Friedman, M. (1962), *Capitalism and Freedom,* Chicago University Press.
43. Friedrich Ebert Stiftung, CED and Association Citoyenne de défense des Intérêts collectives, (2012), *Plaidoyer Pour une Reforme du Régime Juridique des Cession de Terres a grande Echelle en Afrique Centrale*, PUA, Yaoundé.
44. Furon, R. (1961), *Les Ressources Minérales de L'Afrique: Géologie et Mines, La Production Africain dans le Monde, la Production Régionale, les Nouveaux Problèmes,* Payot, Paris.
45. Garnant, R. (1983). *Taxation of Mineral Rents,* Clarenda Press, Oxford, United Kingdom.
46. Garner, B.A. (1999), *Black's Law Dictionary,* 7th Edition, St. Paul, Minn, West Publishing Company, London.
47. Gary, M. (2001), *Large Mines and the Community: Socioeconomic and Environmental Effects in Latin America, Canada and Spain*, World Bank, Washington DC.
48. Gavin, H. (2001), *A contextual Review of the Ghanaian Small-Scale Mining Industry,* Elsevier Press.
49. Grancier, L. (2008), *Aspects Contemporains du Droit de l'Environnement en Afrique de l'Ouest et Centrale,* UNICN, Gland, Suisse.
50. Hamilton, W.C. and Bishop, A.C., (1989), *Minerals, Rocks and Fossils,* 5thEdition, Hamlyn Publishing Group Ltd, London.
51. Harry, D.S. (2012), *The Mining Law: A study in Perpetual Motion,* Amazone, France.
52. Hartman, H.T. (1992), *Mining Engineering Hand Book*, Littleton Publishing C°., United Kingdom.
53. Hatch, F.H. and Wells, A.K. (1961), *Petrology of Igneous Rocks,* Twelfth Edition, Thomas Murby Books, London.
54. Heraud, A. (2003), *Droit des Sociétés : Manuel et Applications,* 10ème Edition, Dunod, Paris.

55. Herring, J. and Cremona, M. (1997), *Criminal Law,* 2nd Edition, Macmillan, London
56. Hohmann, H. (1992), *Basic Documents of International Environmental Law*, Vol. 2, Graham and Trotman Ltd, London.
57. Hudson, T. (1999), *Mining and the Environment,* American Geological Institute (AGI), Alexandra, Virginia.
58. Hunter, D.J. and Durwood, Z. (1998), *International Environmental Law and Policy*, Foundation Press, New York.
59. Ian, B. (2003), *Principles of Public International Law*, 6th Edition.
60. Jaff Bamenjo, N. and Foumena, W.C. (2013), *Artisanal Mining, A Challenge to the Kimberley Process: Case study of the Kadey Division, East Region of Cameroon,* RELUFA.
61. John, R., (1971), *A Theory of Justice*, Oxford University Press.
62. _______ (2003), *Political Liberalism*, Columbia University Press.
63. Kamal Hossain and Subtracte Roy Chowdhurry, (1984), *Permanent Sovereignty over Natural Resources in International Law: Principle and Practice,* Palgrave Macmillan, London
64. Kamto, M. (1996), *Le Droit de L'Environnement en Afrique,* Edicef, Paris.
65. Karl, T.L. (1997), *The Paradox of Plenty, Oil Boom and Petro States,* University of California Press, Los Angeles.
66. Keary, P. B. (2002), *An Introduction to Geophysical Exploitation,* Blackwell Publishing, South Africa.
67. Kettle, B. (1982), *Gold*, Oxford University Press, United Kingdom.
68. Kiss Dinah Shelto, A. (2007), *Guide to International Environmental Law*, Martinus Nijhoff Publisher, Leiden, Boston.
69. Kosciusko-Morizet, N. (2011), *Droit Minier et Droit de L'Environnement*, De Broeck, Paris.
70. Krasner, S.D. (1999), *Sovereignty. Organised hypocrisy*, Princeton. University Press, Princeton.
71. Kubasek, N.K. (2012), *The Legal Environment of Business: A Critical thinking Approach,* 6th Edition, Pearson Publishing, New York.
72. Lacy. W. (2006), *An Introduction to Geology and Hard Rock Mining,* Rocky Mountain Mineral Law Publishing, Indonesia.
73. Lauterpacht, G. (1970), *Private Law Sources and Analogies of International Law,* Aichon Book.
74. Lerat, S. (1971), *Géographie des Mines*, PUF, Paris.
75. Mairet, G. (1997), *Le Principe de Souveraineté*, Gallimard, Paris.
76. Mancebo, F. (2010), *Le Développement Durable*, Armand Colin, Paris.
77. McIntosh, C. (2013), *Cambridge Advanced Learner's Dictionary*, 4th Edition, Cambridge University Press, London.
78. Merrils, J.G. (1998), *International Dispute Settlement,* Third Edition, Cambridge University Press, United Kingdom.
79. Meyer, P. (2002), OHADA: *Droit de L'arbitrage*, Bruylant, Bruxelles.
80. Mohammed Bekhechi, A., and Mercier, J-R. (2002), *The Legal and Regulatory Framework for Environmental Impact Assessments*, The World bank, Washington D.C.
81. Moore, C.D. (2009), *Unified Business Law for Africa: Common Law Perspective on OHADA,* 1st Edition, GMB Publishing Ltd, London.
82. Morand-Deviller, J. (1996), *Droit de L'Environnement*, Éditions Estem, Estem, Paris.
83. Morin, J-Y. (1997), *Les Droits Fondamentaux*, Bruylant, Bruxelles.
84. Mwayila Tshigembe, (2009), *Enjeux Géopolitiques en Afrique Centrale,* Harmattan, Paris.
85. Nazli, C. (1995). *Environmental Challenges and International Responses*, MIT Press, London.

86. Nguiffo, S., and Bamenjo, J. (2014), *Monitoring Local Content and Fiscal Obligations of Mining Companies in Cameroon: Case of the Diamond Mining Project of Cameroon and Korea Mining Incorporation-Mobilong, East Cameroon,* RELUFA and CED, Yaoundé.
87. Ngwafor, E.N. (1989), *Corporate Criminal Responsibility,* 2nd Edition. Institute of Third World Art and Literature, London.
88. Ntep, G.P. (2001), *Ressourcés Minérales du Cameroun*, Société de Presse et d'Edition du Cameroun (SOPECAM) Yaoundé.
89. Ochola, O. (2010), *Managing Natural Resources for Development in Africa: A Resource Book*, University of Nairobi Press, Kenya.
90. OECD, (2004), OECD *Guidelines for Multinational Enterprise*, OECD Publishing, London.
91. Olakunle Orojo, J. (1992), *Company Law and Practice in Nigeria,*3rd Edition, Mbeyi & Associates Ltd, Lagos.
92. Ononio, A. B. (2012), *Lois et Procedure en Matiere Faunique au Cameroun,* 1st Edition, L.A.G.A and W.W.F.
93. Otto Duclaux, C.M. (2013), *Exploitation Forestière et Droit des Populations en Afrique Centrale,* L'Harmattan, Paris.
94. Pougoue, P-G., et al. (1998), *Le Droit des Sociétés Commerciales et Groupement d'Intérêt Economique OHADA*, PUA, Yaoundé.
95. Prieur, M. (2005), *Le Principes Généraux du Droit de L'Environnement,* Edicef, Paris.
96. RELUFA and UNAFAS, (2012), *Extractive Industries in Cameroon: A source Book for Teachers,* Tiffany Fourment, Yaoundé.
97. Robb, L. (2005), *Introduction to Ore forming Process,* 6th Edition, Blackwell Publishing, University of Westersrand, Johannesburg, South Africa.
98. Roseblum, P. et Maples, S. (2009), *Contrats Confidentiels: Pour en finir avec les Accords Secrets dans le Secteur Extractif,* Revenue Watch Institute, New York.
99. Rosenberg, D. (1983), *Le Principe de Souveraineté des Etats sur Leurs Ressources Naturelles,* L.G.D.J, Paris.
100. Rotillon, G. (2005), *Economie des Ressources Naturelles,* Editions la Découverte, Paris.
101. Schreurs, M. (1997), *The Internationalization of Environmental Protection,* Cambridge University Press, United Kingdom.
102. Schrijver, N. (1997), *Sovereignty over Natural Resources: Balancing Rights and Duties,* Cambridge University Press, United Kingdom.
103. Schwart, B. (2006), World Bank Policy: *The Extractive Industries Review and the Chad-Cameroon Pipeline,* SIT, Switzerland.
104. Sean, G. (2002), *The Transparency Evolution: The Environmental Forum, Environmental Law Institute,* Washington D.C.
105. Sheridan, L.A. and George Keeton, W. (1983), *The Law of Trusts*, 11th Edition, Cambridge University Press, UK.
106. Sheriff, R.E. and Geldor, L. P. (1995), *Exploration Seismology,* Cambridge University Press, United Kingdom.
107. Smillie, E. (2009), *Strength of the World Diamond Market*, Alberta Press.
108. Smouts, M.C. (2005), *Le développement Durable: Les Termes de Débat,* Compact Civils, Edition Dalloz, Paris.
109. Sockeng, R.. (2007), *Droit Pénal des Affaires OHADA,* 1st Edition, Presse Minsi le Competing, Douala.
110. Soumah, J. (2007), *Avenir de L'industrie Minière en Guinée,* Edition L'harmattan, Paris.
111. Southalan, J. (1998), *Mining Law and Policy Inter-nation,* Federation Press.
112. Strickler, Y. (2012), *L'arbitrage: Questions Contemporaines,* L'harmattan, Paris.

113. Sutcliffe, S. (2012), *Mining Law: Jurisdictional Comparisms,* Sweet and Maxwell, London.
114. Szablowski, D. (2007), Transnational Law and Local Struggles: Mining, Communities and the World Bank, Hart Publishing, London.
115. Tieguhomg, J.C. and Ingram, V. (2009), *Impact of Artisanal Gold and Diamond Mining on Livelihoods and the Environment in the Sangha Tri-National Park Land Scape,* CIFOR, Indonesia.
116. Tiencheu Njiako, A. (2009), *Le titre Foncier au Cameroun,* Arika.
117. UNEP and IFA, (2013), *Environmental Aspects of Phosphate and Potash Aluminium Mining,* 1st Edition, LIN Publication, Canada.
118. United Nations Environmental Programme, (2005), Selected *Texts of Legal Instruments in International Environmental Law*, Earth Print Limited Orders, United Kingdom.
119. Walker, J. and Howards, S. (2002), *Finding the way Forward: How could voluntary Actions move Mining towards sustainable Development?* , Russell Press Ltd, Nottingham, United Kingdom.
120. Wesphal, C. (2001), *Data Mining for Intelligence*, CRC Press , London.
121. Willy, L.A. (2011), *Whose Land is it? : The Status of Customary Land Tenure in Cameroon*, CED, FERN and the Rain Forest Foundation, UK.
122. Witherel, W. (2002), *Foreign Direct Investment and the Environment: Lessons from the Mining Sector*, OECD Publishing, Paris.
123. World Bank, (1991), *Environmental Assessment Source Book*, Hart Publishing C°., Washington D.C.
124. ___________ ,(2010), *Doing Business Dans les Etats Membres de L'OHADA,* Washington DC.
125. ___________ , (2011), *Les Ressources Minérales et le développement de L'Afriques,* Edilivre, Ethopie.
126. Yanou, M.A. (2009), *Labour Law, Principles and Practice in Cameroon,* REDEF.

B) ARTICLES

1. Akono Minlo, R. (2014), ''*Réflections sur les Droits de l'Exploitant de Mines en Droit Camerounais*'', Revue de L'ERSUMA, N° 4, PP. 363-380.
2. Alana. K. (2008), ''*Judging as Nudging: New Governance Approaches for the Enforcement of Constitutional Social and Economic Rights*'', Columbia Human Rights law Review, Vol. 39, PP.457-476.
3. Aldu, N.P., (2010), ''*Foreign Direct Investment, Economic Growth and Export Performance in Nigeria: An Error Correction Model*'', African Journal of Social Sciences, Vol. 1, N° 2, PP. 53-63.
4. Alemagi, D. Sondo, A.V. and Ertel, J. (2006), ''*Constraints to Environmental Impact Assessment Practice: A Case Study of Cameroon*'', Journal of Environmental Impact Assessment Review, PP.7- 32.
5. Amungwa, F.A. (2011), ''*The Evolution of Conflicts Related to Natural Resource Management in Cameroon*'', J. Hum.Ecol. 35(1), Kamla-Raj, PP.53-60.
6. Appiah-Opoko, S. (2001), ''*Environmental Impact Assessment in Developing Countries: The case of Ghana*'', Environmental Impact Assessment Review, PP.3- 41.
7. Aryeh, N., (2006), ''*Social and Economic Rights: A Critique*'', Human Rights Brief, Vol. 13, PP.1-12.
8. Atangcho Akonumbo, N. (2014), ''*OHADA and Investment Trends in Africa'', African Journal of Law,* Vol. 1. L'Harmattan, Yaoundé, PP.9-60.
9. _____________ ,(2001), ''*Uncertainty of Law in Cameroon: A Diagnosis of the Problem and Prospects*'', Juridis Périodique, N° 47, Juillet-Août-September, PP.62-73.

10. Baker, S.H. (2012), ''*Why the IFC's Free, Prior and Informed Consent Policy does not matter (yet) to Indigenous Communities affected by Development Projects*'', Wisconsin International Law Journal, Vol. 30, PP. 1-32.
11. Bebbington. A. Et al. (2008), ''*Contention and Ambiguity: Mining and Possibilities of Development*'', Journal of Development and Change, Vol. 39, N°. 6, Blackwell Publishing, PP.56-75.
12. Berat, L. (1993), ''*Defending the Right to a healthy Environment: Toward a crime of Genocide in International Law*'', B.U. International Law Journal, Vol. 11, PP.338-356.
13. Berger, T. (1994), ''*The Independent Review of the Sardor Sarovar Projects, 1991-1992*'', Impact Assessment Review, Vol. 12, N° 1, PP. 9- 33.
14. Bichta, C. (2002), ''*Corporate Social Responsible Practices in the Context of Greek Industry*'', Corporate Social Responsibility and Environmental Management Journal, PP.24-53.
15. Boehm, A. (2002), ''*Corporate Social Responsibility: A Contemporary Perspective of Community and Corporate Leaders*'', Business and Society Review, Vol. 107, PP.145-203.
16. Bowen, H. (1953), ''*Social Responsibilities of the Businessman*'', New York, Harper and Row, PP.12- 22.
17. Campbell, B. (2011), ''*Corporate Social Responsibility and Development in Africa: Redefining the Roles and Responsibilities of Public and Private Actors in the Mining Sector*'', Journal of cleaner Production, Elsevier, PP.1- 6.
18. Carroll, A, A. (1979), ''*A Three-Dimensional Conceptual Model of Corporate Performance*'', Academy of Management Review, Vol. 4, PP.505-525.
19. Chayes, A. (1976), ''*The Role of the Judge in Public law Litigation*'', Harvard Law Review, PP.483-515.
20. Chi Muam, A. (2006), ''*When environmental Impact Assessment becomes Peremptory Law*'', Annales of the Faculty of Law and Political Sciences, University of Dschang, Vol. 10, PP. 98-112.
21. Christiansen, E.C. (2007), ''*Adjudicating Non-Justiciable Rights. Socio-Economic Rights and the South Constitutional Court*'', Columbia Human Rights Law Review, Vol. 56, PP.457-481.
22. David Hess and Thomas Dunfee, W. (2000), ''*Fighting Corruption: A Principle Approach*'', Cornell International Law Journal, PP.590-605.
23. David, H. (2001), ''*The Impact of FDI on Host Country Development: The Heritage of Theory and Evidence*'', Journal of Business Ethics, N° 39, Kluwer Academic Publisher, Netherlands, PP.45-69.
24. Davis, K. (1967), ''*Understanding the Social Responsibility Puzzle*'', Business Horizons, Vol. 10, PP.45-51.
25. Deval, D. (2010), ''*Courting Legitimacy: Democratic Agency and the Justiciability of Economic and Social Rights*'', Interdisciplinary Journal of Human Right Law, Vol. 30, PP.35-59.
26. Dinah, S. (1991), ''*Human Right, Environmental Rights, and the Rights to Environment,*'' stan. J. Int'l. L. Vol. 28, PP.103-117.
27. _________ ,(1992), ''*What happened at Rio to Human Rights?*'' Y.B. Int'l. L. J., Vol. 75, PP.77-83.
28. Dounian, A. (2012), ''*La Valeur Juridique des Principes Applicable en Droit de l'Environnement au Cameroun*'', Revue de la Faculté des Sciences Juridiques et Politiques, Université de Ngaoundéré, PP. 82–107.
29. Dowling, J. and Pfeffer, J. (1975), ''*Organizational Legitimacy: Social value and Organizational Behaviour*'', Pacific Sociological Review, Vol. 18,PP.120-145.

30. Durrel, N.H. (2011), ''*Procedures for Granting Authorization and Permit in the Mining Sector in Cameroon*'', Journal de Coalition Camerounaise Publiez Ce que vous payez, N° 03, PP. 3-4.
31. Ekome, E. (2002), ''*Public Issues of Shares under the Companies Ordinance and the Uniform Act of the OHADA Treaty*'', Juridis Périodique N° 50, Avril-Mai-Juin, PP.81-89.
32. Eloi Yao, K. (2011), ''*Uniformisation et Droit Pénal: Esquisse d'un Droit Pénal des Affaires dans l'Espace OHADA*'', Penant, N° 876, Juillet-Septembre, PP. 293-317.
33. Emeka Duruigbo, (2006), ''*Permanent Sovereignty and People's ownership of Natural Resources in International Law*'', Washington International Law Review, N°. 33, PP.11-25.
34. Emeka Duruigbo, (2009), ''*The Global Energy Challenge and Nigeria's Emergence as a Major Gas Power: Promise, Peril or Paradox of Plenty*'', George Town International Environmental Law Review, Vol. 21, PP.11-35.
35. Ewere, A.O. (2012), ''*An Evaluation of the NEITI Act 2007*'', Benue State University Law Journal, N° 1, Vol. 4, Bellan Press, Makurdi, PP.45-63.
36. Fischer, G. (1962), ''*La Souveraineté sur les Ressources naturelles*'', Annuaire Français de Droit International, Vol. 8, PP.83-98.
37. Fitzgerald, E.V.K. (2001), ''*Regulating large International Firms*'', UNRISD Programme on Technology Business and Society, Paper N° 5, PP.15-45.
38. Foko, A. (2010), ''*Analyse Critique de Quelques Aspects du Droit Pénal OHADA*'', Penant, N° 859, Octobre-Décembre, PP. 195-239.
39. Frank, I.M. (2008) ''*Socio Economic Rights in Constitutional Law: Explaining America Away*'', International Journal of constitutional Law, Vol. 76, PP.667-689.
40. Fuller, L. (1978), ''*The Forms and Limits of Adjudication*'', Harvard Law Review, PP. 353- 378.
41. Funwie Tamasang, C. (2008), ''*Sustainable Development: Some Reflections with Regard to the New Constitutional Dispensation in Cameroon*'', The African Law Review, Vol. 5, N° 1, PP.145-165.
42. Gail, H. (2012), ''*Mining Corporations Environmentally Sustainable: The Limits of Responsible Investing*'', German Law Journal, N° 13, PP. 1-23.
43. Garnant, R. (1975), ''*Uncertainly Risk Aversion*'', Journal of Taxation of Natural Resource Projects Economic, Vol. 85, PP.2-19.
44. Garner, E.L. (2012), ''*International Treaties Governing Mineral Exploitations*'', Available at www.Eolss.net.sample-chapters/Co9/E6.65-05-04pdf. Accessed 07/12/2024, PP.1 -34.
45. Garriga. E. and Mele, D. (2004), ''*Corporate Social Responsibility Theories: Mapping the Territory*'', Journal of Business Ethics, Vol. 53, PP.31-53.
46. Ginsburg, N. (1957), ''*Natural resources and Economic Development*'', Annals of the Association of American Geographers, Vol. 47, N° 3, PP.200-219.
47. Gore, A. (2006), ''*An Inconvenient Truth: The Planetary Emerging of Global Warming and what we can Do*'', Available at; www.Ask.com/wiki/Alliance-for-climate-Protection. Accessed on 1/12/2024, PP.1-17.
48. Halleson, D.N. (2009), ''*An Analysis of Natural Resources Related Conflicts in Central Africa and the Gulf of Guinea*'', Cameroon Journal on Democracy and Human Rights, Vol. 3, N°. 1, PP.47-67.
49. Halperin, D.J. (1968), ''*Human Rights and Natural Resources*'', William and Mary Law Review, Vol. 9, PP.12-41.
50. Hector Ferreira, (2010), ''Corporate Crime -Should Corporations be Criminally Liable?'' Available at; http://www.cailaw.org/academy/magazin_101_pdf. Accessed on 09/05/2025, PP.1 -23.

51. Henkin, L. (1976), *''Is there a political Question Doctrine?''*, Yale Law Journal, Vol. 85, 22-45.
52. Hodkova, I; (1991), *''Is there a Right to Healthy Environment in the International Legal Order?''*, Conn. J. Int'L. L, Vol. 7, PP. 65-76.
53. Holme, L. and Watt, R., (2008), *''Making Good Business Sense''*, World Business Council for Sustainable Development, New York, PP.30-54.
54. Hyde, J.N. (1956), *''Permanent Sovereignty over Natural Wealth and Resources''*, American Journal of International law, Vol. 50, PP.854-874.
55. Jaff Bamenjo, N. (2013), *''The Challenge with Mining Projects in Cameroon''*, Extractive Industries Programe, 2nd Edition, N° 2, RELUFA, PP. 2-11.
56. Jean-Marie, B. (1999), *''International Instrument Relating to Human Rights''*, Human Rights Law Journal, Vol. 18, PP. 103-132.
57. Jenkins, H. (2004), *''Corporate Social Responsibility and the Mining Industry: Conflicts and Constructs''*, Corporate Social Responsibility and Environmental Management Journal, Vol. 11, PP.1-34.
58. Jenkins, R. (2001), *''Corporate Code of Conduct: Self-Regulation in a Global economy''* UNRISD Programme on Technology, Business and Society, Paper, N° 2, PP.201-231.
59. Jennifer, C. (2007), *''Enforcing Environmental Human Rights: Selected Strategies of US NGOs''*, NW.U,J. Int'l Hum. Rts. Vol. 6, PP.126-142.
60. Julie Nicholas, E. (2012) *''A Conflict of Diamond: The Kimberley Process and Zimbabwe's Marange Diamond Fields''*, Denver Journal of International law and Policy, University of Denver (Colorado Seminary), PP. 1-37.
61. Juliette, B. (2002), *''Multinational Corporations, Social Responsibility and Conflict''*, Journal of International Affairs, Vol. 55, PP.393-410.
62. Kamphuis, C. (2012), *''Canadian Mining Companies and Domestic Law Reform: A Critical Legal Account''*, German Law Journal, Vol. 13, PP.1-27.
63. Kang Ekome, E. (2015), *''Grappling with the use of Annual Forestry Royalties in Cameroon: The need to look Beyond Legal Rules''*, Annales de la FSJP, University of Dschnag. Tome 17, PP.430-456.
64. Karen, E.W. (2012), *''Conflict Mineral Legislation: The SEC's New Role as Diplomatic and Humanitarian Watchdog''*, Fordham Law Review, PP. 1-37, PP. 1-15.
65. Kéba M'Baye, (1972), *''Le Droit au Développement Comme un Droit de l'Homme''*, Revue des Droit de l'Homme, Vol. 503, PP. 103-132.
66. Kelley. J. (2013), *''China in Africa: Curing the Resource Curse with Infrastructure and Modernization''*, Sustainable Development Law and Policy, Vol. 12. N°. 35, PP.25-42.
67. Kemp, D. (2010), *''Mining and Community Development: Problems and Possibilities at Local Level Practice''*, Community Development Journal, Vol.45, Oxford University Press, PP.198-218.
68. Kitula, A.G.N. (2006), *''The Environmental and Socio-Economic Impacts of Mining on Local Livelihoods in Tanzania: A Case study of Geita District''*, Journal of Cleaner Production, Elsevier, PP.405-414.
69. Kourouma, M. (1994), *''Les Aspects Fiscaux des Convention Perlières en Cote-d'Ivoire''*, Revue Internationale de Droit Africain-EDJA, No 22, Juillet-Août-Septembre, PP.45- 74.
70. Landau, H. (2005), *''Protection of Private Foreign Investments in Less Developed Countries- Its reality and Effectiveness''*, William and Mary Law Review, Vol. 9. Issue 3, PP. 804-823.
71. Lauriol, T. (2015), *''OHADA, Le temps pour un Acte Uniforme Minier''*, Penant, N° 892, Edition Juris Africa, Paris, PP. 112-144.

72. Lee, J. (2000), ''*The Underlying Legal Theory to support a well-Defined Human Right to a Healthy Environment as a Principle of Customary International Law*'', Columbia Journal of Environmental Law, Vol. 5, PP. 283-296.
73. Li-ann Thio, (2002), ''*Battling Balkanization: Regional Approaches Towards Minority Protection Beyond Europe*'', Harvard International Law Journal, Vol. 43, PP. 234-251.
74. Lorne Clark, M. (1977), ''*International Law and Natural resources*'', Syracuse International Law Journal, Vol. 4, PP.377-387.
75. Lukong, A. B. (2010), ''*Corporate Social Responsibility: A Favour or an Obligation?*'' The African law Review, Vol. 7, PP.133-147.
76. Mainguy, C. (2010), ''*Natural Resources and Development: The Gold Sector in Mali*'', Journal of Resources Policy, Vol. 36, Elsevier Ltd, PP.124- 131.
77. Mark, S.P. (2004), ''*The Right to Development: Between Rhetoric and Reality*'', Harvard Human Rights Journal, Vol. 35, PP.137-160.
78. __________, (1981), ''*Emerging Human Rights: A New Generation for the 1980s?*'', Rutgers Law review, Vol. 33, PP.52-61.
79. Marrewijk, M. (2003), ''*Concepts and Definitions of Corporate Social Responsibility and Corporate Sustainability: Between Agency and Communication*'', Journal of Business Ethics, Vol. 44, PP.105-119.
80. Mazalto, M. (2004), "*La Réforme des législations Minières Internationales: La République Démocratique du Congo*", L'Afrique de Grands Lacs, Annuaire Français de Droit International, Vol. 8, PP.10 -34.
81. Mbomeda, J.C. et al.(2012), ''*Impact of Mining Activities on Population in Mbalam, East-Cameroon*'', Available at; http://www.sifee.org/actes/synthese_EE _2009/contenu_formation/ C-EIE_02/003 _mines/024_Tessa.pdf. Accessed 07/12/2024, PP. 45-56.
82. McGraw-Hilland Davis, K. (1960), *"Can Business afford to ignore Social Responsibility?''*, California Management review Vol. 2, PP.23-41.
83. McGuire, J. (1963), ''*Business and Society*", New York, PP.76-98.
84. Moore, C.D. (2005), ''*Harmonizing Business Laws in Africa: OHADA calls the Tune*" Colombia Journal of Transnational Law, PP. 1-63.
85. Mpacko Priso, A. (2010), ''*Où sont passée les Ressources qui Manquent pour le Développement de l'Afriques?*'', Revue Sub saharienne d'Economie et de Finance, PP.119-125.
86. Mungu, M.E. (2002), ''*Regulations Governing the Mining of Gold, other Precious Metals and Stones in Cameroon*'', Juridis Périodique, N° 49. Avril-Mai-Juin, PP.78-85.
87. Munjih, E. (2004), ''*The Regulation of Multinational Companies Operating in Developing Countries: A case of the Chad-Cameroon Pipeline Project*'', Journal of Social Responsibility, PP. 1-56.
88. Nah Fuashi, (2009), ''*Corporate Advantages without Incorporations? – The Case of Société en Participation and Société de fait within the OHADA Zone*'', Annales de la FSJP, University of Dschang, Tome 13, Maryland Printers, Bamenda, PP.67-84.
89. Nah Tetinwe, A. (2016), *"Translating Policies on the rights of Indigenous Communities into concret Practice to Mitigate Conflicts over Natural resource Exploitation in Central Africa: Case study of the Baka people in Eastern Cameroon"*, Studies in Sociology of Science Journal, Vol. 7, N° 6, PP. 1-12.
90. Nana Busia. K.A, and Bibiane Mbaye, (1996), ''*Filing Communications on Economic and Social Rights under the African Charter on Human and Peoples Rights (The Banjul Charter)*'', E. Afr. J. Peace and Hum. Rts. Vol. 3, PP.193-212.
91. Nasi, J. (1997), ''*The Evolution of Corporate Responsiveness. ''An Exploratory Study of Finish and Canadian Forestry Companies*'', Business and Society Review, Vol. 36, PP.301-325.

92. Ndiaw Diouf, (2010), ''*La Place du Droit Pénal dans le Droit Communautaire",* Revue de la Faculté des Sciences Juridiques et Politiques, Université Cheikh Anta Diop de Dakar-Senegal, PP. 161-182.
93. Ndiva Kofele-Kale, (1995), ''*Patrimonicide: The International Economic Crime of Indigenous Spoliation*'', Vand Journal of Transnational Law, Vol. 28, PP.54-72.
94. Nguihe Kante, P. (2011), *Où en est la responsabilité pénale des enterprises en droit camerounais?,* Jurisdis Périodique N° 87, Juillet-Août- Septembre, PP. 53-67.
95. Nji Fogwe, Z. (2014), ''*Anthropo-Environmental Implications of Quarrying of Sedimentary Sand Seams of Douala Estuarine Area, Cameroon*'', African Journal of Social Sciences, Vol. 5, N°. 2, PP.32-43.
96. Nkongho, A.E. (2015), ''*Indigenous Rights in Cameroon and Sustainable Development in an Emerging Economy: A Critical Review*'', African Journal of Social Sciences, Vol. 6, N° 3, PP.81-92.
97. Ntono Tsimi, G. (2012), "*Le devenir de la Responsabilité Pénale des Personnes Morale en Droit Camerounais. Des dispositions spéciales ver un énonce général ?*" , Jurisdis Périodique N° 89, Janvier-Février-Mars. PP. 83-94
98. O'keefe. P.J. (1974),*''The United Nations and Permanent Sovereignty Over Natural Resources,''* Journal of World Trade, PP.56-67.
99. Ocheje, P.D. *''The Extractive Industries Transparency Initiative (EITI): Voluntary Codes of Conduct, Poverty and Accountability in Africa.*" Available at: http:/www.accessdemocracy.org/files/2191_extractive_080807.pdf. Accessed 07/12/2013, PP.1 -11.
100. Opoku, S., and Asure, O.S. (2014), ''*Mining, Environment and Community Conflicts over Gold Mining in the Obuasi Municipality of Ghana*'', Journal of Sustainable Development Studies, Vol. 5, N° 1, PP. 64-99.
101. Oshionebo, E. (2013), *''The OECD Guidelines for Multinational Enterprise as a Mechanisms for Sustainable Development of Natural Resources: Real Solution or Window dressing?''*, Lewis and Clark Law Review, Vol. 17, PP. 1-42.
102. Ososfstry, H.M. (2005), *''Learning From Environmental Justice: A New Model for International Environmental Rights''*, Stan. Envtl. L. J, Vol. 24, PP.109-123.
103. Paillusseau, J. (2004), *''L'Acte Uniforme sur le Droit des Sociétés''*, Petites Affiches, 19-29.
104. Pallemaerts, M. (1996), *''The Future of Environmental Regulation: International Environmental Law in the age of Sustainable, Development: A Critical Assessment of the UNCED''*, Journal of Law and Commence, Vol. 15, PP.642-672.
105. Parance, B. (2013); *''Comment Concilier le Droit des contrats avec les obligations Environnementales pour suivant la satisfaction de L'intérêt général?''*, Recueil Dalloz, N° 10/7547, PP. 231-264.
106. Paul, S. (2003), ''*Resource Impact-Curse or Blessing?'',* Journal or Petroleum and Mineral Law and Policy, University of Dundee, U.K, Vol. 13,PP.1-29.
107. Peg, S. (2005), ''*Mining and Poverty Reduction: Transforming Rhetoric into Reality*'', Journal of Cleaner Production, Elsevier, PP.376-387.
108. Pougoue, P-G. (2006), *''L'Impact de L'Acte Uniforme du GIE sur le Contrôle et le Développement des Entreprise Locale'',* Jurisdis Périodique N° 66, Avril-Mai-Juin, PP.107-116.
109. Prakahs, S. (2005), *''The Effectiveness of Industry-Based Codes in serving Public Interest: The case of the International Council on Mining and Metals'',* Journal of Transnational Corporations, Vol. 14, N°. 3, PP.100- 123.
110. Quazi, A. and O'Brien, D. (2000),*''An Empirical Test of a Cross-National Model of Corporate Social Responsibility'',* Journal of Business Ethic, Vol. 25, PP.51-73.
111. Reed, D. (2002), ''*Resource Extraction Industries in Developing Countries''* Journal of Business Ethics, Vol. 3, PP.199-226.

112. Reisman, M.W. (1989), *''Harnessing International Law to Restrain and Recapture Indigenous Spoliation''*, American Journal of International Law, Vol. 56, PP. 1-30.
113. __________, (1990), *''Sovereignty and Human Rights in Contemporary International Law''*, American Journal of International Law, Vol. 84, PP. 847-900.
114. Render, J.M. (2011), *''Mining and the Indigenous Peoples Issues Review'',* Available at; ww.ICMM.com/document/pdf. Accessed on 7/10/2012, PP.34- 45.
115. Richard N. Kiwanuka. (1988), *''The Meaning of ''People'' in the charter of Human and Peoples' Rights'',* American Journal of International Law, Vol. 82, PP.123-145.
116. Roscoe, W.E. (1971), *''Probability of an Exploration Discovery in Canada'',* Canadian Mining and Metallurgical bulletin, Vol. 64, PP.134-145.
117. Rose D'sa, (1985), *''Human and Peoples' Rights: Distinctive Features of the African Charter'',* African Law Journal, Vol. 29, PP.81-122.
118. Ruth, G. (2003), *''Racing U.S. Foreign Policy''*, Nat'L Black L.J, PP.1-15.
119. Sethi, P.S., (1975), *''Dimensions of Corporate Social Responsibility: An Analytical Framework''*, California Management Review, Vol. 17, PP.75-87.
120. Shadrack Gutto, (1998), *''Beyond Justiciability: Challenges of Implementing/ Enforcing Socio-Economic Rights in South Africa''*, Buff. Hum. Rts. L. Rev., Vo. 79, PP.91-115.
121. Shishi, J.M. (2012), *''The Link Between Democracy and Development Rights in Nigeria'',* Benue State University Law Journal, Vol. 4. No. 1, Bellan Press, Makurdi, PP. 71-88.
122. Siegel, J. (1989), *''A Theory of Justiciability'',* Texas Law review, Vol. 86, PP.57-78.
123. Skinner, B.J. 91979), *''Earth Resources'',* Proceedings of the National Academy of Sciences of the United States of America, Vol. 76, N°. 09, PP. 413-456.
124. Sohn, L.B. (1982), *''The new International Law: Protection of the Rights of Industrials Rather than states''*, American University Law Review, Vol. 32, PP.20-41.
125. Stephen Schwebed, M. (1963), *''The Story of the UN's Declaration on Permanent Sovereignty over Natural Resources''*, Vol. 49. A.B.A.J, PP.463-487.
126. Suchman, M.C. (1995), *''Managing Legitimacy: Strategic and Institutional Approaches'',* Academy of Management Review, PP.598-634.
127. Tabe Tabe, S. (2008), *''Corporate Personality at Common Law and Under the OHADA Uniform Act Relating to Commercial Companies and Economic Interest Groups: A Comparative Study'',* Annales de FSJP, University of Dschang, Tome 12, PUA, Yaoundé, PP.5-31.
128. __________ (2015), *''Contractual Requirements for the Formation of Companies: OHADA and Common Law Compared'',* Annales de la FSJP, University of Dschang, Tome 17, PP.6-28.
129. Toermis, V. and Rabinvovitch, M. (2012), *''Principe de Législation Minière''*, Revue de Réglementation et Formulation'', Vol. 152, Québec, PP.70 -86.
130. Trackman, L. (2010), *''Foreign Direct Investment: Hazard or Opportunity?'',* University of New South Wales Journal, N°. 32, PP. 32-41.
131. Uwafiokum Idemudia, (2007), *''Community Perceptions and Expectations: Reinventing the wheels of Corporate Social Responsibility Practices in the Nigerian Oil Industry'',* Business and Society Review, N° 372, Blackwell Publishing, PP.10-23.
132. Vidal, N.G. and Kozak, R. (2008), *''Corporate Responsibility Practices in the Forestry Sector''*, Journal of Corporate Citizenship. Vol. 31, PP.75-96.
133. Votaw, D. (1972), *''Genius Become Rare: A Comment on the Doctrine of Social Responsibility''*, California Management Review, Vol. 15, PP.31-49.
134. Waddock, A.S. and Boyle, M. (1995), *''The Dynamics of Change in Corporate Community Relations''*, California Management Review, Vol. 37,PP.100-130.

135. Weinthal, E. and Jones, L.P. (2006), *''Combating the Resource Curse: An Alternative Solution to Managing Mineral Wealth''*, Journal on Perspective on Politics, Vol. 4 N°,PP.30-45.
136. Weiss, P. *''Concession''*, Available at; fr.wikipedia.org/wiki/matiere_premiére_minérales. Accessed on 4th February 2013, PP. 12-21.
137. Wieland, P. (2013), *''Going Beyond Panaceas: Escaping Mining Conflicts in Resource-Rich countries through Middle-Ground Policies''*, New York Environmental Law Journal, PP.1- 46.
138. Wilmarth, C.M., (2012), *''Mining Megaliths in the Argentine Andes: Where will Victims of Environmental Degradation Find Justice?''*, William and Mary Environmental Law and Policy review, Vol. 36, PP.1-30.
139. Wood, D., and Lodgson, J., (2002), *''Business Citizenship: From Domestic to Global Level of Analysis''*, Business Ethics Quaterly. Vol. 12. N° 2, PP.56-78.
140. Wood. D. (1991), *''Corporate Social Performance Revisited''*,The Academy of Management Review, Vol. 16, PP.25-40.
141. Yamoah Tenkorang, E. (2013), *''The Impact of Gold Mining on Local Farming Communities in Ghana''*, Journal of Global Initiative, Vol. 8, NO. 1 and 2, PP.25-44.

C) THESES/DISSERTATIONS

THESIS

1. Adamu, I. (2009), ''The Legal Framework for the Promotion and Protection of Foreign Investment in Nigeria'', Ph.D Thesis, University of Jos-Nigeria.
2. Atangcho, N.A. (2008), ''Foreign Direct Investments and Legal Policy options in Cameroon'', Ph.D Thesis, University of Yaoundé II-Soa.
3. Bande, G.M.T. (2014), ''Corporate Social Responsibility and Hydropower Investments under Cameroonian Law'', Ph.D Thesis, University of Yaoundé II-Soa.
4. Batchom, P.E-J. (2010), ''L'Etat, Les Organisations non Gouvernementales et la Transparence des Industries Extractives: La Dialectique de la Souveraineté et la Responsabilité'', Ph.D Thesis, University of Yaoundé II-Soa.
5. Bichta, C. (2000), ''The key Determinant of Environmental Performance- Case Studies from the chemical/Fertiliser and Metal Sectors'', Ph.D Thesis, School of Management, University of Baht-London.
6. Donfack Sokeng, L. (2001), ''Le Droit des Minorités et des Peuples Autochtones au Cameroun'', Ph.D Thesis, Université de Nantes.
7. Kobila, J. (2004), ''Le Cameroun Face á l'Evolution de la Protection Juridique International des Investissements Entrangers'', Ph.D. Thesis, University of Yaoundé II-Soa.
8. Mbetiji Mbetiji, M. (2014), ''Participatory Forest Management: The case of Community Forest under Cameroonian Law'', Ph.D Thesis, University of Dschnag.
9. Mbifi, R. (2012), ''Corporate Human Rights Responsibility and Development in the Oil Industry: The Case of Cameroon'', Ph.D Thesis, University of Buea.
10. Nain, K.V. (2003), ''Oil Exploitation and the State Sovereignty of African States: The Example of Cameroon and Nigeria, An International Perspective'', These de Doctorat de 3ème cycle, IRIC.
11. Penn, G. (1989), ''Legal Aspects of Foreign Investments in Cameroon'', Ph.D Thesis, University of Pennsylvanian, USA.
12. Tabe Tabe, S. (2009), ''Company Formation under the OHADA Uniform Act on Commercial Companies and Economic Interest Groups: Changes in the Law hitherto Applicable in Former West Cameroon'', Ph.D Thesis, University of Yaoundé II-Soa.
13. Tagne Kommegne, S.C. (2015), ''Ressource Naturalles et Processus de construction d'un espace integer en Afrique Centrale'', Ph.D Thesis, University of Yaoundé II-Soa.

14. Tamasang Funwie, C. (2007), ''Community Forest Management Entities as Effective Tools for Local-Level Participation under Cameroonian law: A Case Study of Kilum/Ijim Mounatain Forest'', Ph.D Thesis, University of Yaoundé II-Soa.
15. Titanji Duga, E. (2010), ''Justiciability of the Right of Indigenous Peoples in Municipal and International Law'', Ph.D Thesis, University of Yaoundé II-Soa.

DISSERTATIONS

1. Abessolo Makon, J.F. (2015), ''La Prise en Compt des Exigences Enviromentales dans la Conclusion des Contrats Minier au Cameroun'', Thése de Master, Université de Yaoundé II-Soa.
2. Adjei, E. (2007), ''Impact of Mining on Livelihoods of Rural Households: A Case Study of Farmers in the Wassa Mining Region, Ghana'', Masters Thesis, Norwegian University of Science and Technology.
3. Akumbo Niyeng, R. (2012), ''The Mechanisms for the Settlement of Trade Disputes under OHADA Law'', Masters Thesis, University of Dschang.
4. Anoh Bisong, C. (2016), ''Petroleum Extraction in Ndian Division and its impact on the fishing communities", Masters Thesis, University of Dschang
5. Antwi, F. (2010), ''An Assessment of the Impact of Newmont Gold Ghana Limited (NGGL) on the Socio-Economic Development after six Years of operation in the Birim North District'', Masters Thesis, Kwame Nkrumah University of Science and Technology, Ghana.
6. Arrey Eyong, E. (2015), "The Protection of the Environment and Trade in Cameroon", Masters Thesis, University of Dschang.
7. Baya Nyoh, S. (2012), ''The Place of Land in Foreign Direct Investment'', Masters Thesis, University of Dschang.
8. Boating Owusu, D. (2012), ''The Impact of Golden Star Wassa Limited (GSWL) Operations on its Catchment Communities'', Commonwealth Executive Masters Thesis of Public Administration, Kwame Nkrumah University of Science and Technology, Ghana.
9. Djen Churaen, N. (1999), ''Current Environmental Issues Associated with Mining Wastes in Kyrgyztan'', Masters Thesis, Central European University-Budapest.
10. Djudja, J-C. (2013), ''Le Principe de la Souveraineté Permanenté des Etats sur Leurs Ressources Naturelles a l'épreuve de la Pratique de la Certification minière dans la Région des Grands Lacs'', Mémoire de Master II, Université de Yaoundé II-Soa.
11. Dongmo, R.B. (2010), ''L'Application en Afrique Centrale des Principes de Prévention et de Précaution'', Mémoire de Master 2, Université de Limoges
12. Douala-Ekoko, D.A. (2007), ''Company Meetings as an Aggregate for Members to Exercise Company Powers'', D.E.A Dissertation, University of Yaoundé II-Soa.
13. Edoua Bioko, F. (2014), ''L'Administration et la Direction de la Société Anonyme dans l'acte Uniform Révise du 30 Janvier 2014'', Masters Thesis, University of Dschang.
14. Ehongo Némés, A-B. (2014), ''L'équilibre des Prestations dans les Contrats Pétroliers au Cameroun'' Masters Thesis, University of Dschang.
15. Ewane, M.E. (2010), ''Market and Market Chain Analysis for Bush Mango (Irvingiasp) in the South West and East Region of Cameroon'', Masters Thesis, University of Buea.
16. Fotso Chebou, K.F., (2009), ''Etude d'Impact Environnemental en Droit Français et Camerounais'', Mémoire de Masters 2, Université de Limoges.
17. Foueze Sonfack. R. (2012), ''La Protection des Ressources Minières en Afrique Centrale'', Mémoire de DEA, Université de Yaoundé II-Soa.
18. Gohla Mbinglo, A. (2014), ''Legal Framework of Mining and Environmental Issues in Cameroon'', Masters Thesis, University of Dschang.
19. Jane Hofbaner, A. (2009), ''The Principle of Permanent Sovereignty over Natural Resources and its Modern Implications'', Masters Thesis, University of Iceland.

20. Jemilatu Yaro, J. (2010), ''The Impact of Mining on Livelihoods of Local Communities: A Case Study of Newmount Ahafo South Mining Project of Brong Ahafo Region of Ghana'', Masters Thesis, International Institute of Social Studies, The Netherlands.
21. Kabwe Omoyi Fanny, (2014), ''Ressources Minière, Croissance Economiques et Guerres Civiles en R.D. Congo'', Mémoire de Master II, University of Yaoundé II-Soa.
22. Kebzabo, R. (2016), "La Sécurité au Travail dans le Projet de L'acte Uniforme OHADA Relatif au Droit du Travail", Masters Thesis, University of Dschang
23. Kom Kamsu, M. (1999), ''Le Droit Pénal des Sociétés Commerciales dans L'Acte Uniforme OHADA'', Mémoire de DEA, Université de Dschang.
24. Kouo Nzoko, F.A . (2013), ''Le Propriétaire du Sous-Sol en Droit Camerounais'', Mémoire de D.E.A, University of Yaoundé II-Soa.
25. Kwateng, G. (2012), ''Environmental Impact of Mining and the well-being of the People in Akwatia: A Case Study in Akwatia Town, Ghana'', Masters Thesis, Swedish University of Agricultural Sciences.
26. Lickert, V. (2008), ''Le Ressources Minières au Cameroun: Gouvernance, Prise de Décision et Contre-Expertise'', Mémoire de Master 2, Université Paris 1
27. Malucha Chama, W. (2012), ''International Trade in Forest Products: What Legal Implications on Sustainable Management of Forest for Environmental Protection in Cameroon.'' Masters Thesis, University of Dschang.
28. Mbifi, R. (1994), ''Settlement of Investment Disputes: An Appraisal of the 1965 Washington Convention'', Masters Thesis, Obafemi Awolowo University, Ile-Ife, Nigeria.
29. Mbo'o, J. (1976), ''Encouragement et Protection des Investissements Privée au Cameroun'', Mémoire de Maîtrise, University of Yaoundé.
30. Mbomi, J.C. (2000), ''The Role of Institutions in the Management of Forest-Based Resources in the Mount Cameroon Region'', Maîtrise Dissertation, University of Dschang.
31. Medom, J-D. (2012), ''La Protection de L'Environnement au Cameroun par les ONG: Le Cas du CIPCRE'', Masters Thesis, University of Dschnag.
32. Merino Jimenez, L. (2008), ''Community Right to Participate in Mining Policies with reference to Tintaya and Rio Blanco Mining Conflict in Peru'', Masters Thesis, Institute of Social Studies- The Netherlands.
33. Nchanji Yaah, I. (2014), ''The Doctrine of CAVEAT EMPTOR (Let the buyer Beware) in Contracts of Sale Goods and Land.'' Masters Thesis, University of Dschang.
34. Ncheme Kouotou, I.J. (2014), ''La clause compromissoire dans les contrats conclus par les personnes morales de droit public au Cameroun : Cas des contrats miniers et pétroliers'', Masters Thesis, University of Dschang.
35. Ndukong Nforkwe, M. (2015), ''The protection of the employer's interest under Cameroonian Labour Legislation'', Masters Thesis, University of Dschang.
36. Ndung Mbong, C. (2016), "Environmental and Social Challenges caused by major Investments in the Domain of Infrastructures in Cameroon: Case study of Lom Pangar dam and Kumba-Mamfe Road Project", Masters Thesis, University of Dschang
37. Ngoube, N. L. (2016), "LesEntreprises Miniéres et la protection de l'environement au Cameroun", Masters Thesis, University of Dschang.
38. Ngwome Fosoh, G. (2012), ''The Protection of Foreign Direct Investments under Bilateral Investment Treaties and the Erosion of State Sovereignty-The Case of Cameroon'', Masters Thesis, University of Dschang.
39. Nkuli, G. (2008), ''Effects of Mining Activities at Bulyanhulu Gold Mine (BGM) on the Water quality of Bulyanhulu River: Shinyanga-Tanzania'', Masters Thesis, Univerity of Zimbabwe.

40. Nkumbe, E. M. (2012), ''The Law Regulating the Involvement of Mining Operators in the Exploitation of Hard Mineral Resources in Cameroon'', Masters Thesis, University of Yaoundé II-Soa.
41. Nukuna Zemkwe, N. (2014), ''The Impact of Mining Legislations on Mining Activities in Cameroon since 2001'', Masters Thesis, University of Dschang.
42. Nyingchia Kemei, A. (2015) , ''The influence of Environmental Impact Assessment on Investment in Cameroon,'' Masters Thesis, University of Dschang
43. Opoku-Ware, J. (2010), ''The Social and Environmental Impacts of Mining Activities on Indigenous Communities: The Case of Newmont Gold (GH) Limited (Kenyasi) in Ghana'', Masters Thesis, University of Agder-Norway.
44. Owona Mfegue Kourra, F. (2005), '' La Place des Ressources Naturelles dans les Conflits : Le Cas d La République Démocratique du Congo'', Mémoire de D.E.A. Université de Paris-XII Val de Maine.
45. Randhem, J. (2008), ''Environmental Impacts and Health Aspects in the Mining Industry'', Masters Thesis, Chalmers University of Technology, Sweden.
46. Tamo, (2004), '' La Répression des atteintes à l'environnement au Cameroun", Mémoire de DEA, Université de Yaoundé II – Soa.
47. Tasiki Ntobengwia, D. (2016), "The Protection of the Health and Safety of Mineworkers in Cameroon", Masters Thesis, University of Dschang
48. Tatsadong Tafempa, J-M. (2011), ''Regards sur la Société en Formation (OHADA)'', Masters Thesis, University of Dschnag.
49. Tegha Ekei, V. (2016), "The Protection of Land owners under the Cameroonan Investment Legislation", Masters Thesis, University of Dschang
50. Toukea, D. (2010), ''ONG Internationales et Gouvernance de L'environnement au Cameroun: Les Cas de L'UICN et WWF'', Masters Thesis, University of Dschang.
51. Véronique Christophe, (2012), ''La Malédiction des Ressources Naturelles: Une Question de Dépendance ou de Dispersion?'', Mémoire de Maîtrise, Université du Québec à Montréal.
52. Widerland, A. (2014), ''Environmental Aspects of Mining'', Masters Thesis, Lulea University of Technology, Sweden.
53. Yengue Kamsu, M. (2012) ''The Legal Framework for Environmental Protection and the Effects on Trade: The Cameroon Experience'', Masters Thesis, University of Dschang.
54. Youmbi Fassen, F. (2011), ''Le Cadre Juridique des Investissement Miniéres et Pétroliers Chinois en Afrique: Instruments pour lex Mercatoria Sino-Africaine'', Mémoire de Maîtrise, Université de Montréal.

D) WORKING PAPERS, REPORTS AND PRESENTATIONS

1. Bamenjo, J. ''Mining and Local Development in Cameroon'', A Paper Presented at the Conference Organised by the Centre of Environment and Development on ''Governance des Ressources Naturelles et Droits des Communautés au Cameroun de 1994 à 2014: Billan et Perspective:, Hôtel Mont Fébé, Yaoundé, 13-16 April 2015.
2. Besada, H. and Philip, M. (2013), ''Le Codes Miniers en Afrique: La Montée d'une ''Quatrième'' Génération?, Rapport de Recherché, L'Institut Nord-Sud, Ottawa.
3. Bonnie, C. (2003), ''Factoring in Governance is not enough: Mining codes in Africa, Policy Reform and Corporate Responsibility'', Mineral and Energy, Raw Material Report, vol.18, N°.3.
4. C & K Mining Company Incorporation Sustainability Report (2011), ''Now and Beyond 2011'', A C & K Mining Inc. Publication, Cameroon.
5. Cameroon Population Census of 2005, Rapport de Présentation des Résultat définitifs.
6. Combacau, J. and Perdong, A. (1976), ''La Crise d'énergis au regard du Droit International'', Colloque de Caen-Paris.

7. Commission on Human Rights, ''Prevention of Discrimination and Protection of Indigenous Peoples, Indigenous Peoples', Permanent Sovereignty over Natural Resources'', Final Report of the Special Rapporteur Erica-Irene A. Daes, July 12, 2004.
8. "Corporate Social Responsibility and the Mining Industry'', Report of the International Centre for the Environment, UK, 1998.
9. "Digging in Corruption: Fraud Abuse and Exploitation in Katanga's Copper and Cobatt Mines'', A Report by Global witness, 2006.
10. Ebode, H. ''La Fiscalité des Activités Minieres en Afrique Centrale: Entre Impératif de Développement Socio-Economique et Harmonisation des Législations '', A Paper Presented at the 2nd Cameroon International Mining Conference and Exhibition on ''Developing Central Africa's Sustainable Mining Sector'', Organised by Ametrade and MINMITD, Yaoundé Conference Hall, 27-29 May 2015.
11. European Economic Association, (2005), ''Sustainable use and Management of Natural Resources'', Report N° 9.
12. Eye on EITI, Civil Society Perspectives and Recommendation on the EITI, Publish What You Pay Report, 2006.
13. "Free, Prior an Informed Consent: Two Cases from Suriname. Forest Peoples Programme'', FPIC Working Paper, March 2007.
14. Funoh, K.N. (2014), ''The Impacts of Artisanal Gold Mining on Local Livelihoods and the Environment in the Forested Areas of Cameroon'', Working Paper N° 150, Bogor, Indonesia, CIFOR.
15. Giorgio Brosio, ''Mécanismes de Partage des Recettes: Critères et Bonnes Pratiques Internationales'', Forum Camerounais des Minerais, 29-31 Mai, 2012, Hôtel Hilton, Yaoundé.
16. Halle, N. ''The Legal Framework and Incentives for Mining in Cameron''. A Paper Presented at the 2nd Cameroon International Mining Conference and Exhibition on ''Developing Central Africa's Sustainable Mining Sector'', Organised by Ametrade and MINMITD, Yaoundé Conference Hall, 27-29 May 2015.
17. Hentschel, T. Hruschka, F., and Priester, M., (2002), ''Global Report on Artisanal and Small-Scale Mining'', Mining, Minerals and Sustainable Development (MMSD) Report.
18. Husch, B. (1987), ''Guidelines for Forest Policy Formulation'', FAO Forestry Paper N° 81.
19. "Implementing the Extractive Industries Transparency Initiative: Applying Early Lessons from the Field'', Report of the World Bank and EITI, 2015.
20. "Implementing the Extractive Industries Transparency Initiative: Applying Early Lessons from the Field'', World Bank Report and EITI, 2008.
21. "Integrated Environmental and Social Impact Assessment Guide lines'', Report of African Development Bank, October 2003.
22. International Monetary Fund Guide on Resource Revenue Transparency, 2007.
23. Kenfack, P.E. ''Emergence 2035 et Implications sur le cadre Légal'', A Paper Presented at the International Conference on ''Gouvernance de Ressource Naturelles et Droits des Communautés au Cameroun de 1994 à 2014: Bilan et Perspectives'', Organised by Centre for Environment and Development, Yaoundé, Mt. Fébé, du 13 au16 Avril 2015.
24. Kouokam, R. ''Mines et Dévéloppement: vers la Contribution Effective du Secteur Minier au Dévéloppement Locale'', A Paper Presented at the 2nd Cameroon International Mining conference and Exhibition on ''Developing Central Africa's Sustainable Mining Sector'', Organized by MINMITD and Ametrade, Yaoundé Conference Centre, 27-29 May 2015.
25. Leite, C. and Weidmann, J. (1999), ''Does Mother Nature Corrupt?, Natural Resources, Corruption, and Economic Growth'', IMF Working Paper, 99/85.

26. Maclntosh, J. (2012), ''Special issues on Projects infrastructure in Mining, Energy, and Agriculture: Four ongoing giant projects to boost the economy Business in Cameroon, Strat line Limited, Hong Kong.
27. Mähler, A, et al. (2011), ''Conflict Prevention Through Natural Resource Management?: A Comparative Study'' Work Paper N° 158, German Institute of Global and Area Studies.
28. Martor, B., (2003), ''The OHADA Legal Harmonization Process: The Benefits for Africa's Development'', Proceedings of the OHADA Seminar held at the University of Buea, Cameroon, under the theme: ''The Applicability of the OHADA Treaty in Cameroon''.
29. Mate, K. (2002), ''Communities, Civil Society Organisations and the Management of Mineral Wealth: Mining, Mineral and sustainable Development'', World Business Council for Sustainable Development Report, N°16.
30. Muzong, W.K. ''Governance of the Artisanal and Small-Scale Mining in Africa: Overcoming the Challenges'', A Paper Presented at the 2nd Cameroonlnternational Mining Conference and Exhibition on ''Developing Central Africa's Sustainable Mining Sector'', Organised by AMETRADE and MINMITD, Yaoundé Conferences Hall, 27-29 May 2015.
31. Ndi, E. (2010), ''Lom Pangar dam construction starts March 2010'', The van guard publication.
32. Njilah, I.K. ''Mining and Public Health: Case of HIV-AIDS Prevalence in Mining Communities'', A Paper Presented at the 2nd Cameroon International Mining Conference and Exhibitin on ''Developing Central Africa's Sustainable Mining Sector'', Organised by Ametrade and MINMITD, Yaoundé Conference Centre, 27-29 May 2015.
33. Nkamouna Project Environmental and Social Assessment, Executive summary.
34. Nyuyinui, M. ''Droit Foncier et Droits des Communautés: Les Enjeux de la Reforme au Cameroun'', A Paper Presented at the International Conference on ''Gouvernance des Ressources Naturelles et Droits des Communautés au Cameroun de 1994 à 2014: Bilan et Perspective!'', CED, Yaoundé, Hôtle Mt. Fébe, 13 au 16 Avril 2015.
35. Ouedraogo, F. (2009), ''Diagnostic du Secteur Minier du Cameroun, Rapport final- Diagnostic des Sous Secteurs des Mines et Géologie, ADE, Commission Européenne.
36. PNUE, (2008), ''Afrique: Atlas d'un Environnement en Mutation'', Nairobi.
37. Rainbow Environmental Consult, Cameroon, (2013), ''Environmental and Social Impact Assessment Study for the Proposed Bauxil Mining Project at Minim-Martap and Ngoundal Deposits, Adamawa Region, Republic of Cameroon'', A Report.
38. Reed, E. and Marta, M. (2007), ''Assessment of the Mining Sector and Infrastructure Development in the Congo Basin Region'', W.W.F. Washington D.C.
39. Richard, M.A. (1993), ''Sustaining Development in Minerals Economies: The Resource Curse Thesis''.
40. Schwartz, B. Hoyle, D. and Nguitto S. (2012), ''Emerging Trends in Land-use Conflicts in Cameroon: Overlapping Natural Resource Permits Threaten Protected Areas and Foreign Direct Investment'', Report of W.W.F.
41. Shulika Binlu, S.''The Extractive Industries Transparency Initiative (EITI) Implementation Process in Cameroon'', A Paper Presented at the Parliamentary Awareness Workshop on EITI, Yaoundé Conference Centre, 14 June 2012.
42. Sohn, L.B. (1968), ''A Short History of the United Nations Documents on Human Rights'' In Commission to Study the Organization of Peace, 18th Report, the United Nations and Human Rights.
43. Steven Fox, (2011), ''Opacity: A Socio Economic Study of Diamond Mining in South-Eastern Cameroon'', IST collection Paper N° 728.

44. Tambe Ayuk, E.A. ''Local Content Necessary for Sustainable Hydrocarbon Development in Cameroon'', A Paper Presented at the International Seminar on '' The Sustainable Development of Petroleum Resources in Cameroon'', Organised by Gulf-Field Higher Institute of Petroleum Management and Control-Limbe, held at the SONARA Club House Limbe, 13-15 November, 2014.
45. Tetsopgany, S. Nzolang, C., and Kuepouo, G. (2007) ''Envoronmental and Socio-Economic Assessment of an Artisanal Gold Field: Case of Bétaré-oya, East-Cameroon'', Interrnal Report, Centre de Recherche et d'Education pour le Développement (CREPD), Yaoundé.
46. "The Corporate Responsibilty to Respect Human Rights", United Nations Interpretive Guide, 2012
47. United Nations (1992), Report of the United Nations Conference on Environment and Development (Rio de Janeiro, 3-14 June 1992).
48. United Nations Expert Group, (2006), ''Natural Resources and Conflict in Africa. Transforming a Peace Liability into Peace Asset'', United Nations Expert Group Meeting, Conference Report, Cairo, Egypt.
49. Warhus, A. (1999), ''Mining and the Environment: Case Studies from the Americas'', Report of the International Development Research Centre, Canada.
50. World Summit on Sustainable Development, The Road from Johannesburg: What was achieved and the way Forward, United Nations Department of Public Information Report, 2003.

E) MAGAZINE/NEWS PAPERS ARTICLES

1. ''Dossier Investir: Le Cameroun plus Attractif'', Technopôle N° 005-Août 2013.
2. ''Exploitation Minière: On fait le Point'', Technopôle N° 006-Janvier 2014.
3. ''Quelques Grands Projets et Programmes Miniers du MINMIDT en 2014'', Technopôle N° 008-Décembre 2014.
4. Bainkong, G. (2014), ''Business Climate: Joint Efforts to Better Cameroons Record'', Cameroon Tribune, N° 9803/6004, Thursday, 10 March.
5. Bainkong, G. (2014), ''CEMAC: Difficult Integration Process'', Cameroon Tribune, N° 9803/6004, Thursday, 10th March.
6. Bilingual News Magazine of the Ministry of Mines, Industry and Technological Development, N° 008- December 2014.
7. Cameroon Tribune, Monday 23rd June 2014.
8. Chemete, P. (2014), Mineral Exploitation. Five illegal Companies Unmasked'', Cameroon Tribune N°. 105552/675/, Thursday, March 20.
9. Diamond facts Books, 2010.
10. Diamond Infos; Magazine Trimestriel d'information des Activités du Secrétariat National Permanant du Processus de Kimberley, N° 001, Juillet 2014.
11. Enama Baudouin, (2013), ''Processus ITIE, le Cameroun atteint la Conformité'', le Quotidien de l'économie, N° 0433 du 18 octobre.
12. Foute, J.R. (2014), Climat des Affaires: Ce qui ne va Pas'', Cameroun Tribune N°. 10552/6751, Jeudi, 20 Mars.
13. Joseph Abena, ''Les Villageois barrent la Route aux Engins de la SINOSTEEL CAM'', Le Jour, Vendredi 28 août 2008.
14. Kendemeh, E. (2014), ''London: Cameroon's Investment Potentials Presented'', Cameroon Tribune, N° 10585/16784, Jeudi 08 Mai.
15. Makongo, D. (2011), ''Cameroon's Mining Code is Generous and Friendly to Foreign Investors'', Tenopole, N° 3.
16. Tchakounté A. (2014), ''Climat des affaires: Il faut alléger les Procedures'', Cameroon Tribune, N° 10542/6741, Thursday, March 06.

F) RADIO/TELEVISION SOURCES

1. CRTV, ''Artisanal Mining Activity and Environmental Challenges: Case of Batouri and Bétaré-Oya of the Eastern Region of Cameroon'', Documentary, Thursday 26 March 2024 at 9:00h GMT.
2. CRTV, ''Impacts of Industrial Mining Activity on the Inhabitants of Figuil'', Documentary, Saturday 10th October 2024 at 14:00h GMT.
3. Nico Halle, ''Ntumfor Throws Light about Mining in Cameroon'' CRTV Radio, ''Cameroon Calling'' Sunday 7:00am, June 6th 2024.

www.ingramcontent.com/pod-product-compliance
Lightning Source LLC
LaVergne TN
LVHW052313200926
848481LV00002B/555